The Role of International Institutions in Globalisation

INTERNATIONAL INSTITUTIONS AND GLOBAL GOVERNANCE

Series Editors: John-ren Chen, *Professor of Economic Theory and Econometrics, Department of Economic Theory, Policy and History and Director, Centre for the Study of International Institutions, University of Innsbruck, Austria and* David Sapsford, *Edward Gonner Professor of Applied Economics, University of Liverpool, UK*

Titles in the series will include:

The Role of International Institutions in Globalisation
The Challenges of Reform
Edited by John-ren Chen

International Institutions and Multinational Enterprises
Edited by John-ren Chen

The Role of International Institutions in Globalisation

The Challenges of Reform

Edited by

John-ren Chen

Professor of Economic Theory and Econometrics and Director of the Centre for the Study of International Institutions, University of Innsbruck, Austria

INTERNATIONAL INSTITUTIONS AND GLOBAL GOVERNANCE

Edward Elgar
Cheltenham, UK • Northampton, MA, USA

Published by
Edward Elgar Publishing Limited
Glensanda House
Montpellier Parade
Cheltenham
Glos GL50 1UA
UK

Edward Elgar Publishing, Inc.
136 West Street
Suite 202
Northampton
Massachusetts 01060
USA

A catalogue record for this book
is available from the British Library

Library of Congress Cataloguing in Publication Data
The role of international institutions in globalisation : the challenges of reform /
    edited by John-ren Chen
        p. cm.
    Includes index.
        1. International economic relations. 2. Globalization. I. Chen, John-ren.

HF1359.R65 2003
337—dc21

2003048538

ISBN 1 84376 469 5

Typeset by Manton Typesetters, Louth, Lincolnshire, UK.
Printed and bound in Great Britain by MPG Books Ltd, Bodmin, Cornwall.

Contents

Figures

Tables

Contributors

Professor V.N. Balasubramanyam, International Business Research Group, Department of Economics, Lancaster University, UK.

Professor Peter Bernholz, Professor Emeritus of Economics, Center for Economics and Business (WWZ), University of Basle, Switzerland.

Professor John-ren Chen, Professor of Economic Theory and Econometrics, Centre for the Study of International Institutions, University of Innsbruck, Austria.

Professor Amitava Krishna Dutt, Department of Economics, University of Notre Dame, IN, US.

Professor Peter Egger, Department of Economic Theory, Policy and History, University of Innsbruck, Austria.

Professor Kwan S. Kim, Department of Economics, University of Notre Dame, IN, US.

Seok-Hyeon Kim, PhD candidate, Department of Economics, University of Notre Dame, IN, US.

Professor Kunibert Raffer, Department of Economics, University of Vienna, Austria.

Professor David Sapsford, Edward Gonner Professor of Applied Economics, University of Liverpool, Management School, UK.

Professor Walter S.A. Schwaiger, Department of Industrial Management and Business Administration, Vienna University of Technology, Austria.

Professor John Toye, Department of Economics, University of Oxford, UK.

Preface

The world at the beginning of the twenty-first century is characterised by nearly borderless global economic activity with sovereign national states and multinational companies as the main global economic players in an international political–economic setting. There is no higher authority than a world government. With borders vanishing for transactions of goods, capital and knowledge the markets for these objects have been strongly subject to globalisation.

Sovereign states increasingly seem to run into problems – not only in regulating international economic activities for ensuring economic welfare but also in guaranteeing national security without cooperation with other sovereign countries. In this environment of globalised economies and national politics, sovereign states have to realise that an additional dimension of cooperation is necessary in order to ensure economic welfare and security in their societies. Using economic jargon the public hand has to be active when market failure occurs.

In an international political system without any superior authority, citizens depend on their national governments for the protection of their well-being. Therefore sovereign states remain the most important actors in the international political system. However, in order to effectively fulfil their function and provide essential services to the citizens, cooperation among sovereign states is not only useful but also necessary.

How to effectively and efficiently arrange cooperation with other sovereign states became an important problem of national politics, economics and security. International organisations (both governmental and non-governmental: NGOs), which have existed for more than a century, are one formal way of carrying out international cooperation to provide international (regional and global) public goods.

In the discussion about the necessary reforms, new ideas and research from independent institutions are necessary to overcome deadlocks and prisoner's dilemma situations formed between the divergent interests of governments, bureaucracies, NGOs and special interest groups. The research on international institutions can also be viewed as a public good which the market supplies insufficiently.

Due to their importance, issues need to be studied theoretically as well as empirically. To carry out independent research on international institutions, the Centre for the Study of International Institutions (CSI) was founded at the Faculty of Social and Economic Sciences of the University of Innsbruck, with financial support from the Oesterreichische Nationalbank.

An inaugural conference on 'The Role of International Institutions in Globalisation' was held from 14 to 16 November 2001 in Innsbruck and selected contributions are published in this book. We are indebted to the authors who presented their papers at this conference for their outstanding research work, which has provided essential studies on major issues concerning international institutions and given rise to many suggestions for further research.

We are also indebted to the Oesterreichische Nationalbank for financial assistance to set up the Centre. Without this support it would not have been possible to found the CSI.

We are also very grateful to the Österreichische Forschungsgemeinschaft (Austrian Research Association) who financed the first Conference on International Institutions and supported this publication.

Last but not least we would like to express our deep appreciation to the Tiroler Sparkasse Bank for sponsoring the Böhm-Bawerk Lectures, to the members of the Advisory Board, especially our friends Christian Smekal, Karl Socher (both at the University of Innsbruck), David Sapsford (University of Lancaster) and John Toye (University of Oxford), and to Richard Hule (University of Innsbruck), Gudrun Eder (CSI/University of Innsbruck) as well as Helga Landauer for making the conference such a successful event.

Innsbruck, May 2002

Introduction

The role of international institutions will become more and more important with increasing globalisation for various reasons. To mention just the broad background: it is increasingly difficult for nation states to adapt to the global consequences of market and government failures and different global externalities without cooperation and coordination. As a world government is neither necessarily desirable nor realistic in the near future one of the main solution strategies to such problems is to agree on and work through international institutions.

This volume gathers together several important papers providing theoretical and empirical research that allows a better understanding of the problems related to setting up international institutions and their everyday work. The papers were presented at the first Innsbruck Conference on International Institutions organised by the Centre for the Study of International Institutions (CSI). They stimulated an extensive discussion and, while stating some important results, also pointed to the need for further research.

The agenda of the conference and of future reasearch of the CSI is set in Chapter 1 by John-ren Chen, the Dean of the Faculty for Social and Economic Sciences of the University of Innsbruck and Director of the CSI. After formulating the most important research questions in the field of international institutions, ranging from justification, efficiency and others to evaluation issues, Chen analyses the basic schemes and reasons for the justification of international institutions. Most importantly, he points to different relations between public goods, which have to be taken into account in any theoretically sound investigation of international institutions. On a similar level, in Chapter 2 the Tobin tax is analysed by Kwan S. Kim and Seok-Hyeon Kim. The well-known controversies about the Tobin tax are examined with a special focus on global governance and the desirability, feasibility, effectiveness and revenues of the tax. Kim and Kim propose that the tax could be an important source of financing under global governance by a politically autonomous global institution. They draw the conclusion that the tax could be an effective and technically feasible form of taxation with certain advantages compared to other control devices of capital flows.

The topics of the other chapters have a more concrete research agenda, taking up important global issues where international institutions play an important role. The first topic is trade and foreign direct investment (FDI) and both chapters taking up these issues naturally deal with the World Trade Organization (WTO). In Chapter 3, V.N. Balasubramanyam and David Sapsford examine the case for including FDI on the agenda of the WTO. They argue that FDI is already on the agenda of WTO in the form of TRIMS, TRIPS and services. After dismissing several other reasons for excluding FDI from the WTO they investigate the case of developing countries. The challenge the developing countries face is one of a trade-off between economic sovereignty and the fruits that FDI yields. Based on an evaluation of the impacts of FDI and its regulation either by the developing countries themselves or by the WTO, the authors conclude that developing countries have much to gain and nothing to lose from the inclusion of FDI in the WTO.

In Chapter 4, John Toye is concerned with a similar issue, namely that of reconciling order and justice in the international trade system. Toye finds that in the GATT rules there were more clauses devoted to reneging than there are devoted to free trade. It was a compromise between free trade and various other norms of justice with the notions of fairness in trade. In the new WTO order, however, the institutional innovations have two general effects. They make inroads on what were matters of domestic governance and they 'judicialise' the process of trade cooperation in order to render it more just. But Toye demonstrates that there is still a lack of justice for developing countries. For example, he believes that WTO rules will increasingly prohibit all protection of infant industries in developing countries. His proposition, on the other hand, is an exceptional treatment on 'specific' industrial subsidies for infant industry purposes, provided that these are selective, temporary and performance related. If the path to catch up is blocked for 'legal reasons', the legitimacy of the present hegemonic ideal of embedded liberalism can only erode further, and then world trading arrangements are bound to become more disorderly.

While the chapters just discussed mention developing countries in their discussion of the WTO, those by Raffer and Dutt focus entirely on development issues and international institutions. In Chapter 5, Kunibert Raffer makes some proposals to adapt international institutions to development needs. Most international institutions were not geared to the specific needs of developing countries. With regard to the WTO, proposals for differentiated and preferential treatment based on objective indicators and changes in the arbitration procedures or the voting system are made. In addition, the importance of protecting intellectual property in the case of indigenous knowledge is stressed. The World Bank is criticised for neglecting the default of a country. In general, international institutions should be liable for neglecting membership rights. A body of independent experts should be set up to monitor the implementation of UN summit meetings, as Raffer and Singer proposed in 1997.

In Chapter 6, Amitava Krishna Dutt focuses on the question, whether international institutions can help to mitigate the tendency of uneven development in the global economy in analogy to convergence within countries where governments affect the development process. After reviewing the theories about divergence and convergence, Dutt examines how the mechanisms have been affected by international institutions, namely by the UN and the Bretton Woods institutions. The hope that international institutions can play the role of an international government which can bring about convergence, has not been realised, however. Dutt criticises the contractionary effects of International Monetary Fund (IMF) stabilisation measures and the World Bank for inducing higher interest rates by financial deregulations. Dutt concludes that only a better understanding of the functioning of the global economic system and of feelings of sympathy for human beings everywhere can persuade national governments to push for international institutions striving for equitable global development. In the following chapter, Peter Egger provides a comment on Dutt's chapter.

The final topic of the volume is dedicated to the study of an international institution, namely the Bank for International Settlements (BIS). The three chapters demonstrate how an individual institution and its activities can be analysed and evaluated. In Chapter 8, Peter Bernholz poses the question of justification of BIS activities from a normative economic perspective. He concludes that the main contribution of the BIS is to supply international public goods by the services it provides to the many committees and groups located at the BIS. These include new standards and regulations, which increase international financial stability, gathering financial information and organising training programmes for financial specialists. However, the increasing collaboration with other international financial institutions creates overlapping activities and the bottom-up approach followed by the BIS may come into conflict with the top-down approach of the IMF and the World Bank.

The chapters by Walter Schwaiger and John-ren Chen take up the most recent and quite controversially discussed activity of the Basle Committee of the BIS – namely the New Basle Capital Accord, commonly called Basle II, a set of recommendations and standards for dealing with credit risk for banks. In Chapter 9, Schwaiger investigates empirically the implications of the proposed minimum capital requirements. Using the detailed data of Creditreform, one of the biggest rating companies worldwide, for Austria he shows that the first suggestions were not leading to the intended result. In line with the following chapter by Chen, the empirical results show that these proposals would lead to problems especially for small and medium-sized enterprises (SMEs) and different industrial sectors in Austria. Schwaiger's and similar studies have already led to an update in the suggestions by the Basle Committee.

In Chapter 10, Chen sets up a model to investigate the macroeconomic effects of the new banking standard on the credit markets and its impact for macroeconomic activities. He focuses especially on the key problems of Basle II and the influence on the credit market for SMEs. Therefore his results point to the importance of several structural features of the economy such as transaction costs or the distribution of firm sizes when assessing the impact of Basle II.

Thus, the chapters span the whole range of questions regarding international institutions. Presenting detailed empirical and theoretical analysis, which is needed to assess the effectiveness of international institutions and to criticise and improve measures and actions taken by them, and broad normative and fundamental investigations of the problems behind the institutional curtains, the current volume is an obvious starting point for newcomers to this exciting and complicated field. On the other hand, the book will remain a continuing source of inspiration for those already specialised in specific topics regarding international institutions.

1. Global market, national sovereignty and international institutions

John-ren Chen

1 MAIN ISSUES FOR THE STUDY OF INTERNATIONAL INSTITUTIONS FROM AN ECONOMIC PERSPECTIVE

We are living in a world of global markets for merchandise and capital with global players such as transnational companies and sovereign national states. Economists have had a common understanding that regulations are needed in case of market failure. International institutions (IIs) are needed therefore to regulate global market failures when the sovereign national governments are not able to implement regulation in global markets 'efficiently'. This inability to regulate may stem from the fact that sovereign national governments cannot regulate *global market players* (GMPs), or because of conflicts of interest between the sovereign national states (see Fischer 1999). Therefore, IIs are needed to facilitate collective actions at the global level. In a world of independent sovereign countries (nations) there are conflicts of interest between its members. To reduce the cost of conflict resolution, IIs have been established to set up global rules.

Within a world with sovereign national governments there are not only market failures but also government failures. Some government failures can be solved by introducing markets. However, the market solution cannot be applied to some sovereign government failures, that is, there are both market and government failures, for instance the abuse of human rights by sovereign governments is a failure of both market and government. In this case international organisations (IOs) have been established as private institutions to facilitate global collective actions. As a general rule, the members of such IOs consist of non-governmental organisations (NGOs), such as Amnesty International, Greenpeace and more recently anti-globalisation organisations. IOs have also been set up to assist defence forces, for instance the former Warsaw Pact and the North Atlantic Treaty Organization (NATO).

These rather cursory remarks show that IIs and IOs represent a very complex landscape and can be classified according to various aspects such as:

1. public versus private institutions classified according to whether members are governmental organisations or not;
2. political, economic, military, social, scientific, educational and environmental institutions and organisations classified according to the collective actions for which a specific international institution or organisation is designed for;
3. bilateral and multilateral institutions and organisations rule, respectively, bilateral and multilateral issues; and
4. regional and global institutions and organisations facilitate local collective and global actions (LCAs and GCAs), respectively.

According to a report by Frey (1997, p. 106) there were at least 350 intergovernmental IOs having more than 100 000 employees in 1997, with the growth in their membership taking place primarily since 1939; moreover, the individual organisations have grown very rapidly. Thus, the study of IIs and IOs has become an important field in the social and economic sciences. Following Anne O. Krueger, a former chief economist of the World Bank, an obvious point of departure for the analysis of IIs is the absence of a world government and the proposition that there may be global public goods or externalities which spread beyond national boundaries (Krueger 1998, p. 2005).

While markets are not generally even constrained Pareto efficient, there are also the limitations of governments (Greenwald and Stiglitz 1986). Government and market are seen today more as complements, each providing a check on and facilitating the functioning of the other. The modern theory of collective action is concerned about market failures, and considers whether public regulations can improve welfare and how those regulations can best be designed.

IIs are concerned with collective actions and therefore with global market failures (GMFs). Thus, the concept of global public goods (GPGs) is essential for the study of IIs. From Paul Samuelson's (1954) definition of the concept of public goods, it becomes clear that the benefits of some public goods extend only within a limited geographic region (that is, local public goods: LPGs). Other public goods whose benefits extend well beyond national borders to the global level have been defined as global public goods. There are six broad categories for GPGs often discussed in economic literature: (i) international security, (ii) international economic stability, (iii) environment, (iv) knowledge, (v) humanitarian assistance and (vi) health. Various IIs have been created to facilitate LCAs as well as GCAs in each of these areas. As these six PGs overlap to some degree, so too do the functions of the IIs set up to address the issues.

The following problems have to be considered in the context of the study of IIs and IOs:

1. *Justification for the existence of IIs*   Analysis of IIs has to prove that in the absence of a global government, setting up IIs will contribute to a net improvement in global welfare. Detailed studies of IIs have to identify the conditions under which an II will contribute to a net improvement in global welfare.

2. *How IIs come into being*   To answer the question of framing international rules or institutions one has to examine the incentives for, and potential gains from, cooperation, and the *possibility* and *cost* of designing rules or institutions that can permit the attainment of a desired outcome and are Pareto superior to an international regime of *laissez-faire* (Krueger, 1998, p. 2004).

   Olson's zero contribution thesis in the *Logic of Collective Action* (1965, p. 11) ('unless there is coercion or some other special device to make individuals act in their common interest, rational, self-interested individuals will not act to achieve their common or group's interests') has given rise to much theoretical study and many experiments relating to this issue (Ostrom 2000). The rise in the number of IIs set up by the governments of sovereign national members cannot be explained by Olson's zero contribution thesis, since governments have the mandate and the commitment to look for solutions to global problems and therefore cannot be compared with the NGOs. An example is the Anti-terrorism Alliance initiated by the US government after the attacks of 11 September 2001. However, since NGOs are organised by individuals or private organisations, Olson's zero contribution thesis may explain their rise. In general, the incentives for initiating and framing rules or institutions are high due to the high potential gains from cooperation as well as a high degree of feasibility but low costs involved in framing rules or institutions.

3. *Process for providing GPGs*   IOs have the role of implementing and monitoring the GPGs. Therefore, the study of IIs has to analyse alternative mechanisms for supplying GPGs in appropriate amounts (see Krugman 1997).

4. *Realisation of optimal global institutional design and assignment of appropriate functions to IIs*   Regulations and markets have been seen as complements, each providing a check on, and facilitating the functioning of the other. In general, there are numerous different regulations that could be used to improve matters. Therefore, a main focus of any analysis of IIs should consider how those interventions could best be designed. (Such a study should recognise the presence of agency problems in both the public and private sectors.) How functions should be assigned across related IOs is an important issue of optimal global institutional design which has received little attention (see Krueger

1998). Therefore, the assignment of functions to related IIs is an important topic for the study of IIs.

Since IIs are set up to provide GPGs or to regulate GMFs, the size of an II must also be discussed within the study of IIs. This is similar to the problem of the optimal size of a firm.

5. *How to solve overlapping jurisdiction problems of IIs* There have been many IIs with related functions. Therefore, overlapping jurisdictions and cooperation of IIs is one of the main issues for the study of IIs. The overlapping of jurisdictions can cause over- or underproduction of GPGs and even the implementation of inconsistent measures to rectify GMFs. The problems associated with overlapping jurisdictions are usually caused by several IIs providing related public goods or regulating related market failures. Public goods are said to be 'related' if they are substitutive or complementary for their users, or if they show joint product or input–output relations for their producers. The problem of overlapping jurisdictions has been an important issue between the International Monetary Fund (IMF) and the World Bank (see Fischer 1999; Collier and Gunning 1999). Different IOs dealing with the same issues can be beneficial if it induces some competition among them, and it may increase 'efficiency'. In such a case, the gap created by the failure of one organisation to meet the needs of the international society may be filled by another organisation which is anxious to expand its mandate.

6. *Coordination of global activities between IOs* IIs have had to carry out global actions to solve acute problems, both to improve their effectiveness and to avoid conflicts. Coordination of activities between IIs is not only desirable but also necessary. Such coordination may help to avoid controversial global actions like the 'help program' of the IMF and the World Bank to resolve the crisis in Argentina in the 1990s, for instance.

Recently, the problem of coordinating activities between IOs has received specific attention. Richard Jolly of the Institute of Development Studies at Sussex University has initiated a series of international conferences concerning the relationship between the United Nations and the World Bank, to discuss the question of how to establish better processes for interaction between the UN and the Bretton Woods institutions.

Cooperation between the IOs and coordination of GCAs are necessary to improve their effectiveness and efficiency, especially because of market failures and the monopoly character of most IIs for the functions assigned to them (see Stiglitz 1999b).

7. *Democratic accountability of IIs and IOs* 'Who elected the WTO?' is the topic of an essay published in the *Economist* (29 September 2001).

The most important IIs such as the UN, the Bretton Woods institutions and the World Trade Organization (WTO) are political institutions that are not directly but indirectly accountable to the peoples of the world through the representatives of their governments. The NGOs are private institutions, and they are neither directly nor indirectly accountable to the peoples of the world, but only to their members, who are individuals or private organisations.

Stiglitz criticised the lack of democratic accountability of the IMF and the World Bank:

> In fact, the institutions are not even directly accountable to the chief executives of their 'share-holder' countries: the IMF is accountable to ministries of finance and central banks, while the World Bank is accountable to ministries of finance and either aid agencies (in the case of donor countries) or economic ministries (in the case of recipient countries). Democratic accountability has been further weakened as central banks have increasingly succeeded in achieving greater independence, often with the encouragement of the IMF itself. (Stiglitz 1999b, p. 582)

The democratic accountability of the WTO has been especially criticised with respect to its Dispute Settlement Body.

8.   *Voting systems (decision and power distribution)*   The decisions of IIs or IOs are usually made by a ballot of their members. There are at least two voting systems that have been applied by the IOs since the Second World War, namely the country voting system (each country gets a single vote) and the so-called dollar voting system. The first one has been used in the UN General Assembly while the latter has been used by the Bretton Woods institutions. According to the dollar voting system, voting rights are proportional to the contributions of the countries that support those institutions (which in turn are related to their GDP). The country voting system, on the other hand, does not consider the population differences between the member countries. Therefore, it cannot be seen as a justifiable voting system, since a country with a population of more than one billion has the same vote as one with several thousand people. Although the dollar voting system may reflect the share of contributions made by a member country, the less-developed countries usually contribute only a small share because of their low GDP and therefore their interests cannot be justly represented by this system. Due to these inequalities, the voting systems applied by IIs should be analysed within the study of IIs.

9.   *Ideological background and theoretical principles for the justification of IIs and decisions about GCAs*   The Bretton Woods institutions were set up in a period when the Keynes doctrine was the main strain of economic

thought after the publication of the *General Theory* in 1936. However, since the 1980s, the Washington Consensus has been applied to the design of economic policy and the assignment of functions to IIs as the leading ideological background and standard of theoretical principles.

The main functions for which the Bretton Woods institutions were designed were macroeconomic stabilisation, to arrive at full employment, exchange rate stability, to avoid beggar-thy-neighbour depreciation, and commodity price stabilisation. With the change to the Washington Consensus in the 1980s, the policy objectives of IIs such as the GATT General Agreement on Tariffs and Trade and the Bretton Woods institutions have changed. Trade liberalisation, privatisation, macroeconomic stability with low inflation, liberalisation of international capital movements and so on have become the main concerns of the economic programme followed by the Bretton Woods institutions (see Gilbert et al. 1999).

10. *Evaluation and analysis of the efficiency of IIs and IOs and the effectiveness of GCAs*   The design of economic policy and assignment of functions to the IIs are reasoned on order, justice and efficiency to rectify market failures and to provide GPGs. Not only theoretically but also empirically it is necessary to assess whether the IIs have really fulfilled the conditions of efficiency and have improved global welfare (Rogoff 1999).

The next questions are, obviously: how to improve the effectiveness of these collective actions and measures if they were not effective, and why were the collective actions carried out by an II not effective? Usually several different criteria are used to evaluate the collective actions carried out by an II. The results of such multidimensional evaluations are important for improving the effectiveness of collective actions in the future. The list of questions about IIs is long and could be extended. However, theoretical and empirical as well as experimental research has to be carried out to at least answer the questions mentioned above if we want to arrive at a better understanding of international institutions.

2   PRINCIPLES OF INTERNATIONAL INSTITUTIONS

There are usually several possibilities when it comes to rectification of market failures. In this section we shall discuss the steps necessary for an analysis of international institutions: (i) identification of the reasons for a market failure; identification of the global public good involved; identification of their interaction and relatedness; (ii) assignment of functions; and (iii) design.

Identification of GPGs and Market Failures, and their Interaction and Relatedness

In line with the discussion in the last section, IIs are needed to improve global welfare in the case of global market failures. Market failures may occur when any one of the following is present:

- public goods;
- externalities;
- imperfect markets; or
- incomplete markets.

In the case of global market failures, IIs are needed to rectify them and to improve global welfare. In order to design IIs, these failures first have to be identified.

In his 1986 presidential address, Kindleberger identified the following international public goods: '*trading systems, international money, capital flows, consistent macroeconomic policies* in periods of tranquillity and *a source of crisis management* when needed' (italics added).

More recently, some economists have identified a set of GPGs (see Stiglitz 2000, pp. 9–5). Six areas have been identified in particular as follows:

- global security;
- global economic stability;
- knowledge;
- global environment;
- humanitarian assistance (for example, for famine relief); and
- global health, especially contagious diseases.

A central part of the logic of global collective action is the provision of GPGs by IIs. But the rationale for global collective action goes further and can address any of the market failures.

Similar to global public goods, externalities can also be identified in the six areas mentioned above, as well as market failures due to incomplete markets or imperfect markets. The classification of the GPGs, market failures as well as externalities in the six areas is obviously too coarse since there are different broad categories of GPGs, markets and externalities within each of the six areas. Therefore, in order to achieve optimal policy design we have to make a more detailed identification in each area.

As an example, the identification of GPGs, market failures and externalities with respect to global economic stability is now sketched in more detail (later using the example of Indonesia). First, we identify the markets, that is,

GDP (goods market), money market, capital market and labour market, and the GPGs, for example, following Kindleberger's trading system, international money, capital flows, consistent macroeconomic policies, crisis management, poverty reduction and knowledge. Using terminology from the economics of commodity markets, there is relatedness between GPGs (Chen 1993 and 1994) and private goods.

The trading system is a global public good. A functioning trading system can be used by every country without excluding any other country. A well-performing trading system, which reduces trade barriers and transaction costs, increases the efficiency of global resource allocation. A stable and well-performing international monetary system can also be used by every country without the exclusion of other countries. Such an international monetary system can reduce market failures, prevent financial and currency crises and also improve international trade. Thus, the trading and international monetary systems are complementary. A system of functioning capital flows can also be used by every country, without excluding any other country. The efficiency of international capital markets can be improved by a well-performing international capital market which increases global welfare. Consistent macroeconomic policies can be proposed by IIs and used by every country. Sound macroeconomic policies will reduce market failures such as unemployment, inflation, volatile exchange rates and so on. A sound international monetary system, capital flow and consistent macroeconomic policies prevent crisis. It is generally acknowledged that business cycles can be transmitted to other countries. Increasing trade encouraged by a well-performing trading system can also increase the international transmission of business cycles and easily cause crisis. They might therefore be substitutive. For instance, Basle II will be a global public good for crisis management. It is expected that after its implementation, financial transactions will decrease and international trade therefore might be classified as substitutive rather than complementary. A trading system, which reduces or removes trade barriers for exports of less-developed countries (LDCs) is usually expected to increase their GDP and thus contribute to global poverty reduction. This shows the complementary relationship between the trading system and poverty reduction.

In Table 1.1 we make a proposal about the relatedness and interaction among private goods and global public goods. The private goods money and capital can be considered as highly substitutive and complementary to all other goods. Crisis management and trading systems can be considered as substitutive if protectionist measures are used for rescue operations or rectification in crisis management.

It has recently been proposed that the global lender of last resort and global court of bankruptcy assist in the resolution of financial and currency crises. Both measures can reduce financial fragility and improve the stability of

Table1.1 *Relatedness and interaction among private goods and GPGs*

	GDP	Money	Capital flow	Labour	Trading system	Crisis management	Poverty reduction	Knowledge
GDP		C	C	C	C	C	C	C
Money	h		S	C	C	C	C	C
Capital flow	h	h		C	C	S	C	C
Labour	h	l	l		C	C	C	C
Trading system	h	h	h	m		S	C	C
Crisis management	m	h	h	l	h		C	C
Poverty reduction	h	l	m	h	h	m		H
Knowledge	h	m	m	m	l	l	H	

Note: The relatedness between the objectives on the four markets and the GPGs is either complementary (C) or substitutive (S). The degree of relatedness between the objectives is represented by h: high; m: moderate; l: low.

global financial markets. Therefore, they can also contribute to improved capital flows and economic stability.

There are different degrees of interactions among the GPGs in Table 1.1. On the lower left-hand side of the diagonal, the expected degrees of interactions are shown by l: low, m: moderate and h: high. Both the interactions and degrees of interactions among the different GPGs are relevant for assignment of the functions to specific IIs.

In Table 1.2 the relatedness between or the interaction among the six areas of GPGs proposed by Stiglitz is shown. In comparison to Kindleberger, the GPGs identified by Stiglitz are much more general. For instance, global security is considered as a GPG by the latter but not by the former. In general, global economic stability is a part of global security but not vice versa. But both global security and global economic stability interact in the sense that they are necessary for each other. Policies which increase unemployment or dramatically lower real incomes can lead to civil unrest or ethnic conflict and have often done so. The policies pursued in Indonesia to resolve the financial crisis, including the elimination of food and fuel subsidies just as incomes were rapidly declining and unemployment soaring, predictably led to riots that further undermined the economy (see Stiglitz 2000, pp. 9–23).

Knowledge is a GPG that interacts and is complementary to global economic stability. Policy advice provided by the Word Bank for LDCs may contribute to poverty reduction and also to improving both global security as well as global economic stability. Knowledge can help to improve the effectiveness of economic policy, increase real income and reduce unemployment. Therefore, it can play an important role in reducing poverty. Similarly, knowledge as a GPG can contribute to the resolution of financial currency and debt crises and thus has important implications for crisis management.

Humanitarian assistance can be considered as complementary to both global security as well as global economic stability for similar reasons. But global environmental protection is considered in general as substitutive for poverty reduction and thus for global economic stability. High standards of global environmental protection are seen to undermine the competitive position of the LDCs in the world market and are thus seen as a negative influence on poverty reduction by the LDCs.

High interest rate policies and scarcity of credit in Indonesia after the outbreak of the financial crisis, and elsewhere, have also contributed to a faster exhaustion of natural resources, for example, the cutting down of forests as an easy way of raising cash (as has already been proposed by Hotelling, 1931). Thus, economic policies can have marked implications on the environment. Global health is also seen as complementary to global security and to global economic stability.

Table 1.2   *Relatedness and interaction among GPGs*

	Global security	Global economic stability	Knowledge	Global environment	Humanitarian assistance	Global health
Global security		C	C		C	C
Global economic stability	h		C	S	C	S
Knowledge	h	h		C	C	C
Global environment	m	h	m		C	C
Humanitarian assistance	h	h	l	l		h
Global health	m	h	h	h	h	

Note: The relatedness between GPGs can be either complementary (C) or substitutive (S). The degree of relatedness between the GPGs is represented by h: high; m: moderate; l: low.

Assignment of Functions

After the identification of the GPGs, market failures as well as externalities, the following questions should be answered within the study of IIs:

- What are the functions for providing the GPGs in order to rectify global market failures and externalities?
- Which II or IIs should be assigned the function of providing one or more GPGs?
- How many IIs should take on the function of providing a certain GPG?
- Which GPGs should be provided?
- What amount of every GPG should be provided by global IIs?

To answer these questions we have to consider the following criteria:

- the type of economies of scale of production required to provide a specific GPG;
- which related GPGs can be jointly produced by an II, taking into account cost minimization;
- substitutive GPGs should be provided separately by different IIs, since there is competition among such goods;
- which input factors are needed to provide a GPG and what is the relationship between the output of a GPG and the input of factors.

Design

To illustrate the problem of assigning a function we have used the global lender of last resort as an example. The function of being the lender of last resort has usually been assigned to the central bank which issues the national currency and therefore has unlimited capacity to provide credit to sound financial institutions suffering from a bank run or similar difficulties. In this way it may rescue the sound financial institutions and rectify the financial crisis. In the global financial world, especially after the Asian crisis, the global lender of last resort has been intensively discussed. Is there a need for a global lender of last resort and which II can take over the function of the global lender of last resort? The opinions of economists in relation to this issue are varied.

3 THE ROLE OF INTERNATIONAL INSTITUTIONS IN GLOBALISATION

Characteristics of the Current World Economy

The current world economy can be characterised by the following important facts:

1. Internationalisation of production processes (fragmentation) with increasing international trade of intermediate products which enhances the international transmission of business cycles. The internationalisation of the production process is also a result of foreign direct investment (FDI) and the liberalisation of trade, which are in turn the results of reduced transaction and transportation costs.
2. Increasing use of information and communication technology (ICT) and the international trade of intellectual products.
3. The use of ICT divides the world into dualistic societies: about one-third of the world's population is excluded from access to ICT, which in turn increases the income gap between the rich and poor countries.
4. Globalisation of financial markets and rapid expansion of global financial flows. Global financial transactions have expanded rapidly over the last few decades. The daily amount of international financial transactions has been far higher than the international trade of goods and services.
5. High volatility of exchange rates and the building of currency blocs. Since the collapse of the Bretton Woods system of fixed exchange rates and floating exchange rate regimes have been implemented, exchange rates have become volatile. Because of imperfect markets, small firms have not had access to the derivative markets to hedge against the risk of exchange rate fluctuation.
6. Currency, debt and financial crisis with contagion effects. The world economy has suffered from currency, debt and financial crises, especially as a result of the contagion effects from crises in various countries. More than 100 countries have been confronted with such a crisis. Therefore, crisis management has become an important issue.
7. Highly volatile commodity prices and terms of trade deterioration *vis-à-vis* the developing countries. In recent times, commodity prices have been volatile. Stabilisation of these prices has been an important issue for the LDCs. The long-run deterioration of the terms of trade *vis-à-vis* the LDCs has also been an important topic with regard to poverty reduction.

Trading System and the WTO

Trade liberalisation has significantly increased global GDP since the end of the Second World War. With several rounds of trade negotiations (Kennedy, Tokyo, Uruguay), the GATT has mainly contributed to providing the GPG 'trading system' explicitly mentioned by Kindleberger. The GATT was not an IO but an II which enabled international negotiations that focused on the development of a liberal global trading system. One of the main results of the Uruguay Round was the establishment of the World Trade Organization. The global society took almost 50 years from the Havana Charter to establish the WTO in 1995. This new IO has an expanded mandate and its membership is almost universal. In 1995 the WTO Agreement transformed the GATT into a fully fledged IO. The WTO consists of three mandates (adding services and intellectual property to its existing mandate in goods, that is, GATT, GATS (Agreement on Trade in Services) and TRIPs (trade-related aspects of intellectual property rights) with a binding dispute settlement mechanism (DSM). The WTO together with the IMF and the World Bank are now the three most important IIs providing GPGs such as a trading system, international money and capital flows and global knowledge.

The WTO has the following ordinary functions:

- managing the rule–based trading system;
- the constant process of monitoring the operations;
- application of the full range of WTO agreements consisting of tariff cuts, domestic support and export subsidies;
- dispute settlement;
- monitoring development in individual countries; and
- processing the accession demands of some 30 countries.

This work is done by about 530 staff. The WTO has tried to organise new rounds for trade liberalisation negotiation since its establishment in 1995. The Qatar conference of the WTO in November 2001 started new trade negotiations in order to reduce barriers in goods and services trade, with agriculture on the agenda too (a priority for America and many developing countries). It is expected that a draft declaration will commit WTO members to improving market access for farm products, reducing agricultural export subsidies and cutting trade-distorting domestic support. According to the World Bank forecast of October 2001, the elimination of import tariffs, export subsidies and domestic production subsidies would increase global income by $2.8 trillion over ten years, with well over half the benefits going to poor countries (see *The Economist* 3–9 November 2001, p. 77). There are interactions between the externalities and market failures in the markets of intellectual properties, FDI and the global environment. The WTO negotiation programme must deal with these issues.

International Financial Architecture

More than 100 countries have faced financial, currency or debt crisis since the establishment of the Bretton Woods institutions. The contagion effects of crises, especially since the crisis in Thailand in 1997, have shown not only the failures of financial and money markets but also the externalities involved. Similarly to the debate about the New International Economic Order, in UNCTAD (United Nations Conference on Trade and Development) in the 1970s, the problems of strengthening the international financial system or constructing an international financial architecture have received comparable priority in the discussion of international economic problems and IIs. Issues such as policies for preventing and resolving financial crises have received increasing priority since the Asian crisis.

Asymmetric information, moral hazard, bank runs and so on have been seen as reasons for the failure of financial markets. Credit rating, credit information, deposit insurance, lender of last resort and so on have been used as measures to prevent and to solve a local financial crisis. Bankruptcy law is used in most developed countries to reduce the externalities caused by a bankruptcy. In the current discussion, similar measures have been proposed for strengthening the international financial architecture. The financial markets are characterised by non-symmetric processes for market expansion and shrinking. Usually, the process of expansion to realise the multiplier effect of money creation is much slower than the process of shrinking, especially in the case of bank runs which take place very rapidly and reduce the money volume with a multiplier effect within a very short period, as shown in Figure 1.1.

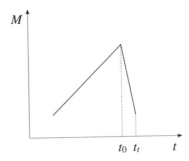

Figure 1.1   Asymmetric money expansion and shrinking process in the case of a bank run

The process of expansion of an initial deposit at a bank from M_0 to M_1 realises the multiplier effect in a period t_0. But the process of shrinking caused by a bank run from M_1 to M_0 will realise the multiplier effect within a period from t_1 to t_0 which is much shorter than t_0. Therefore, the rescue actions provided by the lender of last resort are necessary independently of the soundness of the banking system if a shrinking process is caused by a psychological shock causing a bank run.

A global credit insurance institution, a global court of bankruptcy and a global lender of last resort have been proposed in the discussion about strengthening the international financial system. After identification, we have to examine the assignment of these functions to one or several IIs (either new or already existing ones).

As in the case of the trading system there is an urgent need for a well-performing international financial architecture.

4   SUMMARY

In this chapter I began with the main issues for the study of international institutions on the basis of providing global public goods, to rectify market failures and externalities. They included: (1) justification for the existence of IIs; (2) how IIs come into being; (3) process for providing GPGs; (4) realisation of optimal global institutional design; (5) how to solve overlapping jurisdiction problems of IIs; (6) coordination of global activities between IOs; (7) democratic accountability of IIs and IOs; (8) voting systems; (9) ideological background and theoretical principles for the justification of IIs and decisions about GCAs; and (10) evaluation and analysis of the efficiency of IIs and IOs and of the effectiveness of GCAs.

In Section 2, a general approach was proposed to study international institutions. First, global public goods, market failures and externalities have to be identified. According to Stiglitz there are six areas of GPGs: global security; global economic stability; knowledge; global environment; humanitarian assistance; and global health. The interactions among the GPGs are essential for assigning their functions to one or several IIs. Therefore, before dealing with this latter issue, the relatedness or, in the terminology of Stiglitz, the interactions among the global public goods, externalities and market failures were discussed. Two special forms of being related, namely complementary and substitutive relationships, were identified.

Then the assignment of functions to IIs was considered. The role of IIs in globalisation, which was the general topic of the first conference of the CSI at the Faculty of Social and Economic Sciences of the University of Innsbruck, was discussed in Section 3. In this final section, we began by presenting the main characteristics of the current world economy and then proceeded to discuss the recent development of IIs, especially the role of the WTO, the IMF and the World Bank in globalisation.

REFERENCES

Bordo, Michael D. (2000), 'The International Monetary Fund: its present role in historical perspective', NBER Working Paper 7724, National Bureau of Economic Research.

Chen, John-ren (1993), 'A generalization of modelling for markets of substitutive raw materials: effects if introducing new good on the volatility of price and trade volume of the gross substitutes', *Seoul Journal of Economics*, **6**, 267–82.

Chen, John-ren (1994), 'Modelling of related commodities and its implications for stabilization policy of the world market', *Journal of Agricultural Economics*, **55**, 139–66.

Collier, P. and J.W. Gunning (1999), 'The IMF's role in structural adjustment', *Economic Journal*, **109** (459), 634–51.

Fischer, Stanley (1999), 'Reforming the international financial system', *Economic Journal*, **109** (459), 557–76.

Frey, Bruno (1997), 'The public choice of international organizations', in D.C. Mueller (ed.), *Perspectives on Public Choice: A Handbook*, Cambridge: Cambridge University Press, pp. 106–23.

Gilbert, Christopher, A. Powell and D. Vines (1999), 'Positioning the World Bank', *Economic Journal*, **109** (459), 598–633.

Greenwald, B. and J.E. Stiglitz (1986), 'Externalities in markets with imperfect information and incomplete markets', *Quarterly Journal of Economics*, **101** (2), 229–64.

Hotelling, H. (1931), 'The economics of exhaustible resources', *JPE*, **39**, 137–75.

Kindleberger, Charles (1986), 'International public goods without international government', *American Economic Review*, **76** (1), 1–13.

Krueger, Anne O. (1998), 'Whither the World Bank and the IMF?', *Journal of Economic Literature*, **36** (4), 1983–2020.

Krugman, Paul (1997), 'What should trade negotiation negotiate about?', *Journal of Economic Literature*, **35** (1), 113–20.

Laird, Sam (2000), 'Dolphins, turtles, mad cows and butterflies: a look at the multilateral trading system in the 21st century', Paper presented to the International Economics Study Group 25th Annual Conference, Isle of Thorns, University of Sussex, 8–10 September.

McKibbin, W.J. (1988), 'The economics of international policy coordination', *Economic Record*, **64**, 241–53.

Olson, Mancur (1965), *The Logic of Collective Action*, Cambridge, MA: Harvard University Press.

Ostrom, Elinor (2000), Collective action and the evolution of social norms', *Journal of Economic Perspectives*, **14** (3) 137–58.

Rogoff, Kenneth (1999), 'International institutions for reducing global financial instability', NBER Working Paper 7265, National Bureau of Economic Research.

Samuelson, Paul A. (1954), 'The pure theory of public expenditure', *Review for Economics and Statistics*, **36**, 387–9.

Stiglitz, J.E. (1989), 'On the economic role of the state', in A. Heertje (ed.), *The Economic Role of the State*, Oxford: Basil Blackwell, pp. 9–85.

Stiglitz J.E. (1991), 'The economic role of the state: efficiency and effectiveness', in T.P. Hardiman and M. Mulreany (eds), *Efficiency and Effectiveness*, Dublin: Institute of Public Administration, pp. 37–59.

Stiglitz, J.E. (1995), 'The theory of international public goods and architecture of international organization', United Nations Background Paper 7, Department for Economic and Social Information and Policy Analysis, July.

Stiglitz, J.E. (1999a), 'Knowledge as a global public good', in *Global Public Goods*, New York: United Nations Development Programme.

Stiglitz, Joseph E. (1999b), 'The World Bank at the millenium', *Economic Journal*, **109** (459), 577–97.

Stiglitz, J.E. (2000), 'Globalization and the logic of collective action: Re-examining the Bretton Woods institutions', www.wider.unu.edu/publications/1998-1999-5-1/1998-1999-5-9.pdf.

2. The Tobin tax revisited in the context of global governance on capital markets

Kwan S. Kim and Seok-Hyeon Kim*

1 INTRODUCTION

Capital flight and high volatility in exchange rate markets have been recurrent problems for the global financial system, particularly in the wake of the adoption of floating rate regimes in 1971. Coupled with the enormous size of global exchange markets, the increasing volatility of the exchange rates began to reveal the unstable nature of the flexible exchange rate system. By the mid-1990s, the global volume of daily foreign exchange turnover had reached 1.2 trillion dollars. The annual global transactions in equity markets and in goods and services were, respectively, $21 trillion and $5 trillion and the total reserves of central banks were around $1.5 billion at the end of 1995. The important point to note is the linkage between unregulated cross-border capital inflows and frequent outbreaks of global financial turmoil observed in the past two decades. While such global crises would be the result of many other factors – both internal and external to the domestic economy, excessive short-term inflows far beyond the quantities required for the financing of trade and capital or long-term capital can be seen as an important cause for frequent financial and near-financial crises.

Emerging and transitional markets have been particularly vulnerable to financial crises. In the wake of the drastic devaluations in Europe in 1992/93, there have been a series of major financial crises in eight emerging markets of Mexico (1994/95), Thailand (1997), Indonesia (1997), South Korea (1997), Russia (1999), Brazil (2000), Turkey (2001) and Argentina (2002). The crises in these emerging markets have generally been preceded by either their sudden financial liberalization or unregulated access to global capital markets. As other transitional or emerging economies continue to liberalize their capital market, they will likely make themselves vulnerable to the exposure of speculative global capital attacks.

Various efforts and proposals have been made to address the problems of capital flight and instability in exchange markets. Most significant in this regard is the Tobin tax named after James Tobin in the wake of the breakdown of the Bretton Woods pegged exchange regime in the early 1970s. The proposed tax scheme was a modest one. A tax was to be imposed on the transactions in exchange markets at a rate that would not be excessive in relation to the pretax exchange transaction cost. Its main purpose would be to discourage speculative capital movements. Since speculative capital has large turnovers, this would increase the tax burden. As long as instability of exchange markets is correlated with speculative capital movements, such a tax can be considered effective in reducing the volatility in exchange markets.

Controversies concerning the Tobin tax will be examined in this chapter with respect to four aspects of the tax: desirability, feasibility, effectiveness, and revenue of the tax.[1] The question of desirability of the tax is addressed in Section 2. It explores the perceived benefits and costs of the Tobin tax, also addressing the neoliberal critique of distortionary effects of the tax. Section 3 is about the feasibility of the tax, dealing with the question of how successfully the potential tax evasion can be minimized on technical as well as on political grounds. Section 4 assesses the effectiveness of the tax. The question posed is: to what extent could the Tobin tax prove effective in stabilizing foreign exchange markets? Section 5 examines the revenue impact of the Tobin tax by exploring the potential size and allocation of tax proceeds. The concluding section highlights from the political-economy perspective the issues of global governance in tax administration.

2   DESIRABILITY OF THE TAX

We begin with the question: why is the currency tax necessary? The main objective of the Tobin tax is to reduce or dampen the volatility of exchange markets, which is seen as attributable to unchecked international capital flows. The support for the tax is thus based on the need for a more stable exchange rate regime by constraining international financial mobility.

Neoliberal economists are generally averse to any government intervention on markets. It is argued, for instance, that the Tobin tax would distort markets that otherwise would be more efficient in determining the exchange rates and in allocating capital across national boundaries (Dooley 1996). With only mixed evidence of market distortions from free capital movements, Dooley considers any forms of government intervention or policy as a potential source of distortions in financial resource allocation. He further questions the wisdom of distinguishing between short- and long-term investment, which is the critical distinction in the Tobin tax. Dooley contends that investments based on the economic fundamentals are not necessarily related to long-term projects. Direct investors abroad have many ways to hedge against the risks from a long-term investment. Direct investment does not have to be of any longer duration than short-term investment would be (ibid.: 93–8). Similar opposition to public sector intervention can be found in the typical monetarist (for example, Milton Friedman) view that attributes the instability in exchange markets to erratic monetary policies. Repudiating the monetarist view, the supporters of the Tobin tax rely on empirical evidence. Clearly, the data gleaned from experiences in the European Monetary System (EMS) and a broad range of developing countries fail to substantiate the monetarist claim (Eichengreen and Wyplosz 1996). It is worth noting that the defenders of the tax are concerned more with the hindering effects of exchange rate volatility on multilateral trade and investment than the distortionary effects focussed on by neoliberal critics.

As regards the volatility issue, Arestis and Sawyer (1999) confirm evidence for strong volatility in exchange rates. They further observe that the swings in general tend to be sustained for a long period. Since 1980, the monthly average of the standard deviation of the sterling/DM rates was 3.9 per cent with the ratio of the minimum to maximum per year ranging from 5 to 22 per cent. Mussa's empirical study (1986; also cited in Arestis and Sawyer 1999) shows a strong correlation between nominal exchange rates and real exchange rates in the short term, implying persistent deviations from purchasing power parity. From cross-currency comparisons, he finds that for approximately one-third of quarters the rate of change deviated by more than 5 per cent from the average. This deviation can be viewed as reflecting an asset bubble, which Frankel (1996) explains in the context of a rational bubble model. The model illustrates the process of a bubble formation in exchange markets from the behaviors of two agents: fundamentalist and chartist (technical analyst). While the fundamentalists make a decision based on the economic fundamentals, the chartists who seek short-term profits extrapolate the latest trends in the markets without paying much attention to the long-term fundamentals. As long as the economy rides on the upswing, the chartists enjoy successes. With the profits being sustained, the chartists may dominate market trends while accelerating the bubbles in the process. But sudden events outside the markets can burst the bubble, driving the economy into a deep fall. DeGrauwe and Dewachter (1990 and 1995; also cited in Frankel 1996: 55) similarly demonstrate that such opposite behaviors of two agents generate chaotic price movements, failing to exhibit any convergent trends.

We now take a straightforward look at the issue of the Tobin tax in the context of global governance. We start with a position that the financial crises around the world cannot all be attributed to mismanagement of a national economy, as we observe a number of instances of contagion effects by which a country cannot remain immune from the forces of global capital flows. Despite the enormous costs incurred by the economic crises in the past decade, there is still no assurance that financial crises may recur in future. Rather than exclusively blaming individual country policies, there is a need to search for proper measures of governing global issues in the global context.

There are many control devices that have been suggested for and used in regulating free flows of short-term capital, in particular of the portfolio type. The list includes, for example, the dual exchange rate regime, administrative prohibition and compulsory deposit requirements on bank lending and borrowing from non-residents (Eichengreen and Wyplosz 1996: 16). It is beyond the scope of this chapter to compare the advantages and disadvantages of all these regulations. This chapter looks into the merits of the Tobin tax as a logical candidate from the perspective of global governance on capital flows.

What the advocates of the Tobin tax suspect as an important cause of global financial instability is short-term turnovers of international currency markets that do not move in step with the fundamentals of the real economy. Felix and Sau (1996) summarize the overwhelming expansion of the exchange market, which is inconsistent with other major economic indicators. In particular, the following features that may have contributed to the instability of the exchange market are discernible.

Growth in exchange markets has been driven by financial capital and not by trade financing. In 1998 global exports accounted for a mere 1.5 per cent of the total annual exchange transactions. They fell from 23.6 per cent in 1977 (Table 2.1). The ratio of central banks' foreign exchange reserves to the total exchange transaction volume similarly declined from 13.4 in 1977 to 1.1 by 1998 (Table 2.1). This raises a serious question as to whether central banks could cope with the volatile situation in exchange markets. It is worth noting that transactions among the exchange dealers have exceeded those by non-dealers, with the former accounting for about 64 per cent of global turnover in 1995 and about 59 per cent by 2001. Transactions with the non-financial customers constituted only about 17 per cent in 1998 and about 13 per cent in 2001 (Table 2.2). The huge size and rapid rates of exchange turnover should provide the rationale for the Tobin tax. Tobin originally suggested the tax rate of 1, changing later to a rate less than 0.25 per cent under the recommendation that the tax rate should not be excessive in relation to the transaction fees (Tobin 1996). If the volume of transaction is assumed unchanged, a 0.1 per cent tax rate applied to $312 trillion of annual transactions would generate a revenue of $312 billion (Haq et al. 1996). The Tobin tax is aimed at affecting more the short-term turnovers and discouraging speculative capital movements, thereby stabilizing exchange markets.

Frankel (1996: 62) focusses on inter-dealer dealing in estimating the effects of the tax. With the Tobin tax, the structure of the exchange market is expected to change because the inter-dealer transactions are far more sensi-

Table 2.1 World exports, world reserves and foreign exchange trading volume

	Annual global foreign exchange transaction volume* (US$bn)	Annual world exports (US$bn)	Annual world exports to foreign exchange transaction volume (%)	Daily global foreign exchange transaction volume (US$bn)	Foreign exchange reserves at the end of each year (US$bn)	Foreign exchange reserve/ daily foreign exchange transaction volume (natural unit)
1977	4 575	1 080.5	23.6	18.3**	245.7	13.4
1980	20 625	1 931.7	9.4	82.5**	385.5	4.7
1983	29 750	1 736.0	5.8	119**	340.6	2.9
1986	67 500	2 048.5	3.0	270**	399.6	1.5
1989	147 500	3 008.5	2.0	590	716.5	1.2
1992	205 000	3 713.9	1.8	820	926.1	1.1
1995	297 500	5 099.8	1.7	1 190	1 385.4	1.2
1998	372 500	5 405.8	1.5	1 490	1 635.8	1.1
2001	312 000	6 008.0	1.9	1 200	2 031.6	1.7

Notes:

*   Calculated by the daily volume multiplied by 250 days.

** From Haq et al. (1996: Table A.2).

Sources: IMF (2002), and BIS (2002: Table B.1).

Table 2.2 Daily global foreign exchange turnover by counterparty (US$bn)

	1989*		1992		1995		1998		2001	
	$bn	%	$bn	%	$bn	%	$bn	%	$bn	%
With reporting dealers	436	74	541	69.7	728	64.0	909	63.6	689	58.7
With other financial institutions	—	—	96	12.4	230	20.2	279	19.5	329	28.0
With non-financial customers	154	26	137	17.7	179	15.7	241	16.9	156	13.3
Total	590	100	774	99.8	1137	99.9	1429	100	1174	100

Note: *From Haq et al. (1996: A.3).

Source: BIS (2002: Table B.3).

tive to the tax than the customer transactions. For example, if the ratio of the total transactions to the customer transactions decreases from 5:1 to 2:1, this would result in about a half-size of the total market volume.

Felix and Sau (1996) analyze in detail how finance-oriented exchange transactions can be influenced by the Tobin tax. They argue that any sharp increase in the exchange volume would be due to the covered interest arbitrage. Financial investors could purchase foreign equities – say, those with one month maturity – and simultaneously sell foreign currencies forward due one month later. This way, they could take advantage of small interest rate differentials as long as these are sufficient to cover the transaction cost. Since 1970, interest differentials have been very close to the actual transaction cost. To generate significant profits, the investors need to rely on high volumes of transactions, which may have increased the volatility of exchange rates. Had the Tobin tax been implemented, conceivably small variations in interest rates could no longer motivate financial investors to engage in arbitrage activities.

Reductions in transaction volume generate two additional benefits. First, in a market with reduced transaction volume, financial investors would face increased costs and risks and would be discouraged from arbitrage. Second, the exchange reserves of the national economy relative to the total transaction volume would rise, which strengthens the country's position in defending against currency speculations.

As regards the neoclassical critique against the tax, Arestis and Sawyer (1999) point out that the Tobin tax would be imposed only on the exchange transactions that result essentially in a zero-sum game and are not directly linked to the real sector of the economy. The merits of suppressing excessive capital flows in global markets are best summarized by Dernberg (1989: 459):

> A reform that makes exchange rates more sensitive to current-account conditions should reduce excessive and persistent misalignment, yielding less instability in the trade sectors and a better allocation of resources, even if it is purchased at the price of more short-term 'jumpiness' of exchange rates.

3 FEASIBILITY OF THE TAX

The feasibility issue is examined below in terms of both the technical and political aspects. Some economists are concerned about the possibility of extensive tax evasion, which could defeat the broad goal of the Tobin tax. Technically, the evaders could find or create substitutable ways for exchange transactions or find an alternative exchange marketplace to evade the taxation. While the defenders of the tax agree with the critics' view concerning tax evasion, they see feasible ways to minimize the evasion problem. The defenders see that the major hurdle is not so much in the techniques of reducing the evasion as in the political economy aspect. After discussing the technical feasibility in tax implementation, we shall turn to the political-economy issue.

First, it will be useful to review the working of foreign exchange trade in the currency market. In Appendix 1 the functions of participants, instruments, and types of market in trading markets are explained. As shown in Table 2.2, in exchange transactions the wholesale market (roughly, inter-dealer market, 58.7 per cent in 2001) is typically larger than the remaining retail market. In the wholesale market the dealers quote bid and ask prices. The difference between them reflects the cost of dealers, which constitutes the main part of transactions costs. The spread is normally less than 0.1 per cent, or 10 basis points (Kenen 1996).

Another feature of exchange markets is that most transactions are based on spots, outward forward, and swaps. Futures and options are relatively unimportant in size. Traditionally, spot transactions have dominated, but lately hedges, forwards, swap funds, and other types of derivatives have increased their share (Table 2.3).

The first issue about tax evasion is potential migration of taxation sites. To understand the issue of tax site, we need to distinguish between the booking site and the dealing site. When a deal is made within the same country or between two countries, the dealer can book a deal at his or her office or bank in the country where the deal is made. In this case, the dealing site and the booking site would be the same. If the dealer books the deal at his or her head office in the country which does not have the dealing site, the booking site can be different from the dealing site. Because exchange transactions generally involve two currencies, the exchange trade is cleared in two countries (Kenen 1996: 111–12). Migration can occur since the dealers have a choice of exchange dealing site where no tax is imposed. There are then two possible venues in collecting the tax: one based on the location of dealing and the other on the location of booking. Kenen recommends the dealer site to encourage participation of the countries that have large financial centers or markets.[2]

This idea, however, may run into another possibility of migration. A country may not agree to the Tobin tax and allow for a tax-free zone that attracts exchange dealing businesses to help boost the domestic economy. But this is not a realistic scenario because the tax revenue itself can be more beneficial to the country than hosting a dealing business. To avoid extreme cases of migration, Kenen suggests that all countries that may have the potential to have the tax haven must agree to the tax and that the rates should be low enough (0.05 per cent) to discourage the evasion. This contrasts with Tobin's original proposition that only the advanced industrial countries with their

Table 2.3 Daily global foreign exchange turnover by instrument (US$bn)

	1989		1992		1995		1998		2001	
	$bn	%	$bn	%	$bn	%	$bn	%	$bn	%
Spot	317	53.7	394	48.0	494	41.5	568	38.1	387	32.0
Outright forwards	27	4.6	58	7.1	97	8.2	128	8.6	131	10.8
Swaps	190	32.2	324	39.5	546	45.9	734	49.3	656	54.2
Estimated gaps	56	9.5	44	5.4	53	4.5	60	4.0	26	3.0
Total 'traditional' turnover	590	100	820	100	1190	100*	1490	100	1200	100

Note: * The total may exceed 100 per cent due to rounding.

Source: BIS (2002: Table B.1).

large shares in exchange markets need to agree to the tax. It would be unrealistic to presume that investors depart from the well-established financial centers just to avoid the taxation. In case of migration, the International Monetary Fund (IMF) could coerce some regulations, exerting its influence on these countries (Tobin 1996: xiv).

Recently, Schmidt (1999) and Spahn (2002) have suggested a new possibility in determining the location of the tax. They emphasize technological development in settling international exchange transactions in a more centralized and traceable way. Currently, 12 countries in the euro area are using RTGS (Real Time Gross Settlement) to settle bilateral transactions. Contrary to clearing-house systems where each central bank settles only the balances netted out from the brokerage house,[3] the RTGS system traces the sources of each transaction, keeping intact the gross amounts of transactions.[4]

Furthermore, a multilateral settling system called CLS (Continuous Link Settlement, as an extension of RTGS) was launched in September 2002 (*Financial Times Mandate*, 23 September 2002). These developments have been motivated to reduce settlement risks and to enhance transparency. Ultimately, they could be used in broadening the base for the Tobin tax and in reducing tax evasion. Similar to the CLS model, alternative locations of tax administration are conceived by Schmidt and Spahn, who suggest that a centralized settlement system collect tax revenues into a centralized pool. This would assure much easier and more transparent methods of collecting the Tobin tax.

The other issue regarding tax evasion is possibilities of substitution between different types of transaction instruments. Investors could switch to other tax-free instruments or they could create alternative ones. Thus, it becomes necessary to specify the types of instruments for taxation purposes. While spot and forward markets remain the main targets for taxation, the questions of whether and how the derivative securities should be taxed are controversial. Tobin originally thought that the tax could be confined to spots but accepted Kenen's view that forwards and swaps should also be taxed to prevent tax evasion. But he argues that the derivatives do not have to be taxed until the time when the contract is realized (Tobin 1996: xv).

In the case of futures, Kenen agrees with Tobin because futures should be settled at some point. But in the case of options, the dealers may use an option for tax evasion by taking advantage of the fact that the option contract does not require a settlement for transaction. This could result in disproportionately faster growth in the option markets, rendering the Tobin tax ineffective (Kenen 1996: 118). Tobin and Griffith-Jones, nonetheless, consider that taxing only on the final settlement that accompanies spot transactions would be sufficient (Tobin 1996: xv; Griffith-Jones 1996: 155). Referring to the UK's stamp duty experience,[5] it is pointed out that in the UK with its highly developed financial market full of all kinds of derivatives, stamp duty has been imposed on all financial transactions. Despite many potential loopholes in derivative markets, the authorities have managed to minimize evasion efforts by treating, for example, the exercise of an option as a purchase of ordinary shares at the exercise price.

As for new instruments for tax evasion, Garber (1996) provides an example. If spot transactions are allowed as an exchange of bank deposits subject to taxation denominated in different currencies, investors can choose treasury bonds as a swap instrument to evade the Tobin tax. They could settle the transactions by the treasury bills that are not taxed and then switch from treasury bonds to the bank deposits. On this problem, Tobin and Kenen point out that the swaps for treasury bills would decrease liquidity and that new tax codes could easily be enacted to regulate treasury bond transactions.

Critics of the Tobin tax have thus been mainly concerned with the difficulties in covering all possible loopholes, given the complexity of the exchange market. In reality, however, there is hardly any type of tax even at a local level that could perfectly prevent tax evasion. Domestic tax revenues from financial transactions in many countries have been quite low since multinational firms in the era of globalization easily find loopholes in global tax systems (Kaul et al. 1996: 10). Thus to enhance the base of the Tobin tax, closely coordinated implementation programs must be called for between the financial and the real sectors on a global scale. In general, advocates for the Tobin tax argue that once the tax code is agreed to cover the major categories of exchange transaction, it would become costly and risky to contrive new transaction instruments or derivative products in order to evade taxation. The tax code could easily be updated if tax evasions become frequent.

It seems then that the feasibility issue falls not so much on the technical aspect as on the political one. Given the conflicting interests in the Tobin tax among nations and diverse interest groups, it would certainly be a challenging task even to attempt to build consensus around the broad goal of international taxation. Despite the apparent obstacles, there has recently been growing and widely held interest in the tax not only from academic circles but also from the political arena. Tobin first proposed his idea of the tax in 1972 when the Bretton Woods system with its fixed exchange rate regime collapsed. Amidst the prevalence of optimism for flexible exchange rates during the 1970s and the 1980s, Tobin's proposal had largely been overlooked (Tobin 1996: x). With increased liberalization on capital flows and frequent instances of the currency crisis in the 1990s, discussions on the Tobin tax have re-emerged (Kaul et al. 1996: 2).

Despite the frequent speculative attacks affecting the stability of the currency market in the 1990s, the IMF has, however, shown no particular sign of policy change. During the 1994–95 Mexican crisis, the IMF, which had tried unsuccessfully to eliminate the Articles of Restrictions, began to pay some attention to the limited reliance on taxes and restrictions on selected international financial transactions at the Halifax summit in 1995 (Griffith-Jones 1996: 145). At the conference of the American Economic Association in 1996, Stanley Fisher, First Deputy Managing Director of the IMF, admitted that the Tobin tax could serve as a potentially useful device only if the enforcement problem could be solved (Tobin 1996: xi). Nonetheless, even after the subsequent financial crises in East Asia in 1997–98, the IMF has kept the idea of the Tobin tax at bay. After the meeting with 18 non-governmental groups in September 2001, Horst Kohler, the IMF's new managing director expressed the Fund's ambiguous position about the Tobin tax (*Financial Times*, 11 September, 2001). The Fund's indeterminacy is linked to insensitive reactions of its powerful member countries.

The US disfavored any form of capital restrictions and passed in the Senate a law specifically prohibiting any discussions in the United Nations about the Tobin tax.[6] The British government also explicitly rejected any attempt to introduce the Tobin tax. The European Union's financial ministers also expressed their view that the Tobin tax would not be a workable measure to prevent global financial instability.[7] Other opinions of banks and financial agents in rich countries can be added to the list of the anti-Tobin tax group. According to Patomäki (2001), the US–UK nexus has long evolved by way of the euro-dollar market centered in London since the 1960s. The US provides many advantages to American financial corporations and multinational companies in making financial deals at the London market. As a result, London emerged as the leading financial center in parallel with New York. In order to maintain their roles in the global market, both nations have pushed toward increased liberalization.

The Anglo-American opposition to the Tobin tax notwithstanding, there has been growing dissension among other nations. The Canadian parliament passed a proposal to adopt the Tobin tax in 1999.[8] The Lower House in France endorsed the Tobin tax in 2001 even though the Senate overturned it later. A number of European leaders such as Lionel Jospin – former prime minister of France, President Jacques Chirac of France, and Chancellor Gerhard Schröder of Germany have supported the Tobin tax. The United Nations has taken a supportive position on the tax as a feasible solution to resolve its budget problem (UNDP 1994). The UN's interest in the Tobin tax largely reflects its concern with the economic development of poor countries. The Tobin tax is considered helpful because of its revenue potential for global developmental use as well as its contribution to global financial stability. In addition, civil movement groups or NGOs (nongovernmental organizations) strongly support the Tobin tax. Recognizing that only global-scale solutions can fix global problems, NGOs have spearheaded anti-WTO (World Trade

Organization) movements and have recently been focussing more on the Tobin tax. Such groups as Association for the Taxation of Financial Transaction for the Aid of Citizens (ATTAC) in France, Halifax in Canada, and War on Want in Britain have been putting pressure on both national and international governments to seriously consider implementation of the Tobin tax and have been attempting to build international consensus on this issue (Patomäki 2001: 181).

Recent years have also seen a surge of new ideas for circumventing institutional hindrances to the Tobin tax. Those ideas are specific to individual authors but can be collectively dubbed 'Politically Feasible Tobin Tax' (PFTT), as suggested by Spahn (2002). The key notion of PFTT is to implement the Tobin tax starting with any countries agreeing to the tax scheme. In the context of the contemporary global economy, the particular zone may start with the euro countries. According to Patomäki (2001), about thirty countries could initiate the Tobin tax so long as their exchange transactions cover about 20 per cent of the total size in the global economy. Since London is unlikely to join the first phase of taxation while foreign institutions account for 80 per cent of the total transactions in its market, Patomäki prefers to rely on the national tax base rather than on the market base as suggested by Kenen (1996). The Tobin tax with a low tax rate (for example, 0.1 per cent) within the tax zone and a high punitive tax rate (for example, 2 per cent) for the non-tax area is seen as sustainable.

4   EFFECTIVENESS OF THE TAX

Since the Tobin tax has not been put into practice, it is difficult to determine its effectiveness in stabilizing foreign exchange markets. A few studies point to the stabilizing impacts of the tax based on some reasonable assumptions of the model. There have also been a few observable cases of short-term capital control in emerging markets. Studies of these cases are illustrative of the effectiveness of the Tobin tax as they reveal observable experiences in mitigating excessive roles of capital flows in exchange markets.

Palley (1999) supports the idea of the Tobin tax based on his model of noise-traders. In the model there are two agents: the fundamentalist and the noise-trader.[9] The noise-trader can be bearish even in investment projects viewed as profitable in the eyes of the fundamentalist. The noise-trader may pull out cash from his or her portfolio investment where the fundamentalist stays on. But such a run on cash by the noise-trader works as a negative externality to the fundamentalist. The role of the noise-trader thus forces the fundamentalist to invest at less than the desirable level. Imposition of the Tobin tax can make the cost of cashing-out greater than the noise-trader's bearish estimation of the return and induce him or her not to make a move. The Tobin tax can be viewed as a device to reduce the negative externality and to keep the desired level of investment that would have been lower without the tax.

Jeanne (1996) illustrates the effectiveness of the Tobin tax by applying the target zone model to French franc and German mark movements in 1991–93. In the target zone model, the target exchange rates are established by taking account of international interest rate differentials. In the target zone model, the difference between the foreign interest and some desired domestic rate can be accommodated by exchange rate adjustments. The Tobin tax, however, allows a safe zone where exchange rate adjustments are not necessary. The tax ensures that in the framework of uncovered interest rate parity, the burden of the interest rate differentials need not be borne entirely by exchange adjustments. For instance, if the difference between the foreign interest and the desired domestic rate is less than the transaction cost attributable to the Tobin tax, then the domestic interest can be set exactly at the desired rate without potentially affecting the values of the exchange rate.

The Tobin tax should thus allow the policy makers more flexibility in targetting both the domestic interest rate and the exchange rate. Based on the calibrations on the parameters of the model, Jeanne demonstrates that with small Tobin tax rates the French interest rate could have been substantially lower than the actual one and close to the desired rate. This could have helped to prevent the speculation on the French franc.[10] Of course, the safe zone can be enlarged when either the Tobin tax rate is higher or exchange transactions are more frequent.

Turning to the actual cases of capital control, the recent Chilean experience is illustrative. Amidst the economic turmoil in the 1990s that engulfed many Latin American countries, Chile maintained a relatively healthy position avoiding a balance of payments crisis. The point is that the Tobin tax would have similar effects as the Chilean capital control experience. To reduce the volatility of capital flows after 1991, Chile required a deposit in foreign exchange on capital inflows, along with other regulatory measures. Chile required a 20 per cent deposit with a minimum of 90 days and a maximum of one year. The deposited reserves do not bear interest. As an alternative, medium-term capital inflows are allowed on the condition of paying the amount equivalent to the financial cost of reserve requirements. Either method is aimed at imposing the transaction cost at LIBOR plus 2.5 per cent. The Chilean episode of capital control provides an illustrative example of a workable exchange stabilization policy (Singh 2000: ch. 7).

Colombia also adopted similar measures in 1993. As a result of its capital control measures, Colombia succeeded in escaping from the boom–bust cycle, which had previously been attributed to uncontrolled capital flows. It is to be noted that both Chile and Colombia were able to avoid the contagion effects of both the 1994–95 Mexican crisis and the 1997 Asian crisis. On the other hand, following the liberalization plan advised by the IMF, Mexico has liberalized capital movements without distinguishing between foreign direct investment (FDI) and portfolios since 1989. It is worth noting that among many factors, the massive size of capital flows proved to be a detrimental factor for Mexico.

As shown in Table 2.4, those countries that adopted capital control measures had not only proportionately smaller portfolio inflows in relation to FDI but also more stable patterns in total inflows. Nonetheless, it is worth mentioning that the practice of capital controls is not well received by the neoliberal states. Because of international pressure, small developing countries found themselves in a difficult position to practice the controls. Chile, for instance, lifted the deposit requirements in 2000 and Malaysia also dropped the capital controls in 2001 that were enacted during the Asian crisis. It must be noted that the Tobin tax is not a perfect device to reduce the speculative currency transactions. It can be used as one among other possibilities. It cannot block sudden capital flows when the exchange rate change is anticipated to far exceed the normal transaction costs including the Tobin tax. The tax only helps to reduce the chances of exchange crises. Other measures that can serve

Table 2.4   Net inflows of FDI and portfolio (US$m)

	Chile		Colombia		Mexico	
	FDI	Portfolio	FDI	Portfolio	FDI	Portfolio
1987	885	−8	293	48	1 184	−1 399
1988	952	−8	159	0	2 011	121
1989	1 277	83	547	179	2 785	298
1990	653	361	484	−4	2 549	−3 985
1991	697	189	433	86	4 742	12 138
1992	537	458	679	126	4 393	19 206
1993	600	730	719	498	4 389	28 355
1994	1 672	908	996	87	10973	7 415
1995	2 205	34	713	1 434	9 526	−10 377
1996	3 446	1 100	2 784	1 609	9 186	13 961
1997	3 354	2 365	4 753	892	12 831	4 330
1998	1 840	−829	2 033	1 663	11 312	−1 346
1999	4 366	130	1 352	−701	11 915	10 130

Source: IMF (2002).

similar purposes include: requirement of reserve deposits, and quantitative limits on capital inflows, foreign exchange licensing, and multiple exchange rates. Policy makers can consider all possible options to find the best in a given situation.

5   REVENUE AND DISTRIBUTION OF THE TAX

The revenue from the tax was not the main motive in Tobin's proposal, but as a side-effect it could provide an important funding source for global development. The revenue potentials from the Tobin tax can be estimated using simulation models. To quantify the changes in the volume and composition of exchange transactions, one can simply multiply the global tax base by proposed tax rates. However, since the Tobin tax is aimed at reducing the exchange transactions that are regarded as irrelevant to the economic fundamentals, a better approach is to start with estimating the contraction of the tax base due to the tax, that is, to calculate the elasticity of transaction volume to the transaction cost (including the Tobin tax). The key idea in calculating the elasticity is to project possible contractions of the inter-dealer transactions compared to the customer transactions.

Felix and Sau (1996) elaborate an approach for calculating the elasticities. They deduct a certain percentage (for example, 35 per cent) of the transaction volume from the tax base to exclude such non-taxable components as public and informal transactions. Under the usual assumptions made about the revenue and cost functions applied to exchange transactions, they derive the optimal volume for transactions and the corresponding elasticity with respect to unit transaction cost. Their result shows that the value of the elasticity depends positively on the total volume of transactions (ibid.: 230). Hence, the Tobin tax can be judged as fairly effective with relatively high exchange transaction elasticities that may be assumed for the global capital markets, given the massive size of current capital flows. Postulating, therefore, that the Tobin tax should be adjusted to changing volumes of exchange transactions, they calculate the expected tax revenues for alternative values of the elasticities and tax rates, as shown in Table 2.5.

As for the use and distribution of the tax revenue, three issues must be addressed. First, how much revenue can be projected for the global economy and individual nations? Second, what would be the desirable global strategy in distributing the revenue? Third, what kind of institutional setting would be useful or proper international coordination?

Kaul and Langmore (1996) provide simulated results by selected nations on tax proceeds under alternative Tobin tax rates. They find that the potential revenues are unevenly distributed across nations (Table 2.6). For instance, the

Table 2.5 *Global revenue and foreign exchange turnover effects of a phased-in 0.25 per cent Tobin tax[1]*

Transaction cost	Taxable transaction volume[3] ($ trillions)	Tobin tax revenue ($bn)
Year 1 (tax = 0.1%, E = 1.5)[2]		
t1 = 1.1%	122.4	122.4
t2 = 0.6%	100.8	100.8
Year 2 (tax = 0.15%, E = 1.25)[4]		
t1 = 1.15%	115.5	173.3
t2 = 0.65%	92.4	138.6
Year 3 (tax = 0.2%, E = 1.0)		
t1 = 1.2%	110.6	221.1
t2 = 0.7%	86.9	173.8
Year 4 (tax = 0.25%, E = 0.75)		
t1 = 1.25%	107.0	267.6
t2 = 0.75%	82.2	205.5

Notes:
1. 'Phased-in tax' means that the tax rate is increased steadily many years before reaching the final rate (from 0.1% to 0.25%). Initial tax base is $144 trillion which is the figure arrived at by deducting 35% from $220 trillion (the transaction volume in 1992). The amount 35% is an estimation of the transactions that the Tobin tax is not applied to.
2. E is the elasticity; t1 = the pretax transaction cost (1%) plus the tax; t2 = the pretax transaction cost (0.5%) plus the tax.
3. Taxable volume is obtained by deducting from the tax base the volume which is calculated from: $d\log V / d\log t = -E$, where E is the elasticity and dt is the increase in the effective transaction cost due to imposition of the tax. In year 1 under the pretax transaction cost 1%, transaction volume is reduced from $144 trillion to $122.4 trillion by $21.6 trillion: $21.6 trillion = 1.5 (E) × 0.1 (dlogt) × $144 trillion.
4. Year 2 starts with the base tax of $122.4 trillion which was the taxable amount in year 1 and so on.

Source: Felix and Sau (1996: Table 9.1).

UK's revenue alone amounts to $44 billion (£29 billion) under 0.1 per cent tax rate as of 1995, which would be close to the UK's public sector borrowing requirements (£30 billion) (Felix and Sau 1996: 260). The revenue effect of the tax looms substantial in Singapore and Hong Kong despite their relatively small economic size. Huge sums of tax revenue would constitute a significant portion of government budget in these countries, thereby relieving ever-increasing pressures on government expenditure. As potential tax pro-

Table 2.6   *Annual revenue from Tobin tax by collecting country (1995 foreign exchange volume, US$bn)*

	Tax rate		
	0.25%	0.10%	
Industrial countries			
United Kingdom	89.0	43.7	(29.5)
United States	46.8	23.0	(15.5)
Japan	30.8	15.1	(10.2)
Switzerland	16.4	8.0	(5.4)
Germany	14.4	7.0	(4.7)
France	11.3	5.5	(3.7)
Australia	7.4	3.6	(2.4)
Denmark	5.7	2.9	(2.0)
Canada	5.5	2.6	(1.8)
Netherlands	4.7	2.2	(1.5)
Sweden	3.6	1.8	(1.2)
Other OECD	25.1	12.3	(8.3)
Group total	260.7	127.7	(86.2)
Developing countries			
Singapore	20.0	9.8	(6.6)
Hong Kong	17.1	8.4	(5.7)
South Africa	0.9	0.4	(0.3)
Bahrain	0.5	0.2	(0.1)
Other LDCs	2.9	1.7	(1.1)
Group total	41.4	20.5	(13.8)
Global total	302.1	148.2	(100.0)

Note: Pretax cost is assumed to be 0.5%. Figures in parentheses are percentage of total.

Source: Felix and Sau (1996).

ceeds are highly concentrated in a few countries as shown in Table 2.6, Kaul and Langmore argue that this point must be taken into account in discussions on the burden-sharing under global governance on tax administration. For instance, they suggest the following specific guidelines in dispensing with the tax proceeds for global development: high-income countries could retain 80 per cent of the proceeds; countries in the higher-middle-income bracket retaining 90 per cent of the proceeds; and the poor countries retaining the entire proceeds.[11]

Another point to note is the substantial size of the tax proceeds (Table 2.6). The tax revenues are estimated to exceed the actual United Nations' actual Official Development Assistance (ODA) reimbursement.[12] In this context, Felix and Sau see the urgency of strengthening and expanding the functionalities of the ODA and other global development agencies, as the global economy increasingly needs provisions of public goods on a global scale in such activities as regulating and controlling air and water pollution, preserving public health standards, maintaining international peace and security, and international labor migration and so on. The current way of funding based on the rich donor countries' good will falls far short of meeting the need.[13] The lenders need to see the mutuality of interests since they will also benefit from the global prosperity and stability.

The remaining question concerns the building of institutions to administer the tax proceeds. Kenen (1996) suggests the creation of a new international agency. As the first preliminary step he sees the need for a general agreement by the participating countries about the methods of taxation and distribution of the proceeds. In the subsequent step the new agency plans for the details of administration, which consist of the drafting and implementing tax codes, and the collection of the tax for global usage. The reason for a new institution is that existing institutions are seen to have a strong interest in managing tax proceeds and may fail to serve as an impartial institution.

Griffith-Jones and Tobin see the importance of having an agreement among a few key nations, extending later to other nations at large since reaching any universal agreement on such complex issues as global governance of the tax would be difficult and time-consuming. As for the choice of the agency considered best-suited for administering the tax, they recommend one of the existing institutions, for instance, either the IMF or the BIS (Bank for International Settlements) since these currently deal with international finance issues and thus would be the logical candidate for the new role (Tobin 1996; Griffith-Jones 1996).

In contrast, Patomäki (2001: ch. 7) suggests an alternative institution, dubbed the Tobin Tax Organization (TTO), which should be independent from the IMF. His critique of the IMF is based on two aspects of democracy and transparency. In so far as the decision-making rule of the IMF is 'one-dollar, one-vote', the IMF cannot be regarded as a democratic international institution as it is heavily influenced by economically powerful nations. He also notes that the IMF has been lacking transparency in its own accounting.

6   CONCLUDING REMARK

The massive size and the high volatility of exchange transactions in today's global markets underscore the need for international agreements to have a plan on a global scale to contain speculative capital movements and the attendant instability of exchange. The damaging effects of unfettered capital flows have been seen to affect more severely the transitional and emerging market economies, given their fragile financial infrastructure in defending against massive flows of exchange.

This chapter has shown that the Tobin tax is an effective and technically feasible form of taxation. Compared to other control devices of capital flows it has certain advantages in terms of simplicity and uniformity in implementation under a global governance on tax administration, and the effectiveness in reducing the volatility in exchange transactions. Furthermore, an important side-effect of the tax is the revenue of the tax which would allow substantial funding of many programs for Third World development, human capital development, global environment, and global security, including anti-terrorism cooperation. The Tobin tax could thus emerge as the first and important financing source for global development and financial stabilization under a global governance by a politically autonomous global institution. Despite the overall merits of the Tobin tax and/or other similar devices, there has been to date a lack of political will in rich countries – understandably by the groups of financiers and investors in these countries – even to seriously discuss the tax in international fora. The survey of studies on the tax shows that the main hurdle to the adoption of the Tobin tax placed under global governance has little to do with its effectiveness or technical feasibility but has largely to do with the political will of the international community.

NOTES

*   An earlier version of this paper was presented at the CSI Symposium 'The Role of International Institutions in Globalisation' held at the University of Innsbruck, Austria, 14–16 November 2001.
1. This evaluation scheme draws on Kaul et al. (1996: 2).
2. For the dominance of the UK and the US in foreign exchange markets, see Table 2A2.1.
3. In the UK, such a clearing-house system is called Clearing House Association Payments System (CHAPS).
4. The US uses both clearing systems: Clearing House Interbank Payment System (CHIPS) and Fedwire.
5. A tax imposed on the transfer of ownership in financial instruments.
6. The Helms–Dole Bill passed by the US Senate in 1996 bars the US from participating in the discussion on the Tobin tax.
7. *Financial Times*, 30 August 2001.
8. The parliament overturned it in 2002 under pressure from the US. See CBC broadcasting

commentary on 20 March 2002, downloaded at http://www.halifaxinitiative.org/hi.php/Tobin/255.

9. The fundamentalist makes a decision based on the economic fundamentals. The stock market activity of the noise-trader is influenced by Program Trades and other phenomena not reflective of general sentiment.

10. The author concludes that a 0.1 per cent Tobin tax could have helped avoid the collapse of the EMS.

11. Tobin has a similar idea. He thinks that at least 50 per cent should be retained by each country with 100 per cent for small countries (Tobin 1996: xvii).

12. According to Felix and Sau (1996: 267), under the 0.1 per cent tax rate the tax proceeds allocated to international agencies would amount to $27 billion. This contrasts with ODA aid of $17 billion in 1994.

13. International public spending amounts to a mere 0.3 per cent of the budgets in several donor countries (Kaul and Langmore 1996: 262).

REFERENCES

Arestis, Philip and Malcom Sawyer (1999), 'What role for the Tobin tax in world economic governance', in Mitchie et al. (eds), 151–70.

BIS (Bank for International Settlements) (2002), 'Triennial central bank survey of foreign exchange and derivative market activity in 2001', Basle: BIS, www.bis.org/publ/rpfx02t.pdf, 27 March 2003.

DeGrauwe, Paul and Hans Dewachter (1990), 'A chaotic monetary model of the exchange rate', CEPR Discussion Paper 466, Centre for Economic Policy Research, London.

DeGrauwe, Paul and Hans Dewachter (1995), *Exchange Rate Economics*, Cambridge: Cambridge University Press.

Dernberg, Thomas F. (1989), *Global Macroeconomics*, New York: Harper & Row.

Dooley, Michael P. (1996), 'The Tobin tax: good theory, weak evidence, questionable policy', in Haq et al. (eds), 83–108.

Eichengreen, Barry and Charles Wyplosz (1996), 'Taxing international financial transactions to enhance the operation of the International Monetary System', in Haq et al. (eds), 15–40.

Felix, David and Ranjit Sau (1996), 'On the revenue potential and phasing in of the Tobin tax', in Haq et al. (eds), 223–55.

Frankel, Jeffrey (1996), 'How well do foreign exchange markets work: might a Tobin tax help?', in Haq et al. (eds), 41–82.

Garber, M. Peter (1996), 'Issues of enforcement and evasion in a tax on foreign exchange transaction', in Haq et al. (eds), 129–42.

Griffith-Jones, Stephany (1996), 'Institutional arrangements for a tax on international currency transactions', in Haq et al. (eds), 143–60.

Haq, Mahbub ul, Inge Kaul and Isabelle Grunberg (eds) (1996), *The Tobin Tax: Coping with Financial Volatility*, Oxford: Oxford University Press.

IMF (International Monetary Fund) (1993), *International Capital Markets, Part I*, Washington, DC: IMF.

IMF (International Monetary Fund) (2002), *International Financial Statistics*, Washington, DC: IMF.

Jeanne, Oliver (1996), 'Would a Tobin tax have saved the EMS?', *Scandinavian Journal of Economics*, **98** (4), 503–20.

Kaul, Inge, Isabelle Grunberg and Mahbub ul Haq (1996), 'Overview', in Haq et al. (eds), 1–14.

Kaul, Inge and John Langmore (1996), 'Potential uses of the revenue from a Tobin tax', in Haq et al. (eds), 255–72.

Kenen, Peter B. (1996), 'The feasibility of taxing foreign exchange transactions', in Haq et al. (eds), 109–28.

Mitchie, Jonathan and John Grieve Smith (eds) (1999), *Global Instability: The Political Economy of World Economic Governance*, London: Routledge.

Mussa, M. (1986), 'Nominal exchange rate regimes and the behavior of real exchange rates: evidence and implications', in *Carnegie-Rochester Conference Series on Public Policy*, Vol. 25, 127–214.

Palley, Thomas I. (1999), 'Speculation and Tobin taxes: why sand in the wheels can increase economic efficiency', *Journal of Economics*, **69** (2), 113–26.

Patomäki, Heikki (2001), *Democratizing Globalisation: The Leverage of the Tobin Tax*, London/New York: Zed Books.

Schmidt, Rodney (1999), 'A feasible foreign exchange transactions tax', North–South Institute Working Papers, available at http://www.nsi-ins.ca/ensi/publications/tobin.html.

Singh, Kavaljit (2000), *Taming Global Financial Flows: Challenges and Alternatives in the Era of Financial Globalization: A Citizen's Guide*, London/New York: Zed Books.

Spahn, Paul Bernd (2002), *On the Feasibility of the Tax on the Foreign Exchange Transactions*, Report to the Federal Ministry for Economic Cooperation and Development, Bonn, available at http://www.wiwi.uni-frankfurt.de/professoren/spahn/tobintax.

Tobin, James (1996), 'Prologue', in Haq et al. (eds), ix–xviii.

UNDP (United Nations Development Programme) (1994), *Human Development Report 1994*, New York and Oxford: Oxford University Press.

APPENDIX 1   THE STRUCTURE OF THE EXCHANGE MARKET*

There are four participants in currency trading markets: dealers, brokers, customers, and central banks. The dealers are employed by banks and other financial institutions that need to have a continuing presence in the market and engage in buying and selling foreign exchange on their own accounts. The brokers match orders to buy and sell currencies for a fee. The customers include non-financial corporations as well as some financial institutions that do not maintain a continuous presence in the market as dealers. The customers may speculate, but their main interest is viewed as avoiding exchange risks in trading. Central banks enter the exchange markets both to implement their government policies and to influence the exchange rates.

Foreign exchange transactions are organized at two levels: the wholesale market in which dealers trade with each other and with the central banks, and the retail market, which comprises transactions with the customers. The wholesale market is often called an interbank market since most of the dealers are employed by banks.

Instruments of trade are spot, (outright) forward, swap, futures, and options. Settlement of a spot will require the transfer of two currencies on the value date, which by convention is generally specified as the second working day after the day on which the deal is struck (deal day). Delivery day is called the value day. Forward contracts and most options are sold over the counter, usually between a bank and its customers. Forward contracts are concluded in isolation (so-called outright forward contracts) or in combination with a spot or another forward contract in what is referred to as a swap. A currency swap refers to an exchange of payment flows denominated in different currencies. An outright forward contract is an agreement to exchange specified amounts of one currency for another at some date beyond the spot value date and at an exchange rate specified in the contract. Forward contracts generally come in standard maturities of one month, two months, and so on. Most forward contracts are written as part of a swap arrangement. In their simplest form, an exchange of one currency for another is stipulated on the current spot value date and a reverse exchange on a forward basis. Forward currency contracts entail a single settlement only at the date of maturity. The above two foreign exchange transactions are made at preset exchange rates. Futures and options are of a different category from the previous instruments and are called derivatives. Futures are similar to forwards because actual trade will happen in the future, but are different in that they are traded in standardized quantities on daily exchanges and the exchange rates for contract are not spot values but some specified ones. To net out the purchase and sell, futures need a clearing house which is also in contrast with the over-the-counter market.

Options are similar to futures except that options contracts are not obligatory and most options are traded in the over-the-counter market. The purchase contract is called 'the call option' and the sell contract is called the 'put option'.

NOTE

*   From IMF (1993: 24–30).

APPENDIX 2

Table 2A2.1 *Daily average foreign exchange turnover by country (US$bn)*

Country	April 1992		April 1995		April 1998		April 2001	
	Amount	% share	Amount	% share	Amount	% share	Amount	% share
UK	291	27.0	464	29.5	637	32.5	504	31.1
US	167	15.5	244	15.5	351	17.9	254	15.7
Japan	120	11.2	161	10.2	136	6.9	147	9.1
Singapore	74	6.9	105	6.7	139	7.1	101	6.2
Hong Kong	60	5.6	90	5.7	79	4.0	67	4.1
Subtotal	712	66.2	1064	67.6	1342	68.4	1073	66.2
Others	364	33.8	508	32.4	627	31.6	545	33.8
Total	1076	100	1572	100	1969	100	1618	100

Source: BIS (2002: Table B.7).

3. The WTO system and foreign direct investment: a policy challenge

V.N. Balasubramanyam and David Sapsford*

1 INTRODUCTION

Notwithstanding the anti-globalisation lobby, there is a growing acceptance among both academics and policy practitioners that inflows of foreign direct investment (FDI) into developing countries constitute one *potential* 'engine' of economic growth[1] and thereby offer one route by which living standards might be improved. However, as we have argued elsewhere (Balasubramanyam and Sapsford 2001) there exists, in reality, a degree of reluctance to admit first, that FDI belongs to the World Trade Organization (WTO) system and second, that there is a case for framing a coherent set of rules on the subject. This is perhaps a surprising state of affairs, especially when one recognises that investment is already subject to rules in the WTO system via the agreements reached in the Uruguay Round negotiations of 1986–94 on trade in services (GATS), trade-related investment measures (TRIMs) and the trade-related aspects of intellectual property rights (TRIPs). In our earlier paper we argued that this reluctance might reflect the fact that FDI is, in some sense, doing well and thus does not need to have rules imposed upon it. Alternatively the issue might be being ignored because of the difficult and sensitive issues of sovereignty that it inevitably encroaches on.

In this chapter we revisit our earlier arguments by exploring what appear to be the principal reasons for this apparent reluctance to extend the WTO rules to embrace FDI and making a case for such inclusion. The discussion is then extended to the practicalities of how such an extension might successfully be achieved.

2 LET THE STATUS BE QUO?

The belief that foreign direct investment is doing well is based on the observed growth in such investment flows in recent years. Inflows of FDI amounted to $865 billion in 1999 and the total stock was a sizeable $5 trillion. Save for 1996, annual average rates of growth of FDI flows were in excess of 20 per cent, reaching 39 per cent in 1998. Indeed, the volume of production of goods and services on account of FDI exceeds that supplied by international trade.[2]

Judged solely by the volume of foreign investment crossing borders, and its relatively high rate of growth, FDI is indeed doing well. But it is a judgement that provokes hostility and opposition. It is doing well by multinational enterprises, but what has it achieved for host developing countries? The problem is that most discussion of FDI is centred on its volume, rather than its consequences – *both* positive and negative – for the recipient economy. The attempt in the Organization for Economic Cooperation and Development (OECD) to negotiate a multilateral agreement on investment, which came to grief in 1997, is a case in point. There were a number of reasons for its demise, including the vast range of topics it attempted to cover, but the main one was the widespread perception that its sole concern was with FDI liberalisation and growth.

As already noted, FDI is a potent *potential* ingredient in the development process, being both a conduit for the transfer of technology and human skills, and a purveyor of new ideas. Policy makers in most developing countries appear to be aware of FDI's potential contribution to the development process and many have eagerly sought foreign investment from major enterprises around the world. While they may not always have embraced FDI with open arms, most of them now accept it as 'a necessary evil'. Even so, the OECD's draft multilateral agreement, which intentionally or otherwise appeared to take the virtues of FDI as holy writ and preached it to the developing countries, was inevitably bound to fail.

It is, however, vital to recognise that FDI is *not* a panacea for the development problem. It functions efficiently and contributes to the social product, given certain preconditions, among them a stable macroeconomic environment (including price and exchange rate stability), the presence of distortion-free product and labour markets and the availability of a threshold level of human capital and infrastructure facilities. It is well established that FDI is much more effective in promoting growth and technical change in economies open to competition from both external and internal sources (Balasubramanyam et al. 1996; Silverstraidou and Balasubramanyam 2000).

In short, FDI is a superb catalyst of development, but it is not the prime mover. It functions most effectively as a catalyst only in the presence of the right kind of ingredients in sufficient volumes. Very few developing countries, however, are able to provide all those ingredients. It is for that reason that about three-quarters of FDI flows to developing countries, around $180 billion per annum in recent years, are concentrated in a dozen countries or so, countries with the kind of environment that investment requires.

Thus the claims that 'FDI is doing well' send mixed messages. It is doing well, judged by the growth in its volume; and it is doing well in and for developing countries that are well placed to provide the environment it requires. But FDI is also doing well in a number of countries that provide an array of artificial and transient incentives such as tax concessions and subsidies of various sorts. In these countries, it is doing well in the sense that private rates of return to investment are relatively high, but its contribution to the social product is at best marginal and at worst negative. It is true to say that FDI responds to market forces, but if the markets are distorted its response is not the sort that augments the development objectives of recipient countries.

Should we then rest easy in the knowledge that FDI is a rich-country good, as it were, and is of little significance for the many developing countries that either receive insignificant amounts of FDI or, from a social point of view, squander what little they do receive? The 'do nothing' philosophy suggests as much.

All the same, a framework of multilateral rules that helps to remove or at the very least to delimit various kinds of distortions in product and factor markets, and improves the investment climate in general, should go a long way in promoting the efficacy of FDI. It could also provide the least-developed countries with an opportunity to compete for a rising share of increased FDI flows. It could be argued, though, that the development of poor countries is not the WTO's mandate, explicit or otherwise. In fact, its implicit mandate, strictly speaking, may not even be the liberalisation of trade and investment, but the promotion of a stable institutional environment through rules-based trade and trade-related investment. It is our view that to split hairs regarding such matters is to miss an important opportunity to increase economic welfare in developing countries.

3   DO NOT STEP ON THE SACRED TURF?

By its very nature, any type of commercial transaction between two or more distinct jurisdictions gives rise to issues of sovereignty, broadly defined as the legitimate right of one jurisdiction to protect its citizens against encroachment by others on their general interests, as opposed to sectional or 'special' interests.

In the case of FDI, foreign firms are intimately involved in the operations of the local economy, which is not the case with trade and licensing agreements. When the scale and size of operations of the foreign-owned or-controlled entity and its endowments of money and skills are relatively large, as with affiliates of multinational enterprises, its involvement in the local economy is conspicuous and perceptions concerning its threat to the political and economic sovereignty of nation states are heightened. Such fears were routinely expressed during the 1960s and 1970s when both the advocacy and opposition to FDI went to extremes.[3]

The old debates have re-surfaced in recent years in the context of 'globalisation', with multinational enterprises and FDI being the targets of attack from the anti-globalisation lobby. We have argued that these debates amount to no more than the re-emergence of old wine in new bottles.

1. The familiar refrain is that multinationals are big, their sales exceed the GDP of some African countries, there are no 'trickle down' effects, multinationals pay abysmally low wages and the freedom of policy makers in developing countries is increasingly constrained by the need to cater to the interests of big business.
2. The riposte to these arguments from the pro-globalisation lobby is equally familiar. The relevant statistic to assess the size of multinational enterprises relative to that of the countries in which they operate is not their global sales, but their value added. Multinationals pay higher wages than comparable locally owned firms in developing countries. And it is the electorate, not the multinationals, which dictates the tax and expenditure policies of nation states.

The different camps can produce facts and figures in support of their contentions. But these academic jousts do little to progress the debate. There is ample scope to do so, given that even the most caustic critics of FDI concede its potential to promote development objectives, broadly defined to include the transfer of technology and skills and the creation of employment opportunities with adequate remuneration. The dispute relates to the reasons for the failure of FDI to deliver much more than it has done. Noorena Hertz, of the University of Cambridge, a critic of globalisation, sums up the issue when she writes:

> [T]he point is not that inward investment cannot make people of recipient countries better off. It is why there is not a bigger 'trickle down effect'. Why is globalisation – to quote James Wolfensohn, head of the World Bank – 'not working at the level of the people?' Why has the number of people living on less than $1 a day increased in every developing country outside East Asia? (Hertz 2001, p. 78)

Dr Hertz's answer to the question she poses is that the political process, captured by big business, is unable to protect the interests of the public realm. This may be so, but is it because politicians and policy makers are captured by corporate giants? Or is it because the political process in most developing countries is flawed for reasons that have nothing to do with the multinationals? How come, on Dr Hertz's own admission, the East Asian countries are able to reduce levels of poverty and prosper, while the others are not able to do so? It may be far-fetched to argue that democracy thrives in most East Asian countries and hence their acknowledged success in combating poverty and promoting development goals.

The fact of the matter is that policy makers in these countries have instituted the kind of policies that not only attract sufficient volumes of FDI but also promote its efficient utilisation. The benefits of FDI can hardly trickle down if countries are unable to attract sufficient volumes in the first place and fail to utilise efficiently whatever they attract. As the British economist I.M.D. Little wrote several years ago, 'FDI is as good or as bad as your policies' (Little 1982, p. 182).

None of this is to say that multinational enterprises are entirely blameless in all they do. Admittedly wage rates paid by multinationals in certain areas of activity in some developing countries are abysmally low. Indeed, they do seek low-wage locations for many of their processing activities. But why do multinationals get away with paying abysmally low wages in certain countries but not in others? Here again it is the failure of policy, or the absence of it, that allows profit-maximising multinationals to take advantage of low-wage labour.

In particular, the record appears to show that countries that have failed to institute trade and investment policies designed to create jobs and employment opportunities are also the ones that seek low-wage jobs from multinationals. If this is the case there is little point in railing against multinationals for seeking low-wage locations. It is wishful thinking to expect profit-maximising firms to behave as social service agencies, especially when the domestic market environment is riddled with distortions. Low-wage locations, such as the 'export processing zones' in some countries are, perhaps, little more than a feeble attempt by governments to offset distortions elsewhere in their economies.

All this is familiar landscape dating back to the 1970s. The concern today is with the efficient utilisation of FDI in the promotion of national economic objectives while preserving the economic sovereignty so heavily cherished by nation states. What is the nature of the threat to their sovereignty from the operations of foreign-owned firms that developing countries perceive? This perception of loss of economic sovereignty differs between various influential groups in the host countries.

Writing in 1971 Raymond Vernon, the American trade official who, in a second career at Harvard University, became in his time the leading international authority on the operations of multinational enterprises, identified three influential groups in public discussion of FDI: the government bureaucrats, the local businessmen and the elite sections of opinion.

1. The *bureaucrats* perceive a threat to their power and control over the local economy from the operations of foreign firms.
2. The stance of the *local businessmen* has changed over time. With the growth in their ability to compete with foreign firms they have attempted to cut back the scope of foreign firms. Those businessmen, however, whose activities complement those of the foreign firms seem to tolerate the presence of foreign firms, if not actively encourage their growth.
3. The *elite* is a complex group, consisting of those who are opposed to any form of private enterprise (be it foreign or domestic), those who wish to determine the limits of dependence on foreign firms and those who see foreign firms as a part of the Establishment and thus as a threat to their power and influence.

For the most part, the game plan of the bureaucrats is to voice their concern and opposition to foreign firms in public fora, but to recognise in private negotiations with foreign firms their contribution to development objectives and seek ways and means of attracting FDI. Businessmen, in general, lobby for stringent regulation of foreign firms where they perceive them as a threat; and where they see them as an aid to their power and profits, they seek joint ventures and other avenues of rent sharing. The elite does what they do best, position themselves as critics of foreign firms in the media and provide intellectual support to activists, such as non-governmental organisations.

Arguably, the attitudes and perceptions of the bureaucrats and local businessmen in general towards foreign firms are not entirely unreasonable. At the heart of the matter as they see it is the control over operations that multinationals exercise. Economic sovereignty is all about delimiting the control over operations or power over decision making which foreign firms exercise.

We have argued that, in practice, the problem arises when the interests of the bureaucrats and the businessmen do not coincide with national objectives. If they are intent on safeguarding their private profits and their power base at the expense of the social good that foreign firms, given the appropriate climate, are capable of promoting, they play into the hands of ideologues and the elite. Their actions and the policies they advocate and institute may do more harm than good. According to Vernon (1971) it is this group of businessmen and bureaucrats who, seeing a threat to their power and profits from foreign firms, play the sovereignty card for all it is worth.

4   A MULTILATERAL FRAMEWORK OF RULES

The task of devising multilateral rules on FDI under the aegis of the WTO is much more complex than devising multilateral rules on trade. Nonetheless, the gains from such a compact are potentially quite substantial, both for the recipients and for FDI providers. The problem is that any suggestion of such a compact is immediately seen as one-sided, a set of rules designed to pave the way for unrestrained flows of capital from the developed to the developing countries. Accordingly it is vital that the framework of rules should recognise the concerns of developing countries, as discussed above, while also shifting the emphasis away from the objective of easing the passage for multinational enterprises.

Possible Objections

Before discussing the form and nature of the compact that is likely to be acceptable to the recipients of foreign investment, especially the developing countries, several objections to its inclusion on the WTO agenda require discussion.

The first of them is that the WTO is not the appropriate forum for framing a compact on FDI because its mandate does not extend to investment. It is concerned with trade. This was one of the objections to the inclusion of services on the GATT (General Agreement on Tariffs and Trade) agenda. This has no basis in fact because a substantial proportion of world trade is on account of multinational enterprises. If rules can be devised for trade, there is no reason in principle why they should not be extended to the entities that generate trade. The latter is unlikely to flourish in the absence of the former. It is established that trade and FDI are complements and not substitutes. A set of rules that facilitate both the flows of FDI and its efficient operations is more than likely to promote the growth of trade.

In any case, trade and investment in the services sector are on the WTO agenda and, except in the case of so-called long-distance services, efficient delivery of most services requires the presence of the producer in the locale of the consumer. Here production and trade are coterminous. More often than not the presence of the service producer in the locale of the consumer is established through foreign investment. Again, the TRIMs Agreement, a product of the Uruguay Round negotiations, is about the polices of host countries towards foreign firms (Balasubramanyam 1990; Greenaway 1992). TRIMs impact on the production decisions of foreign firms, including the sourcing of inputs. Admittedly, the justification for the inclusion of TRIMs in the WTO is that all such measures, at one remove or the other, impact on trade. But then there are very few policy measures that do not impact on trade in one way or another.

What Can a Compact on Foreign Direct Investment Achieve?

As argued earlier, the twin objectives of the compact should be to provide access to FDI for developing countries that receive relatively low volumes, and to help resolve the economic sovereignty dilemma the developing countries face in utilising FDI. The first of these requires not only increased volumes of FDI, but also much more widespread distribution of FDI. Both of these objectives, especially the second one, essentially involve creating competitive market conditions that foster efficient operations of foreign firms.

The first of the objectives poses much more of a challenge than the second. The literature on the determinants of FDI identifies (i) macroeconomic stability, including exchange rate stability, distortion-free product and labour markets that allow for the play of comparative advantage in resource allocation, (ii) a stable policy framework and (iii) resource endowments, including a threshold level of human capital. No compact on FDI, however ingenious it may be, can promote macroeconomic stability or the provision of human capital. These belong to domestic policy in the host countries.

A compact on FDI, though, may serve to promote the establishment of a stable policy framework and the elimination of distortions in product and labour markets. There is a strong suggestion in the literature that when foreign firms seek political stability, what they look for is *policy stability*. In fact, economic stability may more often than not promote political stability. Here the enshrined principles of the WTO relating to trade, notably most-favoured-nation (MFN) treatment, transparency and national treatment, may serve to promote policy stability. Non-discrimination between differing FDI providers, explicit regulations that are agreed and bound and the guarantee that there would be no discrimination in the policy framework between foreign and local firms should achieve the policy stability that foreign firms seek.

Feedbacks

Some of these factors relating to determinants also influence the efficient utilisation of FDI, which in turn are intimately related to the economic sovereignty issue, as discussed earlier. The first of these is the presence of distortion-free markets, defined as markets where prices of factors of production and products reflect social opportunity costs. In most developing countries, especially those that receive relatively low FDI volumes at present, there are pervasive distortions in factor and product markets. These last arise from tariffs and quotas on trade, stringent labour laws designed to protect jobs and assorted subsidies including export subsidies. It is now the received wisdom that such distortions do not attract large FDI volumes and that which is attracted, such as the tariff-jumping type, serves in large part to bolster rents and the private returns to foreign investments. They also impair the efficiency of operations.

Multilateral Rules and Distortions

What can a set of multilateral rules achieve to reduce if not eliminate these distortions? To the extent that agreed rules pertaining to trade serve to lower artificial barriers to trade, they also serve to reduce product market distortions. Especially relevant in the context of FDI are TRIMs, which encompass not only local-content requirements but also equity regulations tied to exports and so-called incentives such as tax holidays, tax concessions and assorted subsidies. The economic sovereignty issue is also bound up with TRIMs. This complex animal is supposed to serve several objectives: garner the maximum possible benefits from the operations of foreign firms to the host countries, satiate the desire of bureaucrats to retain power and control, provide local businessmen with a complementary role in the operations of foreign firms and, in some cases, protect locals firms from foreign competition.

TRIMs were included on the Uruguay Round agenda on the grounds that they had an impact on trade. Initially, there was a push by the United States to negotiate multilateral rules on international investment, but this was resisted by developing countries and so they settled for a codification of existing GATT rules. So the Uruguay Round accord on TRIMs relates to local-content requirements and incentives such as tax concessions tied to exports. Domestic regulations in both areas violate the principle of national treatment (laid down in GATT Article III) and the prohibition of quantitative restrictions (laid down in GATT Article XI). Thus the TRIMs Agreement reaffirms the need for WTO member countries to conform to GATT rules within a specified period.

But the TRIMs Agreement was no more than a Pyrrhic victory. It only addresses local-content requirements and export obligations. It has nothing to say about other trade-related investment measures such as the subsidies and tax incentives that host countries offer foreign firms. Nor does it include regulations relating to employment of nationals and the requirement of some developing countries that foreign-enterprise participation has to be in the form of joint ventures with locally owned firms. The agreement is much weaker than the one concluded in the North American Free Trade Agreement (NAFTA). Even so, the fact that an agreement of sorts was reached in the Uruguay Round negotiations, involving developing countries, is a major achievement.

Building on the Uruguay Round

A multilateral framework on FDI would inevitably reopen the issue of TRIMs. The developing countries would seek ways and means of preserving their economic sovereignty, as discussed above, and are unlikely to consent to a blanket ban on all TRIMs. But then any suggestion that each and every TRIM should be assessed for its trade-distorting effects, as was proposed by the developing countries in the run-up to the Uruguay Round negotiations, would only serve to muddy the waters. The case-by-case approach, so dear to the hearts of bureaucrats, would only result in protracted negotiations, delay and red tape.

The alternative would be to formulate general rules designed to preserve those aspects of TRIMs that do promote development objectives. Instead of imposing a ban on all local-content requirements, developing countries could be allowed to require foreign firms to increase gradually their purchases of locally produced components over time. This would allow foreign firms time to search for indigenous suppliers and impart the technology required to such suppliers. In any case, most multinational enterprises would seek indigenous sources of supply of components, rather than incur heavy transport costs that imports involve, especially so if the former are cost competitive. The problem they face is the heavy search costs of locating competent local suppliers. Local-content requirements would act as a catalyst for the search process (Balasubramanyam 1990).

TRIMs such as those that tie equity participation to exports, though, are much more problematic. They are imposed for narrow balance of payments reasons and not for broader development objectives. In the presence of distortion-free markets, comparative advantage and market forces would guide the investment allocations of foreign firms. Equity-oriented export requirements are put in place to offset distortions elsewhere in the economy and provide artificial incentives for production oriented towards domestic markets.

These restrictions hardly fulfil development objectives. A foreign firm, which does not wish to comply with equity restrictions, may dilute its equity in favour of indigenous suppliers and opt to produce for the protected domestic market. And indigenous capital, whose social opportunity costs could be considerable, will also be oriented towards the protected domestic market. The net result is the creation of rents in protected markets for both the foreign- and domestic-owned firms, and it would also result in a reduction in trade.

There are also instances where foreign-owned firms are allowed 100 per cent ownership of equity if their entire output is exported. Suppose that export prices are lower than those prevailing in domestic markets and the foreign firm services both markets. In that case the foreign firm operating in the protected domestic market would have an incentive to bridge the price difference between the two markets by raising prices on the domestic market. In essence, domestic consumers would provide an export subsidy to the foreign firm. All this and other distortions and social costs that these measures impose have been rehearsed often (see Greenaway 1992). These are not measures that promote development objectives and have no place in a compact on FDI.

Then there are the assorted incentives offered by developing countries to attract foreign investment. These include tax holidays, tax concessions and subsidies of various kinds. Most of them are tied to performance requirements of one sort or another. It is doubtful whether they weigh heavily in the investment decision-making process of foreign firms. The evidence on the issue is not conclusive. Developing countries may be compelled to offer such incentives only because their competitors offer them. If none of the countries offer such incentives, the location decision of FDI would be based on the resource endowments of host countries and the climate they provide for efficient operations. Given the nature of these incentives, and the fact that each of the host countries offers such incentives only because others do so, it is likely that they are yet another source of distortions in the market for FDI. It could be in the interests of developing countries to do away with such incentives that only serve to transfer incomes to foreign firms. At the very least, they should consent to a set of WTO rules that would limit the distortions that incentives generate and eliminate competition between developing countries based on artificial incentives.

Although local-content requirements, equity and export regulations and investment incentives are frequently seen as instruments devised to transfer rents from multinational enterprises to host countries, they often extend into other areas such as competition policy. Regulations that limit the operations of foreign firms to designated regions and areas of host countries, prohibit them from entering designated areas of economic activity and stipulate conditions governing joint ventures, acquisitions and mergers all fall into the arena of competition policy. These policies go beyond the objective of transferring rents from multinationals to host countries. Here the objective is the preservation of economic sovereignty or the retention of national control over production facilities.

No-go Zones?

This is the principal issue that policy makers are reluctant to discuss and opponents of globalisation like to emphasise. Admittedly debate on these issues cannot be confined to narrow economic considerations such as their impact on resource allocation and economic efficiency of operations of FDI.

The concerns of the developing countries have to be heard and rules and regulations devised with a view to preserving the economic sovereignty of developing countries. While exceptions to the general principles of national treatment may have to be conceded, there is no reason why such policies should not be subjected to rules relating to transparency and stability of policy regimes.

In developed countries, such as the UK, there are tried and tested procedures for the adjudication of disputes concerning mergers and acquisitions, including cross-border ones. Cases referred to the Competition Commission in the United Kingdom are adjudicated on the basis of the impact of mergers on consumer interests and, lately, on whether they interfere with competition in the marketplace. Admittedly when the concern of the policy makers is not so much with consumer interests, or with the impact on competition, but with loss of control exercised by national governments over the operations of foreign firms, the problem is much more complex. In such cases, exceptions to the general framework of rules governing FDI have to be allowed, albeit in the knowledge that host countries may be sacrificing economic objectives for the sake of non-economic objectives.

It is worth noting in this context that the GATS, which is essentially an agreement related to FDI since services necessarily entail presence and establishment, provide a framework for a multilateral agreement on FDI more generally. The GATS takes account of many of the concerns of developing countries while, at the same time, subjecting trade in services to MFN treatment, national treatment, market access and transparency.

Perhaps the next step could be to extend GATS to cover FDIs in other sectors. In the past, suggestions for a separate agreement on FDI have been made. It may be judicious, though, to aim at one cohesive set of rules and regulations on FDI that encompasses the GATS accord. The new set of rules to be incorporated could include TRIMs and other national regulations relating to FDI discussed earlier. It would be neither necessary nor practical to establish a separate framework of rules for FDI when one already exists in the form of GATS framework.

5   PROBLEMS OF IMPLEMENTATION

Admittedly the formulation of a pragmatic competition policy which is universally acceptable is no easy task. Inevitably compromises have to be forged, concessions made and the policy framework should be incremental with a gradualist approach. The WTO principles of non-discrimination, national treatment and transparency of policies should form the building blocks for a multilateral compact. National treatment implies not only non-discrimination in policies between locally owned and foreign firms but also market access. In fact national treatment is coterminous with market access. Here again, because of considerations of national sovereignty exceptions may have to be allowed as in the case of the Agreement on Trade in Services. GATS, in fact, provides an ideal framework for a compact on competition policy, especially so as most trade in services entails the presence and establishment of foreign firms or FDI. Arguably the GATS framework in place constitutes a multilateral compact on competition policy. All that is required is the addition of the agreements on TRIPs and TRIMs with due recognition of development objectives, and provisos relating to mergers and acquisitions.

The WTO with its existing accords on trade and promotion of rules-based trade, which for the large part are designed to promote non-discrimination or market access to both domestic and foreign firms, may be ideally placed to promote market access in the wider sense of the term now known as contestable markets. In addition, it may also be capable of promoting competition without actually intervening but with credible threats of intervention.

6   CONCLUDING REMARKS

This chapter has outlined the case for a multilateral accord on FDI under the aegis of the WTO. The one principal conclusion worth emphasising is that such an accord should be centred on the development objectives of developing countries and it should not be an instrument for facilitating increased flows of FDI. It is also worth noting that a multilateral accord on FDI should be designed to streamline and coordinate existing national policies on FDI and not supplant national policies. The main role of the accord should be one of monitoring and coordinating existing policies with the proviso that it should have the principles of non-discrimination, national treatment and transparency as its building blocks.

NOTES

*   Revised and extended version of the paper presented at the CSI Symposium 'The Role of International Institutions in Globalisation' held at the University of Innsbruck, Austria, 14–16 November 2001.
1. See Greenaway and Sapsford (1994) for a critical review of trade as an engine of growth literature.
2. United Nations, *World Investment Report, 2000*, New York and Geneva: United Nations, 2001.
3. See MacBean and Balasubramanyam (1978) for a review.

REFERENCES

Balasubramanyam, V.N. (1990), 'Putting TRIMs to good use', *World Development*, **18**, 684–97.

Balasubramanyam, V.N. and D. Sapsford (2001), 'Foreign direct investment in the WTO system', International Business Research Group Discussion Paper, Department of Economics, Lancaster University, December.

Balasubramanyam, V.N., D. Sapsford and M. Salisu (1996), 'Foreign direct investment and growth in EP and IS countries', *Economic Journal*, **106**, 92–105.

Greenaway, D. (1992), 'Trade related measures and development strategy', *Kyklos*, **45**, 49–68.

Greenaway, D. and D. Sapsford (1994), 'What does liberalisation do for exports and growth?', *Weltwirtschaftliches Archiv*, **130** (1), 152–74.

Hertz, N. (2001), 'Decrying Wolf', *Prospect*, August–September, 78–82 (reply to Martin Wolf, 'The infantile leftist', *Prospect*, July 2001, review of Noreena Hertz's book, *The Silent Takeover*).

Little, I.M.D. (1982), *Economic Development: Theory, policy and international institutions*, New York: Basic Books.

MacBean, A. and V.N. Balasubramanyam (1978), *Meeting the Third World Challenge*, 2nd edn, London: Macmillan, for the Trade Policy Research Centre.

Silverstraidou, K. and V.N. Balasubramanyam (2000), 'Trade policy, foreign direct investment and convergence', *Review of Development Economics*, **4**, 279–91.

Vernon, R. (1971), *Sovereignty at Bay*, Harmondsworth: Penguin Books.

4. Order and justice in the international trade system

John Toye

1 THE IDEA OF RECONCILING ORDER AND JUSTICE

The reconciliation of Order and Progress (including social justice) is a nineteenth-century agenda. Its intellectual parents were the Saint-Simonians, Auguste Comte and the Positivists, and the scientific socialists. The aftermath of the French Revolution convinced them that, while progress was desirable and reaction was impossible, *the pursuit of social justice was politically and socially disruptive of order.* Therefore, people with special knowledge of society should be empowered to direct what should be done for the good of all.[1] However much today, after the end of the Cold War, democracy and its triumph are trumpeted, this older ideal of technocracy – that power should be exercised by experts, who know how to reconcile justice with order – is still alive and well in political affairs. The spread of democracy has been accompanied by a growing interest in 'agencies of restraint', devices by which certain aspects of economic policy can be removed from the regular political arena, and by which democratic governments try to commit themselves to refrain from acting on matters of economic importance, and leave decisions to supposedly impartial experts.[2]

Technocracy is also on the rise in international affairs, including in international trade. The new World Trade Organization (WTO), which has been created since the end of the Cold War, is distinguished from its predecessor, the General Agreement on Tariffs and Trade (GATT), in part by the greater scope of decision making it allows to various kinds of legal technocrats. Most academic observers have regarded this change as a self-evident improvement. This chapter asks: will this recent judicialisation of trade disputes lead to the reconciliation of justice and order in the international trade system? Its conclusion is that the great economic and political inequalities between nations prevent this (a) when formal justice is dispensed in an incomplete legal system and (b) when the rules to be administered do not recognise these inequalities as a difference relevant to the issue of substantive justice.

I begin with a fundamental distinction between justice as an ideal and justice as a legal organisation, that is, as a system of legislature, courts and sanctions. Historically, I think that justice as an organisation came first. At least in mediaeval England, 'justice' meant a form of organisation, whose purpose was the enforcement of law and the promotion of public order. The law was mainly custom and practice, and the decisions that the justice organisation enforced, while somewhat effective in relation to order, were arbitrary in relation to any modern ideal of justice. The ideal of justice in public organisations became influential, even insistent, centuries later, as an intellectual critique of the actually existing justice organisations. Its key exponents were John Locke, Cesare Beccaria, Jean Jacques Rousseau and Jeremy Bentham. The fruits of this critical spirit can be seen in eighteenth-century constitutions that enshrined 'due process', outlawed compulsory self-incrimination, double jeopardy and the widespread use of cruel and unusual punishments.

Initially, the main point upon which I wish to insist is that ideals of justice in society, having started out as criticism, in the end require their own justice organisations if they are to have an effect in the world. For the US constitution, for example, the new justice organisation was the Supreme Court.[3] The new ideal of justice could realise itself (or not) according to the institutional features of this new justice organisation – how its judges are appointed, whether they can be dismissed, whether decision is by simple majority, what rules of interpretation they adopt (for example, strict construction, role of precedents), whether the costs of supplicants are paid by the court, and so on. It is these factors that determine what, in the real world, any ideal of justice actually delivers. No ideal of justice in society can be worth more than the new justice organisations to which it gives birth, and the devil is always in the detail.

Andrew Hurrell (2003) has said that, from the point of view of justice, all international organisations suffer 'particular deformity'. It is certainly true that they are incomplete as legal systems, lacking a legislature, courts that can compel recognition and centralised sanctions, and that this affects the quality of the justice that they deliver. However, additionally, *all* justice organisations, regardless of whether they are municipal or international, have common features that put them at a distance from most ideals forms of justice. They all

- use up resources for which someone, somewhere, has to pay, and in regulating these costs legal technocrats face a clear problem of moral hazard;
- take time to come to judgment, during which time the offence continues unpunished;

- generate judgments that are unpredictable, even under a legal regime of strict precedent, because of the open texture of legal rules;
- produce miscarriages of justice, from time to time finding in favour of the violator of the law, instead of for the victim of the violation; and therefore
- operate with least success when the parties between whom justice is to be done are unequal in resources, power or culture.[4]

So, in discussing order and justice in the international trade system, I shall look not only at ideals of justice in international trade, but also at the justice organisations that these ideals have entailed. In particular, I shall consider the justice arrangements of the WTO, embodied in its dispute settlement understanding (or DSU).

2　FREE TRADE: JUSTIFICATION AND CRITICISM

'Free trade' is one of those brilliant eighteenth-century ideas that contained a powerful moral principle that was critical of old practices. The moral justification of free trade was utilitarian. It was that, regardless of differences between countries in natural and human resources, unrestricted trade between them would necessarily generate a higher level of welfare in all the trading countries. Subsidies to national producers, navigation laws and all the paraphernalia of mercantilism were not only harmful to the welfare of other countries (that was intended and to be expected) but were *also harmful to the welfare of the country that employed them*. That was something that mercantilists neither intended nor expected.[5] This, incidentally, is one of the most robust of economic theorems.[6] It was made the intellectual foundation for British policy in its period of world hegemony, namely, *unilateral* removal of tariff barriers, followed up by bilateral free trade accords (Goldstein 1998: 139).

'Justice' as an abstraction has at least three layers. One layer is simply the notion of there being some appropriate assignment of rights and duties within societies, including international societies. Another layer is that of general theories of how such an assignment might be determined, and this includes utilitarian, contractarian, intuititionist and other theories. Yet another layer is that set of distinct and partially overlapping common-sense norms of justice, all of which seem quite reasonable in themselves, but which in part conflict. They cause both the moral dilemmas that we encounter in everyday life and the difficulties of judges in coming to just legal judgments. Now, the justice of free trade is argued from a well-elaborated utilitarian general theory, based on the principle of maximising aggregate net benefits.[7] That theory, however, does not always sit well with the other principles of justice from the third layer of specificity – norms such as non-discrimination, distributional equality, universality, reciprocity and maximum liberty, all of which can be applied as ideals of justice in international trade. Utilitarians regard these justice norms as socially useful rules, but as essentially subordinate to the principle of utility. In contractarian theories of justice, however, these specific justice norms are both more prominent and more integrated into the theoretical structure. Unfortunately, in many discussions of trade, this somewhat complex layering of theories and norms of justice is often reduced to the misleadingly simple dichotomy of free trade versus fair trade.[8]

In response to the free trade argument, Friedrich List proposed that *the case for free trade had to be modified if some nations were still developing.* He completely accepted the case for free trade in the context of universal peace, a global moral community and a world government, that is, if the world could be treated as a single society. However, he argued that the existence of nations had to be taken seriously in considering the justice of free trade.[9] According to List, the moral communities of civilisation were embodied in nations. True prosperity was not the possession of material wealth, but the ability to support invention, the arts and the sciences (List 1977 [1885]: 208–9). It was these that would underwrite the sustainability of material wealth, *and they could be gained only if agrarian states became industrialised, if necessary behind tariff barriers.* In his own words,

> [T]he system of protection, inasmuch as it forms the only means of placing those nations which are far behind in civilisation on equal terms with the one predominating nation ... appears to be the most efficient means of furthering the final union of nations, and hence also of promoting true freedom of trade'. (ibid.: 127)

Without protection for the less developed, List claimed that free trade would serve best the purposes of the most economically advanced nation. It was a doctrine that would perpetuate any hegemonic nation's political and economic dominance, because it would allow the emerging industries of any potential antagonist, on which its safety would depend in wartime, to be destroyed by the economic competition that free trade would permit.[10] The morality of free trade was the morality of cosmopolitanism, but, in a world of unequal and potentially antagonistic national states, it was a doctrine that would entrench the national interests of the one predominating nation.

List challenged the doctrine of free trade by challenging the utilitarian norm of maximum aggregate net benefit. His argument rested on an implicit appeal to the norms of distributional equality and maximum liberty. He thereby opened up the debate on the variety of principles of justice that could be applied to international trade. This variety itself further suggested that there was a possibility of self-interest entering into the adoption of a particular principle. List suggested that the choice of justice norm by the hegemonic state could be, and indeed was, self-interested. There are three prongs to his argument:

- first, that nations do not confront each other as economic equals, but in a world where one nation exercises hegemony,
- second, that the hegemonic nation gains legitimacy for its dominance by prescribing an ideal of a just world order to the economically weaker nations, and
- third, that any such ideal must be limited by the economic (and military) interests of the hegemonic nation.

He therefore concluded that the ideal of a just world order propagated by a hegemonic state could not and should not be accepted uncritically by the non-hegemonic states.[11]

3 NATIONAL LABOUR STANDARDS AND THE ILO AS A JUSTICE ORGANISATION

In the late nineteenth century, Germany's national development – partly under List's influence – involved both industrial tariffs and the creation of a welfare state.[12] Bismarck created social security systems intended to recruit workers into the national endeavour of industrialisation. This produced a major problem of justice in the international trading system. The greater the nation's efforts to create a truly national economic community at home, the less competitive it became in international trade.[13] Germany was bound to lose out in international trade to countries like the United States, which also adopted industrial protection, but did not provide social security for its workers, and had no need to, as long as millions of continental European workers wanted to emigrate to America.

The continental European states, by contrast, faced revolutionary political movements that threatened political order in the name of liberating the working class, and had to address the injustice that the more vigorous they were in legislating social reform, the more they placed their national firms at a disadvantage in international trade. Only if all nations would agree to level their labour standards upwards could revolution in Europe be staved off, and free international trade be reconciled with 'fair' international trade, according to norms of reciprocity and non-discrimination. The new orgnisation to tackle this injustice was the International Labour Organization (ILO). Adumbrated before the First World War, it was established as part of the Versailles postwar settlement, under the threat posed by the Bolshevik revolution in Russia.[14]

Compared with the League of Nations, the ILO was a successful international organisation.[15] Its work was, however, overtaken by events. In the inter-war years, the emergence of much greater distortions in the international trade system overshadowed the problem of unequal labour standards.

On 8 July 1916, Democratic Congressman Cordell Hull had argued in the House of Representatives for the establishment of 'a permanent international trade congress'. Its function would be to consider

all international trade methods, practices, and policies which in their effects are calculated to create destructive commercial controversies or bitter economic wars, and to formulate agreements with respect thereto, designed to eliminate and avoid the injurious results and dangerous possibilities of economic warfare, and to promote fair and friendly trade relations among all the nations of the world. (Hull 1948: 81–2)

This vision united order and justice in trade relations, but it was based on the idea – reflected in the third of President Woodrow Wilson's Fourteen Points – of the removal, so far as possible, of all economic barriers to trade. The Great Crash began a decade of tariff raising, starting with the infamous Smoot–Hawley tariff in the US, plus discriminatory trading arrangements organised around regional currency blocs that practised the beggar-my-neighbour tactics of competitive currency devaluation. This experience destroyed popular confidence in the possibility of a return to the previous automatic and self-regulating arrangements. It provoked new ideas on the reconciliation of economic order with economic justice, and of the justice organisation that could best deliver it. After 1933, '(t)here began to crystallize ... a conception of "economic order" that included norms, rules and frameworks for ... decision-making on a multinational level – this to supply the deficiency of the liberal ideal, in which the key legal, institutional and 'moral' context was simply taken for granted' (De Marchi 1991: 144).

The ILO served as a model for the American designers of the new United Nations system.[16] To regulate international trade, a new specialised agency, the International Trade Organization (ITO) was negotiated at Havana in 1947. It did not come into being because the United States government failed to ratify it. This was because what the US government negotiators agreed to in Havana was not in the end acceptable to its own domestic business community, and the Truman administration belatedly realised in 1950 that, without business support, ratification was politically impossible. In this curiously accidental way, the GATT – which was only a temporary agreement pending the ratification of the ITO – became the main justice organisation in the field of international trade for nigh on fifty years. The ILO continued its task of seeking voluntary harmonisation of national labour legislation, but that of rolling back discriminatory trade taxes (tariffs) was left to GATT.

4   GATT AS A JUSTICE ORGANISATION

What ideal of justice inspired GATT? The purposes of GATT reflected the new American world hegemony. The US was much more ambivalent about unadulterated free trade than Britain had been when it exercised world hegemony. This ambivalence produced a distinctly different ideal of justice and order in international trade from free trade. It is known as 'embedded liberalism'. The moral basis of the new ideal was open multilateralism, derived from the norms of non-discrimination and reciprocity. Its claim to 'fairness' was that it required sharing both the benefits of any other country's tariff reductions *and* of the burdens of any other country's 'need' to re-impose tariffs to safeguard its domestic industry. It inclined to free trade in that it aimed to facilitate multilateral and reciprocal tariff reductions. At the same time, 'contingent protection' was also provided for, that is to say, opportunities for individual countries to renege on tariff concessions under pre-specified conditions, to avoid 'injury' to domestic industries adversely affected by tariff reduction. (There were indeed more clauses of GATT devoted to reneging than there were devoted to free trade!) In short, 'embedded liberalism', made manifest in the GATT rules, was from the start an attempted compromise between the application of utilitarian theory and of other norms of justice, and between free trade and various different notions of fairness in trade.[17]

Existing levels of tariffs were intended to be reduced by mutual agreement in successsive GATT 'Rounds' of multilateral negotiations.[18] These agreements did indeed reduce industrial tariffs substantially, and this, as Table 4.1 shows, contributed to the expansion of world trade at a rate 1.6 times faster than the expansion of world output between 1950 and 1994.[19] GATT tariff reductions were achieved by reaching a consensus among the near-equal rich countries.[20] The developing countries remained outside this virtuous circle (Ruggie 1982: 413). From 1955, special treatment was granted to developing countries, allowing them to protect particular industries and to plead balance of payments reasons for adding to quantitative restrictions on trade (Pangestu 2000: 1285–9). They were glad to do this at the time. The tragedy was that, in general, they were not using these exemptions to carry out an effective

Table 4.1   Comparative growth of world output and trade, 1950–94

	1950–74	1974–94
Rate of growth of output (%)	5	2
Rate of growth of trade (%)	8	4

development strategy, but only opportunistically, to promote some visible but chronically uncompetitive industries. They were rarely using them to shield a time-phased programme of development that would create competitive industries with the capability to export. There were a few, but hugely significant, exceptions to this – after 1965, the Asian economic 'tigers'. These apart, the developing world suffered static losses to their economic welfare inflicted by their own tariffs, but did not reap the dynamic gains that would have been possible from their more intelligent use.

Furthermore, the arena of tariff reduction among the developed countries was limited to industrial products. Until 1987, agricultural tariffs were never even on the tariff-reduction agenda, since developed countries were agreed on protecting their own agricultural sectors. This was the legendary era of butter mountains and wine lakes in Europe and huge grain surpluses in the United States, the result of the foolish policies of the EEC (European Economic Community) and the US of subsidising farm production rather than farm incomes. The excess production had to be disposed of, and the methods of disposal often forced down the world prices of food products and damaged the livelihoods of farmers in developing countries.

From the justice perspective, it is noteworthy that GATT's free trade disciplines were mild, since its rules were (mainly) based on negative prescription. They did not require states to do something that GATT specified. It required them to refrain from actions contrary to the twin GATT principles of eliminating discrimination in trade and halting tariff increases. GATT never insisted on a maximum tariff rate or on a particular rate of indirect tax on imports. It asked states only to refrain from increasing tariffs and from taxing imports differently from domestic production. In addition, the clauses in GATT that permitted countries to renege on tariff reductions included safeguard measures against serious injury, and other measures against material injury. Anti-dumping and countervailing duties (AD/CVD)[21] were permitted, the intention being to penalise trade-distorting practices, according to the norm of reciprocity. They were quickly adapted by the US and a few other leading industrial countries to be instruments of unilateral protectionism. The Tokyo Round tried to eliminate this by greater legal clarification, but the use of the AD/CVD mechanism for protection grew rapidly in the 1980s, with the US, the EC (European Community), Australia and Canada between them bringing 96 per cent of all cases, and some of the larger middle-income countries getting in on the act in the 1990s (Tharakan 1995: 1551; Bhagwati 1994: 237). It seems that this surge of abusive AD/CVD actions was stimulated because the very legal clarifications that were designed to eliminate them in fact conferred some legitimacy on them (Marvel and Ray 1995: 1593).

Contrary to Hull's vision of the union of justice and order, the abuse of reneging provisions helped to swell the number of trade disputes. Overall, legal proceedings in GATT were initiated in over two hundred cases. However, the legal force of the GATT rules remained moot. There was no provision for disputes to go to a World Court, and enforcement in national jurisdictions was impossible except in the few countries that had incorporated the GATT rules into their domestic laws. What remained was legal proceedings within GATT. These could be stymied by the countries found to be in contravention of the rules, who could block the adoption of the panel reports that found them guilty and thereby prevent their own punishment. Enforcement came from periodic unauthorised unilateral retaliation by large countries, especially US Section 301, but this blatantly breached the norm of non-discrimination.[22] For the rest, order in international trade depended on members' sense of being under a legal obligation, and/or care for their national reputations.

The mere threat of AD/CVD actions had a harassment value, because they were costly to contest.[23] It was used to secure so-called 'voluntary export restraints' on textile exports from developing countries.[24] The textile industry is the obvious first step on the path of industrialisation, but poor countries were denied the economies of scale that they could have gained by exporting to developed-country markets. Restraints on textile exports were exceedingly damaging to the economic welfare of the developing countries, but they were either untouched or positively recognised by GATT. This breach of the non-discrimination norm was accepted by developing countries themselves as part of a larger implicit bargain, in which their balance of payments deficits – worsened by trade restriction – were met by offsetting flows of official financing from OECD (Organization for Economic Cooperation and Development) country donors, or, in more familiar terms, by foreign aid.

Perhaps it is too sweeping to say that the injustice was accepted by the developing countries. In the euphoria of de-colonisation, there was one moment when an alternative seemed feasible, and when List's argument that free trade was not optimal when some of the world's nations still had to develop was given an organisational basis. In 1964, UNCTAD (the UN Committee on Trade and Development) was established, but in a curious form. This new international organisation was largely financed by developed countries (Group B) in order to support the claims of injustice of all the others – the Group of 77 developing countries. Then, during the 1980s, the instrument of redistribution chosen by UNCTAD – international commodity agreements (ICAs) – proved to be something of a broken reed.[25] It turned out that petrol power was, and is, the only effective economic lever to move the OECD countries, and the oil producers lacked solidarity with the non-oil-producing developing countries. That is why Adam Roberts could describe UNCTAD headquarters in Geneva as 'the temple of a failed religion'.[26]

5 THE TRANSITION FROM GATT TO THE WTO

The bargain between the OECD and developing countries of balance of payments support in exchange for trade access restrictions broke down in the 1980s, in the wake of the oil price shocks, the debt crisis and the arrival of Ronald Reagan, Helmut Kohl and Margaret Thatcher. A ceiling was put on foreign aid, and when private capital flows dried up after the 1982 Mexican debt crisis, the balance of payments gaps of developing countries had to be contracted by means of internationally inspired stabilisation and structural adjustment policies.

The Uruguay Round, the last GATT Round, was launched in 1986. Part of the work of this Round remained in the traditional mode, namely further major industrial tariff reductions and a strengthening of non-discrimination in government procurement. In addition, a start was made, at long last, on bringing agriculture and textiles into the arena of tariff reduction negotiations, albeit in the form of writing a post-dated cheque. Moreover, a host of new issues of interest mainly to the developed countries were introduced into the international trade regime, even though agriculture is still far from being fully liberalised. Finally, the Uruguay Round engineered the birth of a new trade system under the aegis of a new justice organisation, the WTO.

How does the WTO differ from its predecessor?

1. One strand of the change concerns the nature of the agenda. The overall aim has broadened, from non-discrimination and the reduction of trade barriers to the adoption *of policies in support of open markets generally*. New agreements have been added concerning trade in goods, such as agriculture, sanitary and phyto-sanitary (plant hygiene) standards, textiles and clothing, technical barriers to trade, and trade-related investment measures. Other agreements on 'new issues' apply to trade in services, and to intellectual property rights, and the removal of various non-tariff barriers.

2. The WTO is potentially much more intrusive on national policies, because it is now *making rules* across this substantial new agenda, whereas before GATT used only negative prescription.

3. These rules now over-ride the pre-existing national laws of members. GATT 1947 required countries to comply with its provisions only to the extent that they were not incompatible with domestic law at the date that the Agreement came into force. (This is known as 'the GATT grandfather clause'.) The WTO now requires countries to change existing domestic laws that conflict with the obligations of WTO membership.

4. A new Trade Policy Review Mechanism requires members to give regular public accounts of the state of their compliance with their obligations.

5. Under GATT, trade disputes perforce had to be dealt with by informal diplomacy, with the aim of dispute avoidance and reconciliation. Now the WTO has a strengthened dispute settlement mechanism (DSM).[27] The status in international law of the reports of dispute investigation panels has changed. Under GATT, it remained obscure. It is now much clearer that any ruling obliges all WTO members to bring their practices into conformity with the rule upheld by the adjudication. There will, therefore, now be an accumulating case law where observance will be mandatory on all members (Jackson 1998: 85–9). Members are not allowed to discuss the Appellate Body's decisions, but must abide by them under the threat of trade sanctions.[28]

These five institutional innovations, taken together, have two general effects. First, they make considerable inroads on what were matters of domestic governance before the coming into force of the Uruguay Round agreements, and second, they further 'judicialise' the process of trade cooperation, in the expectation that this will simultaneously improve order in the trade system, and render it more just.

6   THE WTO DISPUTE SETTLEMENT UNDERSTANDING

That a more powerful mechanism for the settlement of international trade disputes should have blossomed in the early 1990s is somewhat surprising. It has been argued that an open world trade structure is most likely to occur during periods when a hegemonic state is in its ascendancy (Krasner 1976: 323). Given that the relative dominance of the US has declined since 1945, this would imply that the trade dispute settlement mechanism would tend to weaken, not strengthen. To all appearances, the opposite has happened. GATT's dispute settlement process broke down in the 1950s, when America was at the height of its relative power. In fact, the US itself had a very bad record of failing to comply with GATT panel judgements.

The new DSM restores and strengthens the original GATT dispute settlement process by making it more automatic, and introducing specific time limits on procedures. Requests for panels on alleged violations are approved more automatically, as are the panel reports, the appellate body reports and the authorisations of retaliation. Instead of requiring a positive consensus to proceed, they now need a negative consensus to fail to proceed (Das 1999: 7; Sampson 2000: 1112–13). These changes have allowed about 160 cases to be handled during the first five years of the WTO, roughly three times the previous level. Developing countries have been involved in more cases, about 25 per cent of the new total (Das 1999: 7; Sampson 2000: 1112–13). This has been taken as a sign that the DSM is working well. However, although the formal justice of the institution has improved, formal justice can be at odds with substantive justice, and this I claim has been the case with regard to one issue of fundamental importance to developing countries.[29]

Where then is there any lack of justice for developing countries? Let me begin with the formal justice of the WTO, as it impinges on developing countries. For them, there remain serious deficiencies at every stage of the WTO dispute settlement process, from inception through judgment and granting remedy to enforcement. These deficiencies arise from the interaction of the standard features of a legal process – its cost, absorption of time and uncertainty of outcome – with the incompleteness of international legal machinery and the great inequalities of wealth and power that currently exist between nations. In particular,

- Given the substantial cost of bringing a WTO case, in terms of legal and diplomatic person time, poor countries are deterred disproportionately from doing so.
- Only governments can bring cases to the DSM, and poor governments will be disproportionately deterred by the prospect of antagonising more powerful countries, on whom they depend in non-trade matters, such as defence or foreign aid.
- By convention, no compensation is paid by the loser for a violation, after a process that can still take over two years to complete, a fact that bears more heavily on poor states than on rich ones.
- If a country does not take measures to comply with its WTO obligations, there is no centralised sanction. The only sanction is retaliation. Since all economic sanctions are costly to the initiator, the ability of a poor country to sanction a rich one is much less than in the reverse.[30]

Thus even if we assume an identical propensity to violate WTO rules as between developed and developing countries, and perfect formal justice in the panels in reaching their judgements on cases, developing countries will win fewer cases than they lose, and will be less able to be sure of remedy in those that they do win. The norms of distributional equity, universality and reciprocity are not satisfied in this outcome.

This effect would be reinforced if, in addition, the developed countries were to be tempted to exploit the advantages that they enjoy in this legalistic environment. Wealthy states can better afford to hazard their resources in the hope of a successful outcome to the dispute process, even when there is no actual violation. We have already seen how a few advanced countries were able to create harassment under the GATT rules on anti-dumping and CVDs. More extensive rules plus increased judicialisation widens the scope for oppresssive litigation by rich countries, which the poorer party cannot afford to contest, and for which there is no remedy.[31] While most of such suits would not be upheld, given the open texture of all legal rules, some surely would.

The fact that the improved administration of formal justice in the WTO nonetheless produces an outcome biased against developing countries is one reason to doubt the benefits of its recent judicialisation. More serious is the coincidence of judicialisation with the adoption of new rules that, on one key issue, embody substantive injustice. The Uruguay Round introduced new rules on the use of countervailing duties.[32] In a further attempt at legal clarification, reneging is now permitted in the face of some subsidies, but not others. Three kinds of subsidies, to R&D (research and development), to disadvantaged regions and to the costs of complying with environmental regulations, if available to all firms or industries regardless of their status as exporters, are now not actionable with CVDs. The remainder are actionable, according as they inflict 'material injury'. If subsidies are 'specific' – to an exporting enterprise or industry, or to an exporting group of enterprises or industries – they can be countervailed if they cause material injury. The definition of 'material injury', already weak, was further diluted (Baldwin 1998: 311). Participation in this subsidies code, which developing countries could and did decline to join under the Tokyo Round rules, has now ceased to be voluntary. It is now mandatory on all WTO members, although some have fixed transition periods before full compliance.

The effect will be to outlaw the sorts of industrial subsidies that have been used successfully in the past to accelerate the growth and develpment of poor countries. It has been said that the Asian miracle growth of the 1965–95 period could never occur again under WTO rules. It seems clear to me that the phenomenal growth of the Asian tiger economies did depend on selective departures from pure free trade regimes. Contrary to the opinion of most orthodox economists, the Asian 'miracle' demonstrated that an intelligent long-term development strategy – based on interventionist departures from free trade that are genuinely selective and temporary – can be made to work. Indeed, if the right conditions can be created, it can be made to work spectacularly well (Wade 1990; Chang 1994: 91–129). What is not so clear, however, is that the Annexes to the WTO Agreement absolutely prohibit *all* the instruments of such a strategy. The change from GATT to WTO does bring tighter restrictions, particularly the clear outlawing of specific subsidies, but it also leaves some gaps unplugged that an imaginative and ingenious developmental state might want to try to exploit for its own purposes (Akyuz et al. 1998: 30–32). Much will depend on how the DSM actually works, and it is in the hands of the legal technocrats how activist they decide to be.[33]

My concern is that, even if they do not choose to be legal activists now, as time passes and as the DSM gets into high gear, they will take that route, which the WTO rules would clearly permit. If and when they do, *the interpretation of the Annexes will increasingly prohibit all protection of infant industries in developing countries.* This will slam the door on a vital means of economic catching up, which at least some poor countries are capable of using, and so serve to solidify the existing unequal worldwide distribution of wealth and income. Although perfectly consonant with criteria of reciprocity and non-discrimination, the consequences will be unjust in terms of distributional equity, universality and maximum aggregate net benefit.

7   THE WTO AS A MEMBERSHIP ORGANISATION

When critics raise this issue, or other issues concerning the substantive justice of the WTO rules, they are often answered with an implicit appeal to the norm of reciprocity. The WTO arrangements cannot be unjust, it is said, since every nation voluntarily agreed to them when applying to join the WTO, and voluntary agreement to an act implies that the gain and the loss from it are at least equivalent. Is this an adequate reply?

In weighing this rebuttal, one must bear in mind the evolution of the community of nations. For all the talk of the demise of the nation state, they have in fact been multiplying fast. The members of the United Nations in 1945 were 51. Now there are about 190. Moreover, as a result of that quadrupling, the disparities between the strongest nations and the weakest nations have multiplied. These new states necessarily emerge on to a stage where the international action is already well advanced. They do not face a moral or legal tabula rasa on which they can, jointly with others, inscribe a new compact. To believe otherwise is to take fiction for fact.

In fact, every member nation did not participate in shaping the constitution of the WTO. Formally, it was agreed between the 76 nations that negotiated the Uruguay Round. Others have had to queue to join a done deal, and in negotiating their admission, and are forced to take the rough with the smooth. As of November 2000, a further 63 nations had been admitted, and applications from a further 30 were still outstanding. It is significant that these negotiations for admittance do not take place with the membership as a whole, but with individual existing members. The entry of China into the WTO was negotiated by the US administration, for example.

Did all of the 76 nations that were GATT members in 1994 shape the WTO rules? Well, yes and no. They may have been formally in the Uruguay Round negotiation, but the actual leverage that any state can exert in such negotiations differs vastly. A few states or groups of states had negotiating strength, but most of them had little, and sat on the sidelines. That was the situation at the birth of the WTO, and it continues to be the case. Formally, all WTO members are equal. Unlike the IMF and the World Bank, the WTO does not have an unequal voting structure, in which rich countries control a share of the vote that is much greater than their numbers in the world community. It appears that the poor countries, who form the majority, *could in principle outvote the rich countries*. Why does this not happen? Because the WTO, like the GATT before it, does not take decisions by voting. Instead, it 'finds consensus'. Finding consensus is an informal procedure in which the Director-General invites some members to participate in a 'green room consultation'. These discussions with selected members go on until the Director-General thinks he has found a basis for consensus, which he brings for approval to the WTO Council plenary session. At this stage countries decide that a consensus exists, or not, as the case may be.

This informal procedure allows the inequalities that exist between members to come into play. There are two main sources of disparity – information about what agreements will benefit your country, and the power to influence the outcome of the informal negotiation.

1. The information access problem comes down to a simple economic question: can your country afford to maintain an embassy in Geneva? If it cannot, it is unlikely that you will be able to follow the trade negotiations, let alone take part in them (Sampson 2000: 1100).
2. Then, if your country's resources are inadequate, what international help is available to assist it to acquire and process trade related information? There is in fact very little. The regular WTO budget provided $741 000 in 1998 for technical assistance and training, about $7000 for each developing country member (ibid.: note 7). Of aid donors' total expenditure on technical assistance, only about 2 per cent is trade related.
3. Since the inauguration of the WTO in 1995, the problem of understanding which outcomes will be more in your interests is aggravated by the great broadening of the trade agenda. The effects on a country of a round of mutual tariff reductions is fundamentally calculable – albeit by economists using general equilibrium models. The effects of a change of standards, by which a whole range of a country's export products may be suddenly deemed substandard, is very much harder to forecast, to calculate, and to negotiate.

A country's informal negotiating influence or power depends on the extent of its trade. In a negotiation based around tariff reduction, bargaining power depends not only on how far you are willing to cut your tariff, but on the size of the trade flows to which the proffered tariff cut will apply. Small tariff cuts on big trade flows are worth much more as bargaining chips than big cuts on small flows. So even a country that knows where its interest lies may not be able to achieve it because of lack of negotiating influence.[34] This is very frustrating for countries with small trade sectors. However, it is *unjust* only if a country's trade sector is being deliberately kept small by others' denial of market access.[35] While true of some countries, the external trade of others, notably in Africa, is constrained not by lack of access to markets, but by unresolved difficulties of supply. These do not involve global injustice, only misfortune. They cannot be helped by trade negotiations, however they are arranged. They need other remedies, including financial aid and technical assistance.

8   IMPLICATIONS FOR JUSTICE VERSUS ORDER

How would the nineteenth-century figures with whom I began have assessed the new WTO? Saint-Simon would have been gratified to see the international legists at work on the adjudication and enforcement of the rules of trade, now removed from the hurly-burly of diplomacy and political pressure and entrusted to the decisions of dispute panels, the Dispute Settlement Body and the Appellate Body of the WTO. He would have been disappointed that there are still no 'scientists' to direct the work of the legists, and wonder why a group of independent economists is not called in to re-write the rules. To Bentham, too, it would have been self-evident that such an international judicial establishment, if capable of calculating the greatest happiness of the greatest number, would be the appropriate framework for achieving global prosperity. At the same time, he would have criticised roundly the host of particular WTO rules that do not derive from the utilitarian theory of justice.

If List had been present at Seattle, he would have recognised in the proceedings the arrogance of the hegemonic state in its insistence in pressing ahead without an agreed agenda, its unwillingness to pursue any agenda, of procedure or substance, but its own, and its abuse of its position as chair of the meeting to pander to its domestic interest groups. He might well have reflected on the difficulties of China in cutting a deal with the US on entry into the WTO.[36] China has invested much in building up its own national strategic industries, which are highly unlikely to withstand the US and European competition that WTO entry would unleash (Nolan 2001: 159–232). So List would have sympathised with China's repeated 'last minute' hesitations in clinching the long-drawn-out membership deal.[37]

Nevertheless, US hegemony has produced a distinctly different trade system from that evolved under British hegemony, whose ideal of justice List first criticised. In response to concerns that free trade can cause social instability within nations, the ideal of embedded liberalism is of a balance between free trade and protection, rationalised by a mixture of different norms of justice.[38] The political reality behind this is that the behaviour of the hegemonic nation in international trade, the US, is driven by the disparate interests of two groups of great domestic business corporations, which are united only by their willingness to pay the bills of the major US political parties. US exporters want other countries to liberalise and provide them with more markets, while those selling into US domestic markets want to block out foreign competition. For both their sakes, the US government would like to have it both ways. The ideal of embedded liberalism, when constrained by US national interests, produces the asymmetric liberalism of the hegemonic power.[39]

Some think that increased judicialisation of international trade will be bad because it will tilt the US political balance in favour of more protection (Goldstein 1998: 149–51). That is valid up to a point, but their argument assumes that the DSM will be effective in striking down existing administered protection, whereas in fact it cannot touch abuse of the AD provisions (Baldwin 1998: 310–11; Das 1999: 425). I have argued that increased judicialisation, or even the achievement of perfect formal justice, will not prevent a systemic bias of outcomes against developing countries. To me, it seems naïve to believe that mere judicialisation, the streamlining of formal justice, can remove injustices in the world trade system, as long as gross economic inequalities between nations remain.

I have argued further that the combination of the new rule on countervailing duties and judicialisation will eventually outlaw performance-related industrial subsidies in the developing countries, striking down one of their most important policies for rapid development. Judging the WTO rules on subsidies as substantively unjust requires clarity about what resemblances and differences between nations are relevant to the treatment of like cases alike, and different cases differently. I believe that the existing inequalities of economic and political power between developed and developing countries do constitute a relevant difference for the purpose of deciding the substantive justice of these rules. If any reneging from multilateralism is to be legitimised, it should be in favour of the economically weak, not the economically strong. The substantive injustice of disregarding a country's stage of development is actually worsened by an improvement in formal justice. Judicialisation tightens the screws of unjust rules.

How then might List's 'true freedom of trade' be achieved in the twenty-first century? The Uruguay Round promises made to developing countries must be fulfilled. Then the overall process of trade liberalisation on a multilateral and non-discriminatory basis must continue. Tariffs on industrial goods of special export interest to developing countries must be reduced. The failure of the Uruguay Round to eliminate administered protection in a wide range of intermediate industries must be rectified. The heavy protection of developed countries' agricultural sectors must be reduced. Neither developed nor developing countries should be contemplating a retreat into protectionism, rather the reverse. At the highest level of generality, it is not free trade, but its absence, that they should beware.

Nevertheless, if in the end both justice and order depend on the possibility of removing existing gross economic inequalities by the successful development of the developing countries, both goals will be ill-served by quasi-judicial attempts to block off the most promising (for some countries) fast track to development. I believe that there is a morally compelling case for developing countries to be given exceptional treatment on 'specific' industrial subsidies for infant industry purposes, provided always that these are selective, temporary and performance related. The idea of 'special and differential treatment' of developing countries, which was added to GATT and survives in different forms in the WTO Agreements, needs to be re-visited, simplified and given greater precision.[40] It is in every nation's interest that late developers succeed in catching up, because that is the only route to a world of less poverty and conflict. If their path is blocked 'for legal reasons', the legitimacy of the present hegemonic ideal of embedded liberalism can only erode further, and then world trading arrangements are bound to become more disorderly.

NOTES

1. Comte refers to such people as 'scientists', but he held that 'legists' had a supporting role to play within the scientific elite, because they had the skill of making regulations, which was indispensable in the construction of a new social system (see Jones 1998: 74, especially note e).
2. The most famous example of this in trade matters is the 1934 decision of the US Congress to delegate the setting of tariff levels to the office of the President, who was less accountable to particular electoral constituencies (Destler 1986: 1–4; Goldstein 1998: 140–45, but see also Cupitt and Elliott, 1994 which takes a different view of the impact of constituency economic interests). Similar measures after the Cold War include safeguarding the independence to central bankers, thereby taking national interest rate policy out of the hands of the elected politicians.
3. Bentham described the United States as 'that newly-created nation, one of the most enlightened, if not the most enlightened, at this day on the globe', although he also criticised the looseness of the drafting of the Declaration of Independence (1970 [1780]: 309–10).
4. On the sense of injustice, and the role that inequality plays in sustaining it, see Shklar (1990: 83–126).
5. On the problems of using the term 'mercantilism' in historical studies, see Coleman (1969: 92–117).
6. It does, however, assume that market prices reflect social costs, so that theoretical debates about free trade centre around possible cases of market imperfection (Bhagwati 1994: 232). There is also the question of how equally the gains from trade are distributed between the countries that trade.

7. 'An action then may be said to be conformable to the principle of utility ... (meaning with respect to the community at large) when the tendency it has to augment the happiness of the community is greater than any it has to diminish it' (Bentham 1970 [1780]: 12–13. This principle of 'maximum aggregate net benefit' does not take account of the distribution of benefits and disbenefits, or the equality of rights or liberty (Rawls 1972: 22–33).

8. For a discussion of legal justice, see Hart (1961: 153–63). For a useful review of norms of fairness in international trade, see Suranovic (2000).

9. Similarly, modern contractarians have argued that persons have to be taken seriously when defining social justice. 'Utilitarianism does not take seriously the distinction between persons' (Rawls 1972: 27).

10. See List (1977 [1885]: 130–32. This view is also to be found in Krasner (1976: 322). It is quite odd that the 'polarisation effect' is often cited as a potential drawback of creating a regional free trade area, but it tends to get lost in discussions of global free trade. A notable exception to this is Deardorff (2001).

11. See List (1977 [1885]: 397–8). List's view here differs from the most familiar Marxist formulation of the role of the state, as a mere emanation of a capitalist world order (Fisk 1989: 219–22). Marx thought that the worldwide expansion of bourgeois society and its capitalist mode of production, under the banner of free trade, was unstoppable – except by proletarian revolution. 'The cheap prices of its commodities are the heavy artillery that batters down all Chinese walls ... in one word, it (bourgeois society) creates a world in its own image' (Marx 1973 [1848]: 71). Unlike List, Marx never took nations seriously, or their international organisations.

12. There was a positive correlation between the adoption of tariffs and economic growth for ten countries, including Germany and the US, in the period 1875–1914 (O'Rourke 2000: 456–7). Correlation does not imply causality, but this scepticism also applies to modern correlations of growth with trade openness.

13. This is one of the sources of the free trade versus fair trade debate (DeMartino 2000: 203–15).

14. The function of the ILO was to raise 'the common standard of the conditions of life, so that those nations which lead the world on social reform may not be placed at an undue disadvantage by those which compete with them by the exploitation of their labour' (Shotwell 1934: xix). Despite its defeat in 1918, Germany was extremely keen to be allowed to join the new ILO, for obvious reasons.

15. It had a unique structure, in that international negotiations were conducted through a tripartite mechanism, which involved representatives not only of national governments, but also of each country's employers and trades unions. This built up a national consensus for change in the course of an international negotiation. The disadvantages of the ILO were that progress was very slow, and the labour standards conventions agreed often pertained to highly specific working practices and technologies that were, in any case, rapidly becoming uneconomic.

16. The idea of a small central UN Secretariat, and a large number of specialised agencies arose from favourable perceptions of the ILO compared with the failed League of Nations.

17. Goldstein (1998: 139, 146–9). According to Ruggie (1982: 398), 'that multilateralism and the quest for domestic stability were coupled and even conditioned by one another reflected the shared legitimacy of a set of social objectives to which the industrial world had moved, unevenly but "as a single entity". Therefore, the common tendency to view the postwar regimes as liberal regimes, but with lots of cheating taking place on the domestic side, fails to capture the full complexity of the embedded liberalism compromise'. Ruggie borrowed the term 'embedded' from Polanyi (1957 [1944]). The treatment of tariff reductions as 'concessions' which must be reciprocated is a vestige of mercantilist thinking.

18. The eight GATT Rounds were Geneva (1947), Annecy (1949), Torquay (1951), Geneva II (1956), Dillon (1960–61), Kennedy (1964–67), Tokyo (1973–79) and Uruguay (1987–94).

19. Tariff reductions were only one of several favourable factors in output growth, however, as the slowdown of growth in the second sub-period indicates. Fixed exchange rates, national full employment policies and cheap petrol prices were also important favourable influences in the period up to 1974, and falling transport costs were present throughout. The growth

of trade faster than output is evidence that tariff reduction stimulated a more refined specialisation within industrial sectors and even within industrial firms (Ruggie 1982: 400–401).

20. Developing countries did not participate actively in any of the GATT Rounds until the Uruguay Round (Krueger 1998: 5, note 9). While developed countries have greatly reduced tariffs on products of mutual interest, they maintain tariffs that are comparatively high on products of export interest to developing countries (Das 1999: 69).

21. Duties that 'countervail' subsidies granted by the government of the exporting country, deemed to be a non-tariff barrier to trade.

22. It has been argued that being bound by 'international obligation may reduce the incentive to punish a cheater outside GATT, thereby raising the gain from cheating ... It is possible for international obligation to exert forces reducing cooperation' (Kovenock and Thursby 1992: 151–70).

23. 'Frequent investigations, even if the complaints are finally rejected, amount to a kind of harassment of the defendants because of the uncertainty and expenses such actions create' (Tharakan 1995: 1551). See also Marvel and Ray (1995: 1583–4) and Destler (1986).

24. Ruggie (1982: 411). 'Most governments ... [negotiated] a "voluntary" export restraint with the presumably reluctant exporter who had been previously "softened" by threats of emergency action under GATT (Article XIX). The 1962 Cotton Textiles Arrangement (later the Multi-Fibre Agreement) was a VER (voluntary export restraint) administered by the GATT, although it was clearly a new form of trade discrimination' (Johnson 1967: 21–2). After nearly 40 years, it still has not been fully phased out, although it is now planned to end in 2005 (Laird 2000: 4–5).

25. Gilbert (1996: 17) suggested that ICAs are not infeasible *per se*, but that the collapse of the International Tin Agreement in 1985 led to a loss of confidence in ICAs among producers, and that this undermined their willingness to work at resolving the operational difficulties of ICAs.

26. Another excessively dismissive evaluation of UNCTAD is in Henderson (1998: 110–11).

27. The full text of the Understanding on the Settlement of Disputes is given in Jackson (1998: 145–69).

28. 'The last resort ... is the possibility of suspending the application of concessions or other obligations under the covered agreements on a discriminatory basis *vis-à-vis* the other Member, subject to the authorization by the DSB [Dispute Settlement Body] of such measures' (Article 3, Clause 7).

29. Formal justice is the equal application of the existing rules of an institution in its legal or adminstrative processes (Hart 1961: 156–8; Rawls 1972: 58–60).

30. Das (1999: 397) regards this as a 'serious limitation of the DSU'. On these major systemic deficiencies, see Hoekman and Mavroidis (2000: 529–32).

31. The fact that developing countries have started to bring disputes to the DSM does not detract from this point if, as seems to be so, these are disputes mainly with other developing countries (Jackson 1998: 74).

32. Although ADs and CVDs are analytically and legally distinct, they are linked in practice. In most US cases they are sought jointly by the complainant industry, and granted together by the US International Trade Commission. This is evidence that they are being used for protection and not for their original purpose of removing trade distortions (Marvel and Ray 1995: 1587–8).

33. Amsden (2000) argues that the new WTO rules leave ample room for developing countries to pursue industrial strategies that use subsidies. This is true, but the problem is that the developmental use of subsidies requires them to be temporary, selective and conditional on the performance of the beneficiary firm (see Kaempfer et al. 1989: 272). If the selection criteria include *export performance*, it will be difficult to avoid the charge of giving a 'specific' subsidy.

34. '[P]owerful countries have far more bargaining chips to use ... to leverage less powerful countries into "agreeing" on the preferred "consensus decision"' (Sampson 2000: 1101).

35. This would breach norms of non-discrimination and universality.

36. This is not so fanciful as it sounds. List used the case of China, along with Ireland, to illustrate the dangers to weak countries of participating in free trade (Yaffey 1996: 87).
37. As described in 'Prospect of WTO entry looks distant for China', *Financial Times*, 14 March 2001, p. 14.
38. Thus Krasner's 1976 argument that hegemony *as such* leads to an open structure of trade seems to be too simple. See Lipson (1982: 453–4).
39. The idea of asymmetric liberalism is captured in the following remark of Alan Winters: 'The 1980s saw increased numbers of VERs, tighter MFA restrictions, and more anti-dumping actions, but this did not prevent (liberal) opinion from covering trade policy when (industrial) countries offered development policy advice' (Winters 2000: 5).
40. The present position where 'special and differential treatment' (SDT) consists of an arbitrary deadline for full compliance, unenforceable promises of technical assistance for transitional difficulties and a wish to confine SDT to the 48 least-developed countries is highly unsatisfactory. See the discussion of SDT in Pangestu (2000).

REFERENCES

Akyuz, Y., H-J. Chang and R. Kozul-Wright (1998), 'New perspectives on East Asian development', *Journal of Development Studies*, **34** (6), 4–36.
Amsden, A. (2000), *Industrialization under New WTO Law*, Geneva: UNCTAD.
Baldwin, R.E. (1998), 'Imposing multilateral discipline on administered protection', in Krueger (ed.), pp. 297–328.
Bentham, J. (1970 [1780]), *An Introduction to the Principles of Morals and Legislation*, London: Athlone Press.
Bhagwati, J.N. (1994), 'Free trade: old and new challenges', *Economic Journal*, **104** (423), 231–46.
Chang, H.-J. (1994), *The Political Economy of Industrial Policy*, Basingstoke: Macmillan.
Coleman, D.C. (1969), 'Eli Heckscher and the idea of Mercantilism', in Coleman (ed.), *Revisions in Mercantilism*, London: Methuen, 92–117.
Cupitt, R.T. and E. Elliott (1994), 'Schattschneider revisited: Senate voting on the Smoot–Hawley Tariff Act of 1930', *Economics and Politics*, **6** (3), 187–99.
Das, B.L. (1999), *The World Trade Organisation. A Guide to the Framework for International Trade*, London: Zed Books.
De Marchi, N. (1991), 'League of Nations economists and the ideal of peaceful change in the thirties', *History of Political Economy*, **23**, Annual Supplement: 143–78.
Deardorff, A.V. (2001), 'Rich and poor countries in neoclassical trade and growth', *Economic Journal*, **111** (470), 277–94.
DeMartino, G.F. (2000), *Global Economy, Global Justice. Theoretical Objections and Policy Alternatives to Neoliberalism*, London: Routledge.
Destler, I.M. (1986), *American Trade Politics: System under Stress*, Washington, DC: Institute for International Economics.
Fisk, M. (1989), *The State and Justice. An Essay in Political Theory*, Cambridge: Cambridge University Press.
Gilbert, C. (1996), 'International commodity agreements: an obituary notice', *World Development*, **24** (1), 1–19.
Goldstein, J. (1998), 'International institutions and domestic politics: GATT, WTO and the liberalization of international trade', in Krueger (ed.), pp. 133–52.
Hart, H. (1961), *The Concept of Law*, Oxford: Clarendon Press.

Henderson, D. (1998), 'International agencies and cross-border liberalization: the WTO in context', in Krueger (ed.), pp. 97–130.

Hoekman, B.M. and P.C. Mavroidis (2000), 'WTO dispute settlement, transparency and surveillance', *The World Economy*, **23** (4), 527–42.

Hull, C. (1948), *The Memoirs of Cordell Hull*, Vol. One, London: Hodder & Stoughton.

Hurrell, A. (2003), 'Order and justice in international relations: what is at stake?' in R. Foot, J.L. Gaddis and A. Hurrell (eds), *Order and Justice in International Relations*, Oxford: Oxford University Press, pp. 24–48.

Jackson, J.H. (1998), *The World Trade Organization. Constitution and Jurisprudence*, London: Pinter for Royal Institute of International Affairs.

Johnson, H.G. (1967), *Economic Policies Towards Less Developed Countries*, London: Allen & Unwin.

Jones, H.S. (ed.) (1998), *Auguste Comte. Early Political Writings*, Cambridge: Cambridge University Press.

Kaempfer, W.H., E. Tower and T.D. Willett (1989), 'Performance contingent protection', *Economics and Politics*, **1** (3), 261–75.

Kovenck, D. and M. Thursby (1992), 'GATT, dispute settlement and cooperation', *Economics and Politics*, **4** (2), 151–70.

Krasner, S.D. (1976), 'State power and the structure of international trade', *World Politics*, **38**, April, 317–47.

Krueger, A.O. (ed.) (1998), *The WTO as an International Organisation*, Chicago: Chicago University Press.

Laird, S. (2000), 'Multilateral market access negotiations in goods and services', CREDIT Research Paper No. 00/4, University of Nottingham, Nottingham.

Lipson, C. (1982), 'The transformation of trade: the sources and effects of regime change', *International Organization*, **36** (2), 417–55.

List, F. (1977 [1885]), *The National System of Political Economy*, Fairfield, NJ: Augustus M. Kelley.

Marvel, H.P. and E.J. Ray (1995), 'Countervailing duties', *Economic Journal*, **105** (433), 1576–93.

Marx, K. (1973 [1848]), 'The Communist Manifesto', in D. Fernbach (ed.), *The Revolutions of 1848*, London: Penguin, pp. 67–98.

Nolan, P. (2001), *China and the Global Economy*, Basingstoke: Palgrave.

O'Neill, H. and J. Toye (eds) (1998), *A World Without Famine? New Approaches to Aid and Development*, Basingstoke: Macmillan.

O'Rourke, K.H. (2000), 'Tariffs and growth in the late 19th century', *Economic Journal*, **110** (463), 456–83.

Pangestu, M. (2000), 'Special and differential treatment in the millennium: special for whom, and how different?', *The World Economy*, **23** (9), 1285–1302.

Polanyi, K. (1957 [1944]), *The Great Transformation. The Political and Economic Origins of Our Time*, Boston: Beacon Press.

Rawls, J. (1972), *A Theory of Justice*, Oxford: Oxford University Press.

Ruggie, J.G. (1982), 'International regimes, transactions and change: embedded liberalism and the postwar economic order', *International Organization*, **36** (2), 379–415.

Sampson, G.P. (2000), 'The World Trade Organisation after Seattle', *The World Economy*, **23** (9), 1097–117.

Shklar, J.N. (1990), *The Faces of Injustice*, New Haven, CT: Yale University Press.

Shotwell, J.T. (1934), *Introduction to The Origins of the International Labour Organization*, Vol. 1, New York: Columbia University Press.

Suranovic, S.M. (2000), 'A positive analysis of fairness with applications to international trade', *The World Economy*, **23** (3), 283–307.

Tharakan, P.K.M. (1995), 'Political economy and contingent protection', *Economic Journal*, **105** (433), 1550–64.

Wade, R. (1990), *Governing the Market. Economic Theory and the Role of Government in East Asian Industrialization*, Princeton, NJ: Princeton University Press.

Winters, A. (2000), *Trade Policy as Development Policy: Building on Fifty Years Experience*, Geneva: UNCTAD.

Yaffey, M. (1996), 'Friedrich List and the causes of Irish hunger', in O'Neill and Toye (eds), pp. 84–106.

5. Some proposals to adapt international institutions to developmental needs

Kunibert Raffer

1 INTRODUCTION

Most international institutions were not drafted for the specific needs of so-called 'developing countries', even those meanwhile providing their services practically only to this group. The Bretton Woods institutions are prime examples of this latter category. The Organization for International Cooperation and Development (OECD 1985, p. 140) describes their initial tasks: 'The IBRD [International Bank for Reconstruction and Development] was there to guarantee European borrowing in international (North American) markets; the IMF [International Monetary Fund] was there to smooth the flow of repayments'. Originally, not much attention had been paid to development problems. The presence of delegations from what is nowadays called the South, mainly Latin American countries, but also an Indian delegation (*pro forma* led by British officials as India was in transition to independence) insisted on resources financing development as well as European reconstruction (Raffer and Singer 2001, pp. 3ff). Thus 'and Development' was added to the original name International Bank for Reconstruction. Reconstruction soon became relatively unimportant for the IBRD, because of aid programmes for Greece and Turkey, the Marshall Plan, the large US loan to the UK negotiated by John Maynard Keynes towards the end of his life, and the newly-created UN Relief and Rehabilitation Administration (UNRRA), which took over some of the Bank's intended functions.

European economic recovery was – rightly, one may assume – seen as necessary for a non-communist future of Western Europe. In contrast to hard IBRD loans, the Marshall Plan operated almost entirely on a grant basis. IBRD loans were seen as inappropriate for the task of reconstructing Europe successfully, which raises questions about their appropriateness for fostering development in much poorer countries. After the demise of the Bretton Woods system the IMF shifted totally to the South. During the last two decades no industrialised country drew on its resources. Nevertheless it has not adapted to the new situation.

Although created in the 1990s and with large participation by Southern countries (SCs), the WTO (World Trade Organization) framework accommodates Northern needs and wishes much better than those of the South. A certain selectivity of liberalising where the North, notably the US, could hope to conquer markets created resentment. Present complaints by SCs show that they feel sidelined, not least by the way the treaties are implemented.

Adapting the main international institutions in the fields of trade and finance to developmental needs is strongly indicated. Also drawing on proposals made by Raffer and Singer (2001), this chapter presents ideas for change regarding the WTO and international financial institutions (IFIs). It argues that some main principles of any market economy must be introduced into North–South relations. Finally, a body where SCs can draw attention to infringements on their rights is necessary. This body could also monitor the implementation of UN summit meetings, such as Copenhagen, international commitments such as the reduction of extreme poverty and malnutrition by one-half by the year 2015, or of the famous 0.7 per cent target of aid.

2   TRADE: REFORMING THE WTO

The new WTO framework denies SCs important policy options to foster development. After complaints in Singapore, and the deadlock of Seattle, SCs seemed determined to foil a new round at Doha because the WTO had not taken their legitimate interests properly into account. It was argued that the implementation of clauses in favour of SCs had not been satisfactory, and that poor countries were overburdened with implementing all rules, a respite would be necessary before any further steps should be taken and a 'development Round' would be needed. The results of Doha, however, do not suggest a fundamental change in favour of development needs so far.

The OECD has repeatedly pointed out that Northern trade policies often obstruct Southern diversification efforts by tariff escalation, suddenly imposed new trade barriers, anti-dumping actions, and other selective trade-restricting provisions, when SC exports start to take off successfully. Average tariffs on manufactured imports from poor countries are a multiple of those on imports from other Northern countries. As a first step this discriminatory trading system described in detail and repeatedly by the OECD (cf. Raffer and Singer 2001, pp. 250f.) must be abolished. Market access must be equal irrespective of whether the exporting country is Northern or Southern. Non-discriminatory barriers, particularly equal tariffs for all goods imported by OECD countries regardless of their origin is an absolutely minimal demand. It could easily have been negotiated into the relevant WTO agreements, but the North apparently chose not to do so. The economic doctrines which OECD countries use to advocate liberalisation are forgotten when it comes to discriminating against Southern suppliers. Abolishing this discrimination is therefore an important demand.

Differentiated and Preferential Treatment

But to encourage development trade policy should go further. Differentiated and preferential treatment within the WTO based on objective indicators such as GDP/head was therefore proposed (ibid., pp. 251f.). Some clauses demanding preferential treatment of SCs exist, most of them not very concrete. Concern has been voiced by many SCs that not much preferential treatment has actually been forthcoming. One could even speak of a certain de facto rollback of a principle once established within GATT (General Agreement on Tariffs and Trade) by the WTO.

To allow SCs to develop their economic structures their right to protect their economies at least as strongly as the North must be built into the WTO agreements. This system could be differentiated by stages of development. One possible way of integrating infant industry protection into the WTO framework would be to establish a right of any SC to obtain a given number of waivers for industries the country specifies, and for a specified time, depending on the country's stage of development. To avoid petrification, protection would be calculated to equalise differences in productivities between SCs and the global market. Protection would be reduced over time, either because Southern producers have reduced productivity gaps or because they have failed to improve their productivity within a reasonable period of time. Liberalisation would have to be sequenced. Time spans considered necessary by the North are informative. Regarding the textiles and clothing sector, the first protectionist step by the US occurred in 1935. In 2001 no industrialised country yet feels fit to liberalise this small sector, while all advise and make SCs open their whole economies quickly.

In the case of textiles the North took protective steps explicitly against the market, not against government action. The Decision of 19 November 1960 on the Avoidance of Market Disruption explicitly referred to 'market disruption' as a situation where 'price differentials do not arise from governmental intervention in the fixing or formation of prices or from dumping practices' (Blokker 1989, p. 365). Restrictions on trade in textiles and clothing were thus explicitly introduced by industrialised countries against the effects of the world market. The argument that trade reflected comparative advantages did not carry much weight when used by SCs (ibid., pp. 72 and 76).

When the GATT Secretariat sent out a questionnaire in December 1960 to collect information on concrete cases of market disruption, member states could either not provide the necessary information or were unwilling to do so (ibid., p. 80). A clear definition of 'market disruption' was not given, nor did this expression appear in the GATT Treaty. Opaqueness served importing industrialised countries to claim that they suffered from market disruption, whenever they chose to. This is clearly at odds with the principle of the Rule of Law. Even this was not considered sufficient: to make protectionism easier, 'actual' market disruption – whatever it might be – was not necessary, potential import increases sufficed. Without any clear rules of how to assess their likelihood, potential disruption can always be claimed, even in the case of countries presently unable to export at all. Regarding textiles and apparel, measures violating the GATT Treaty could be taken by the North with impunity. Providing an institutional base for protectionism regarding these manufactures, the GATT provided assistance in breaking its own basic rules.

Developmental protection can easily be combined with measures that would raise funds for development. Rather than lowering tariffs in line with productivity changes, SC governments could keep tariffs constant but levy taxes on protected domestic production that increase slowly in line with productivity, thus abolishing incentives to producers to establish themselves comfortably behind high protectionist walls. The money obtained would have to be used to finance diversification, but also for redistributive measures in favour of the poor. Obviously, TRIMs (trade-related investment measures) should be waived for SCs, except possibly for a few very advanced SCs, where one might discuss fairly similar treatment to that of OECD countries. TRIMs bar any possibility of pursuing industrialisation drives like those of the successful Asian Tigers or the OECD countries themselves.

Although space prohibits a theoretical discussion on markets, one should acknowledge that the academic mainstream strongly opposes any protectionism, basing their arguments on the Heckscher–Ohlin theory of trade. The practical example of industrialised countries would not cut any ice either. It is indeed difficult to find economists of some renown with mainstream colleagues, who openly oppose this ruling view, for example, by writing:

> The obstinate conservatism with which the classical comparative cost thinking has been retained in theory as something more than a pedagogical introduction – or a model for the treatment of a few special problems – is evidence that, even today, there is in many quarters an insufficient understanding of this fundamental fact.
>
> It follows that not only the comparative cost model but also the factor proportions model can only be applied in special cases and used as a general introduction to illuminate the character of trade in some essential aspects ... It is characteristic of *the developing countries* that a good many factors do not exist at all and that the quality of others differs from factors in the industrialized countries. This means that a simple method of analysis – such as the factor proportions model – which does not take this into account is to some extent unrealistic. (Ohlin 1967, pp. 308f., stress in original)

Eli Heckscher (1950, p. 275; stress added) explicitly found his theory '*in full accordance with List's point of view, since his criticism of the "school" was directed only at the dynamic factors*' – a view fully shared by List (1920, pp. 234f.). Nevertheless the Heckscher–Ohlin theory is used to advocate liberalisation and to 'disprove' List's infant industry protection argument. While shunned by most economists knowledgeable about the Heckscher–Ohlin trade theory, the advice to SCs to diversify and to protect temporarily and selectively, also derived from the Prebisch–Singer thesis, would at least meet Eli Heckscher's and Bertil Ohlin's approval.

A Food Import Facility

When the WTO agreements were about to be signed, OECD countries apparently perceived a need to assure SCs that relief measures against expected higher food prices would be financed. Once the agreement was signed no relief was granted. The WTO tried to help SCs in this matter, but without success. Meanwhile a WTO list of Net Food Importing Developing Countries exists. However, being listed does not confer automatic benefits but donors and international organisations see this as another possibility to exercise leverage. Unlike negative effects corrective benefits do not result automatically from the treaty. The 'alternative' offered to these countries – using existing facilities of the Bretton Woods institutions – is not economically sensible. It means that consumption is financed by loans carrying interest. Even under IDA (International Development Association) conditions this still means 0.75 per cent a year in hard currency which countries have to earn. In the case of Sub-Saharan Africa, for example, a region paying only one-fifth or one-sixth of what they should pay every year, the rest accumulating as arrears, even such soft loans increase the debt overhang.

To compensate poor net importers of food for price increases a Food Import Facility established at the WTO was proposed (Raffer 1997). It should be a contractual insurance scheme without conditionality – like the original Stabex in Lomé I. Payments should depend exclusively on statistical facts, on observed price changes. Conditionality must not creep in eventually as it did with Stabex or the IMF's Compensatory Financing Facility.

Due to the asymmetry between export earning shortfalls and food import costs, transfers cannot be modelled precisely as in Stabex. Compensating increases in food import costs (price times quantity bought) over those of a base period would be problematic. Rising prices and falling quantities could even out at constant expenditures. Heavily affected net importers would receive no support, although they cannot afford to buy the same quantity any longer and have to pay higher prices. Therefore a formula is needed, which –

in line with initially voiced official intentions – compensates negative effects on availability, securing adequate access to food.

As food imports can be fairly inelastic, Raffer (1997) proposed to compensate price increases rather than compensating quantity reductions in kind. Transfers could thus be either

$$q_b(p_i - p_b) \tag{5.1}$$

or

$$q_i(p_i - p_b), \tag{5.2}$$

the price difference times the quantity of the base year(s) or multiplied by the current quantity. The indices b and i indicate the base year(s) before and the year for which compensation is claimed after the change respectively. Naturally q_b or p_b could also be averages of several years, as in the concept of the base period in the Agreement on Agriculture. Both variants have the theoretical advantage that price differences are easier to determine than changes in quantity due to price changes. Theoretically they are not elegant solutions, because observed differences can partly result from other factors than Uruguay Round induced price effects as well. Compensation might be higher than these price effects. However, when helping the hungry one should prefer erring on the safe side. No transfers arise if the price falls below that of the base period.

Both variants would allow compensating poor net importers for Uruguay Round induced increases in import costs. Transfers would be effected if price effects can be proved, either in the form of grants or of grants and loans depending on the development stage of the countries entitled to transfers. Loans – if there are any – should carry no interest not to overburden already overindebted countries. The money should be used for diversification measures or for poverty alleviation, another ODA (Official Development Assistance) goal of the OECD's at the moment. The Food Import Facility would allow OECD donors to pursue this particular goal much more effectively. Knowing that transfers are temporary should be an incentive to use them properly.

Both variants of calculating transfer payments would be acceptable. Variant (5.1) implies an element of petrification and cannot react properly to cases when imports increase beyond q_b due to natural or human-made disasters. Variant (5.2) would do well in this respect, but produces too low transfers in the normal case of negatively sloped demand curves, where higher prices reduce q_i and thus transfers. Net importers would get no compensation although they cannot afford to import as much as before. Under the assumption that increased imports because of disasters would usually be covered by emergency aid, one could prefer (5.1). A safer and more generous solution is using formula (5.1) when $q_i < q_b$, but (5.2) whenever $q_i > q_b$. For the poorest countries this option seems strongly indicated, in spite of the formulae's built-in safety margin.

Some form of phasing out is necessary to induce net importers to stimulate domestic food production. This would correspond to economic reasoning as well as to the intentions of the Decision on Possible Negative Effects. The amounts received would be slowly reduced after some years according to a predetermined time schedule. The scheme would be temporary, giving net importers time to adjust, the kind of breathing space considered so essential by the North for adjusting in an orderly manner avoiding disruptive effects in the case of textiles and clothing. The time needed by the North to adjust in this sector could serve as an indicator for the period envisaged.

The WTO's Committee on Agriculture has the mandate to monitor the follow-up to the Decision on measures in favour of net importers pursuant to Article 16(2) of the Agreement on Agriculture. This strongly suggests that the Food Import Facility should be established at the WTO. As a measure against abuse of funds, recipients themselves could monitor their use in the way the US allowed self-monitoring by recipients under its Marshall Plan. This successful precedent should be copied (Raffer and Singer 1996, pp. 197f.).

Dispute Settlement

It was one of the main incentives to convince smaller and weaker countries to sign the WTO treaties, promoted as a rule-based system, protecting the rights of the weak. Arguably the most enlightening illustration of reality is the European Union's complaint against the US Helms–Burton Act. According to the US 'the WTO panel process would not lead to a resolution of the dispute, instead it would pose serious risks for the new organization' (WTO 1996, p. 2). Following US 'advice' to 'explore other avenues' (ibid.) the European Commission 'requested' the panel to suspend its work in April 1997.

The dispute between Canada and Brazil on subsidies to their small aircraft industry also proves that the WTO does not enforce its own rules against powerful members. Canada, a G7 country, simply refused to provide the information requested by the panel. Declining Brazil's demand to infer that the information withheld was prejudicial to Canada's position, the panel stated that Brazil's evidence was insufficient. The Appellate Body found that Canada had violated its obligation to respond promptly and fully (Article 13(1) of the Understanding on Rules and Procedures Covering the Settlement of Disputes), remarking that 'a party's refusal to collaborate has the potential to undermine the functioning of the dispute settlement system' (WTO 2000,

p. 59). The Appellate Body 'might well have concluded that the facts on the record did warrant the inference that the information Canada withheld ... included information prejudicial to Canada's denial that the EDC [Export Development Corporation] had conferred "benefit" and granted a prohibited export subsidy'. Nevertheless the panel's finding was upheld as it was felt Brazil had not done enough to produce evidence. The Appellate Body did 'not intend to suggest that Brazil was precluded from pursuing another complaint against Canada' (ibid.), without specifying, however, why Canada should then provide prejudicial information that it had previously withheld.

The following changes to the WTO's dispute settlement are suggested:

- Compensation should be paid if an industrial country brings a complaint against an SC and loses. Both the SC's legal costs and damage compensation should be paid by the plaintiff.
- Non-negligible damage would have to be proved to be at least likely to have been done by the SC if a Northern member starts a complaint. Differentiation according to income levels, development stages and so on can be discussed.
- Collective retaliation by the whole WTO membership against an offender is needed to change the present situation where powerful countries can decide not to implement decisions – or even prevent them – with impunity. This suggestion (Raffer 1995) was formally brought up by India in 1999.
- The Textiles Monitoring Body (TMB) should be abolished for two reasons. First, its two-tier system differs from the normal process of WTO dispute settlement. As it is required to take all decisions by consensus (members appointed by countries involved in the unresolved issue are exempted) effective and speedy dispute resolutions are likely to be prevented, especially so as there doubtlessly exists Northern solidarity with regard to impeding Southern exports. The fact that the transparency and impartiality of the TMB has come under heavy criticism corroborates the view that it would be better not to have this two-tier procedure.
- The 'Green Room' should be abolished. The expression refers to the practice of backroom negotiations to which only a few countries are invited, whose results are then presented to the rest for 'consensus', sometimes under time pressure. Since the WTO's Northern members in particular have repeatedly declared themselves to be in favour of transparency, open decisions, accountable democracy and so on, this change cannot but reflect their own interests.

TRIPs (Trade-related intellectual property rights)

Leaving local indigenous knowledge totally unprotected, the TRIPs Agreement strictly speaking does not protect intellectual property, only specific intellectual property defined according to Northern criteria, and needs. Historical parallels exist. In Europe the adoption of Roman Law was used by the higher nobility to claim peasants' land as their 'property'. Colonialism, when land and property were taken from 'natives' by introducing Northern law voiding autochthonous legal systems, is another example of pillage under a thin legal cloak – protected by the sword of colonial armies not the WTO's dagger.

It would be very easy to protect Southern knowledge. It is easily established whether specific procedures or specific knowledge exist or not in any given region. Mechanisms to protect indigenous knowledge in the proper way are easy to design and should be used. Unfortunately the TRIPs Agreement does exactly the opposite by no longer demanding an inventive step. Article 27 first speaks of the involvement of an 'inventive step' as a condition. But the pertaining footnote 5 redefines it as 'non obvious'. If someone applies tribal or traditional knowledge to problems in the North, this may be considered non obvious. The WTO confers to Northern interests a licence to take other people's intellectual property. In parentheses its might be said that the WTO itself appropriated the acronym of the World Tourism Organisation (WTO) in clear breach of Article 15 of its own TRIPs Agreement.

The disadvantage of Southern producers is compounded by Article 34 of the TRIPs Agreement shifting the burden of proof in the case of process patents onto the defendant. Thus it is easy to create a lot of nuisance and considerable costs simply by accusing a competitor, particularly poorer Southern competitors. SCs already face an array of problems in WTO dispute settlement procedures, not least costs. Therefore Article 34 must go, at least for SCs.

The effects of TRIPs on human lives have been felt particularly severely in the case of medical drugs. In April 2001 a group of African countries demanded a special session of the TRIPs Council to discuss the Agreement's effects on access to medicines, particularly for treating AIDS. They pointed out that TRIPs had enabled pharmaceutical companies to raise prices of their products far above the levels that can be afforded by a great number of people, claiming the existing model of protecting intellectual property rights to be too heavily tilted in favour of right holders and against public interest. The Republic of South Africa was sued by pharmaceutical companies on the grounds that it violated international patent regulations by facilitating access to low-cost medicines. Under strong public pressure the companies ultimately withdrew the lawsuit. Providing the 'cocktail' of needed drugs free of charge, Brazil reduced AIDS mortality from 10 592 Brazilians dying from AIDS-related causes in 1995 to 1 700 in 2000. The US filed a WTO complaint on behalf of its pharmaceutical industry against Brazil, one of the promoters of a declaration on access to low-cost pharmaceuticals to be presented at the WTO. The US complained against provisions in Brazil's patent law requiring local production of a patented product within three years under threat of compulsory licensing.

The TRIPs Agreement contains a wide range of safeguards to protect public health, including the possibility of overriding patents through compulsory licensing or parallel imports, a flexibility, which – according to the World Health Organization is not being used. 'Parallel imports' means importing from countries where the product is sold more cheaply without approval of patent owners. Under compulsory licensing, governments are authorised to grant the use of patents without the patent-holder's consent, especially in cases such as public health emergencies. The *Financial Times* (20 June 2001) explains why safeguards are not used. For years the US threatened trade sanctions against countries such as Thailand and South Africa, revising their legislation to incorporate TRIPs safeguards. After AIDS activists dogged Al Gore's presidential campaign, the Clinton administration announced it would no longer oppose TRIPs-consistent measures, a policy President George W. Bush pledged to continue. Health groups, however, say that the US is still exerting pressure on countries to forgo or weaken TRIPs safeguards, for instance in negotiations on the Free Trade Agreement of the Americas. Over 100 non-governmental organisations (NGOs) urged the WTO to adopt a seven-point strategy including a moratorium on dispute settlement action, an agreement not to put pressure on SCs to forgo TRIPs rights, and an extended TRIPs implementation deadline for the poorest countries.

Threatening to override Bayer's patent, the US meanwhile forced Bayer to sell its Cipro tablets at roughly a fifth of its market price. Canada had already placed large orders with the local company Apotex for a copy of Cipro, reopening the debate about patent protection for essential medicines. On the same day (25 October 2001) the *Financial Times* reported both about the US enforced price cut and fierce opposition by a US-led group including Canada against SCs led by Brazil and India, insisting on a declaration by ministers at Doha that 'nothing in the TRIPs agreement shall prevent governments from taking measures to protect public health'. This is another fine example illustrating the nature of TRIPs and the real value of membership rights guaranteed under the WTO's rule-based system if members are not the US, the EU, or Japan. The WTO has a built-in ratchet effect: its obligations bar SCs from reverting to options of the past, but massive pressure is exerted to prevent them from enjoying 'guaranteed' membership rights. This underlines the need to reform dispute settlement procedures as proposed above to prevent their being used to harass weaker members. The WTO rightly presents itself as a rule-based system – apparently with one rule for the rich and another one for the poor.

3 REFORMING MULTILATERAL INSTITUTIONS AND FINANCIAL COOPERATION

Arguably, the problem that contractual rights of SCs are not respected in practice is even more pronounced in the case of IFIs, most notably the IMF. IFIs have repeatedly caused damage to their clients by violating their own constitutions. Introducing the Rule of Law to these institutions is thus a legal, economic, and developmental necessity.

Respecting Membership Rights of All Members

Pursuant to its presently valid Articles of Agreement any member of the IMF has the right to choose policies differing from the usual, fairly uniform IMF prescription. Article IV(3)(b) states 'These principles [General obligations of members pursuant to Article IV(1)] shall respect the domestic social and political policies of members, and in applying these principles the Fund shall pay due regard to the circumstances of members'. Similarly paragraph 7 of Schedule C demands: 'The Fund shall not object [to changes in par values] because of the domestic social or political policies of the member proposing the change'.

In contrast to conditionality foisted onto members in distress, the IMF's constitution not only allows capital controls, but even explicitly restricts the use of Fund resources to finance outflows. Article VI(3) establishes the right of members to 'exercise such controls as are necessary to regulate international capital movements, but no member may exercise these controls in a manner which will restrict payments for current transactions'. These are defined by Article XXX(d) as 'not for the purpose of transferring capital'. They include 'Payments of *moderate* [emphasis added] amount of amortization of loans or for depreciation of direct investments', or '*moderate* [emphasis added] remittances for family living expenses'. Even restricting such flows is a member's right.

Article VI(1)(a) goes further, stating that

> [A] member may not use the Fund's general resources to meet a large and sustained outflow of capital except as provided in Section 2 of this Article [this refers exclusively to reserve tranche purchases] and the Fund may request a member to exercise controls to prevent such use of the general resources of the Fund.

Current transfers can be restricted with the approval of the Fund. Although the Fund may, but is not obliged to, request controls, these regulations clearly show that the IMF is not supposed to press for liberalisation of capital movements in the way it has actually done. However, when it comes to protecting Southern rights, legal regulations and obligations are apparently insignificant. Clearly, not only had Asian countries the right to control capital outflows – as the IMF had to admit when Malaysia exercised it (cf. Raffer and Singer 2001, p. 157) – but the Fund's forcing members to finance large and sustained outflows by speculators is definitely a violation of the IMF's own constitution.

Corrective measures affecting the balance of payments should be done 'without resorting to measures destructive of national or international prosperity' (Article I(v)). This would have been easily possible in Asia, but speculators would then not have been bailed out by socialising their losses. Article IV(1)(ii) requests the IMF to foster stability and a monetary system that does not produce 'erratic disruptions'. The policy of high real interest rates forced on clients did the opposite. Real interest rates skyrocketing beyond 40 per cent are no doubt erratic disruptions, as bankruptcies of domestic corporations and entrepreneurs prove. A price tag can be put on such policies. According to Standard & Poor's, non-performing loans would have risen to above 30 per cent of total loans, computed on a three-month basis, if Malaysia had not cut interest rates sharply.

There might even be some awareness that crises are in the institutional self-interest of IFIs. During the Asian crisis the IMF's first deputy managing director still argued – using Thailand and Mexico as supporting evidence – that the prospect of larger crises caused by capital account liberalisation would call for more resources for the IMF to cope with the very crises the IMF's proposal would create in the future (Fischer 1997). This is easily explained by the present lack of financial accountability, which is at severe odds with any market-friendly incentive system. From the narrow point of view of institutional self-interest such crises make more sense than the use of contractual rights to capital controls, an option that would not require increased IMF resources.

The IBRD, too, violates its own constitution to the detriment of its Southern members. By simply refusing to acknowledge default, even if countries have not paid anything for six or seven years (Caufield 1998, p. 319) it creates damage by delaying a solution. In 1992, when the end of the debt crisis was proclaimed and one could argue that insolvency relief was no longer necessary, the IBRD (1992, pp. 10ff., original emphasis) acknowledged insolvency as the cause of the crisis, arguing '*In a solvency crisis, early recognition of solvency as the root cause and the need for a final settlement are important for minimizing the damage. ...* protracted renegotiations and uncertainty damaged economic activity in debtor countries for several years'. It was conveniently forgotten that the Bank itself as well as the IMF had ardently lobbied against relief, arguing that countries would 'grow out of debts', supporting this with highly optimistic forecasts of future export earnings.

Claiming no default as long as countries stay 'in mutual respectful contact' (Caufield 1998, p. 319) with the Bank, the IBRD not only mocks all acceptable accounting rules, but breaches its own Articles of Agreement recognising default as a fact of life. Article IV(6) demands a special reserve to cover what Article IV(7) calls 'Methods of Meeting Liabilities of the Bank in Case of Defaults'. The statutory procedure is described in detail. As the Bank is only allowed to lend either to members or if member states fully guarantee repayment (Article III(4)) the logical conclusion is that default of member states was definitely considered possible, maybe even an occasionally needed solution. Unaware of any preferred creditor status, a legal concept which cannot be found in its Articles of Agreement and does not formally apply to the IBRD (Caufield 1998, p. 323), the IBRD's founders wanted it subject to some market discipline rather than totally exempt from it. Mechanisms allowing the Bank to shoulder risks appropriately were designed. Thwarting its founders' intentions, the IBRD has refused to use them, wrongly claiming that this would make development finance inoperational. The IBRD's very statute proves that financial accountability is necessary and possible. The European Bank for Reconstruction and Development (EBRD) writes off losses, and submits to arbitration (also foreseen for the IBRD), proving that multilateral development banks can survive financial accountability and market risk.

To force IFIs to respect membership rights and to abide by their own constitutions in order to avoid damages to poor countries it is necessary to introduce damage compensation. Violations of membership rights must have appropriate, not least financial, consequences. Like anyone else, IFIs must be liable for damage illegally inflicted. At present IFIs gain from their wrong behaviour. New and larger crises increase their importance. The record since 1982 illustrates this quite clearly. Negligently designed and implemented projects creating damage may lead to new loans to redress this damage, leaving the SC with more debts and the IFI with a higher income stream, increasing the importance of the IBRD and the IMF as troubleshooters: 'IFI-flops create IFI-jobs' (Raffer 1993, p. 158). This is a wrong incentive structure in severe need of correction, creating huge moral hazard problems. Minimal standards of the Rule of Law and of economic reason are urgently needed.

Introducing Minimal Professional Standards

One main shortcoming of present development cooperation is that aid recipients are denied any form of protection usual in all other cases. This shows in cases of violation of membership rights as well as regarding professional best practice. Damage done by grave negligence has to be compensated in all cases unless this is done in the context of development cooperation. Donors and IFIs are totally exempt from any liability. The increased role of IFIs in international capital markets since 1982 contrasts sharply with a total lack of financial accountability. They may and often do gain institutionally and financially from crises, but also from their own errors and failures, even if they cause damage by grave negligence. Another loan may be granted to repair damage done by the first loan, increasing the IFI's income stream (cf. Raffer 1993). This is a severe moral hazard problem and an economically totally perverted incentive system.

Like consultants, IFIs give economic advice – to the point that 'ownership' becomes a problem – but unlike consultants they cannot be held liable. This victim-pays-principle is a unique arrangement, which cannot be justified by economic or legal reasoning (ibid.). Under market conditions, international firms do sue their consultants successfully in cases of wrong or negligent advice. Damage compensation is even awarded to private individuals in the Anglo-Saxon legal system if a bank goes beyond mere lending. A British couple borrowing money from Lloyds sued the bank successfully, because its manager had advised and encouraged them to renovate and sell a house at a profit. The High Court ruled that the manager should have pointed out the risks clearly and should have advised them to abandon the project. Because of its advice, Lloyds had to pay damages when prices in the property market fell and the couple suffered a loss (*Financial Times*, 5 September 1995). With comparable standards regarding Southern debtors there would be no multilateral debt problem.

Raffer (1993) therefore argued that IFIs must be held financially accountable for what they do. There must be a court or an arbitration panel where they can be sued. To increase IFI efficiency and to improve their role in capital markets, market incentives must be brought to bear. The international public sector must become financially accountable for their own errors in the same way that consultants are liable to pay damage compensation if/when negligence on their part causes damage, or OECD governments are if they create damage by negligence or violating laws. By contrast, the IMF has been allowed to violate its own statutes with impunity. The present privileged position of international public creditors discriminates unfairly against private creditors suffering avoidable losses because of IFI privileges when countries are unable to service their debts.

In discussing financial accountability, one needs to differentiate between programmes and projects. In the case of projects, errors can often be isolated and proved with less difficulty. IFIs should be liable for damage done by them in the same way that private consulting firms are liable to their clients. If a project goes wrong the need would arise to determine financial consequences. In the simplest case borrower and lender agree on a fair sharing of costs. If they do not, the solution used between business partners or transnational firms and countries in cases of disagreement could be applied: arbitration. This concept is well established in the field of international investments. If disagreements between transnational firms and host countries can be solved that way, or the International Chamber of Commerce offers such services, there is no reason why disputes between IFIs (or donors) and borrowing countries could not be solved by this mechanism as well. Ironically, the IBRD's own *General Conditions* (Section 10.04) foresee arbitration to settle disagreements with borrowers, be they members or not, *inter alia* for 'any claim by either party against the other' not settled by agreement. Incidentally, the procedural provisions on how to establish the panel are nearly identical to my proposal of debt arbitration based on the principles of US Chapter 9 insolvency (Raffer 1990).

A permanent international court of arbitration – different from *ad hoc* arbitration panels which are preferred for practical reasons in the case of debt arbitration – would be ideal. If necessary this court might consist of more than one panel. It decides on the percentage of loans to be waived to cover damage for which IFIs are responsible. The right to file complaints should be conferred on individuals, NGOs, firms, governments and international organisations. As NGOs are less under pressure from IFIs or member governments, their right to represent affected people is particularly important. The court of arbitrators would of course have the right and duty to refuse to hear apparently ill-founded cases. The need to prepare a case meticulously would deter abuse. The possibility of being held financially accountable would act as an incentive for donors and IFIs to perform more efficiently and protect the poor from damage done by ill-conceived projects.

Financial accountability can also be brought to bear in the non-project sector. As it is practically impossible to determine the fair share of one or more IFIs in failed programmes, Chapter 9 based arbitration (ibid.) provides a clear and simple solution, finally 'bailing-in' the public sector. All private and official creditors including IFIs should lose the same percentage of their claims. This would automatically introduce an element of financial accountability of IFIs. An accumulation of bad projects financed by loans or a string of unsuccessful programmes would eventually lead to insolvency, reducing all official creditors' claims. As IFIs – like donors – control the use of loans, this would be highly positive. This point is also occasionally stressed by private creditors. In their publication *Emerging Markets this Week* no. 26/ 1999 (15 October) the German Commerzbank sees the IMF and the IBRD as more concerned with protecting their own balance sheets than with fair burden sharing – to the detriment of other creditors. This publication rightly demands that multilateral institutions 'accept accountability for their past lending', by sharing the burden of debt reduction via arbitration in cases of extreme borrower distress.

While the importance of decisions by official creditors may vary, it has always been particularly great in the poorest countries on account of the lack of local expertise to participate appropriately in decision making as well as the high dependence on aid. This is a fundamental difference to private creditors who usually limit themselves to lending without any additional consulting activities. As the share of multilateral debts is relatively higher in the poorest countries, protecting IFIs from losses is done at the expense of particularly poor clients, often extremely dependent on solutions elaborated by IFI staff.

The urgent need for change is clearly shown by Stiglitz (2000). Using an example from the IMF:

> Country teams have been known to compose draft reports before visiting. I heard stories of one unfortunate incident when team members copied large parts of the text for one country's report and transferred them wholesale to another. They might have gotten away with it, except the 'search and replace' function on the word processor didn't work properly, leaving the original country's name in a few places. Oops.

Legal implications – including consequences under penal law in most countries – are absolutely clear in the case of 'normal' consultants. The IMF's reaction to the so-called Blumenthal Report, often quoted by NGOs, is another example. In his 1982 report, the German expert Erwin Blumenthal, seconded by the Bretton Woods institutions to Zaire's central bank, gave explicit warning that Zaire should not get any further money because of the prevalent corruption of Mobutu's clique. In 1983 the IMF allowed Zaire the largest drawing by an African government so far. As predicted, the money disappeared. In the period between the publication of the Report and 1989, the IMF trebled the volume of Zaire's drawings. Under the existing biased anti-market system it was good business for the Fund and marvellous for Mobutu's clique, but not for Zaire.

Arguably an even more cogent point is connected with the Asian crisis of 1997. Until the crisis broke, both the IMF and the IBRD encouraged further liberalisation of capital accounts. Until the meeting of the Bretton Woods institutions in Hong Kong the IMF wanted to change its Articles of Agreement to allow it to continue what it had been doing in open breach of them that far. Wade (1998) gives examples that warning signs were ignored. IBRD staff trying to sound the alarm were overruled by superiors. During a visit to Indonesia in the autumn of 1997, IBRD President James Wolfensohn himself removed a passage written by the resident mission that warned of serious problems, replacing it with an 'even more fulsome endorsement of Indonesia as an Asian miracle' (Wade 1998). According to Wade, one typically did not want to hear news that went against one's ideological preferences – free private capital markets had to be proved right by the Asian example.

In 1999, though, the IBRD (1999, p. 2) acknowledged having been aware of 'the relevant institutional lessons' since the early 1990s. An audit report by its Operations Evaluation Department (OED) 'on Chile's structural adjustment loans highlighted the lack of prudential supervision of financial institutions in increasing the economy's vulnerability to the point of collapse' (sic! ibid.) The OED's 'key lesson' that 'prudential rules and surveillance are necessary safeguards for the operation of domestic financial markets, rather than unnecessary restrictions' (ibid.) did not make 'policy makers and international financial institutions give these weaknesses appropriate weight'. In spite of what was already known they encouraged the same policies in Asia. According to the Bank they were 'guided' by 'the lessons of the general debt crisis' (whatever that might mean), not by the 'more relevant' cases of Chile and Mexico in 1994–95. The neglect of proper sequencing and institution building 'featured prominently in the Chile and Mexico crises' (ibid.) Briefly, the problem was known years before the crash, and the unfolding of the Asian crisis could be observed like a movie whose script is known. The Argentine crisis of 1995 goes unmentioned in this source, although it was of a similar variety as Asia, namely triggered by private sector debts. Why did the Bretton Woods institutions (both not normally known for their restraint in giving advice) not warn those countries to proceed more slowly with cautious sequencing – as they do now – pointing at already available evidence, instead of once again applauding too quick liberalisation and those inflows of volatile capital? Before 1994–95, the IMF and the IBRD had welcomed and encouraged inflows to Mexico, presenting them as a proof that the debt crisis was over. As in the case of Asia, official euphoria must certainly have fuelled inflows further. In the case of any consultancy, courts would decide whether the firm had complied with its professional duties by not making essential knowledge it had available to the client – with fairly foreseeable results. The same market discipline of connecting actions and risk must be brought to IFIs. In parentheses it should be added that Northern regulatory measures increased speed and volatility, thus fostering crises. The risk weight given by the Basle Committee to short-run flows to banks outside the OECD region, or regulatory changes necessary to allow institutional investors to invest in Mexican *tesobonos* before 1994–95 illustrate this point. The costs of these changes had to be borne mainly by SCs.

4   MONITORING BY INDEPENDENT EXPERTS

Raffer and Singer (2001, p. 255) proposed an independent body within the UN to monitor divergence and suggest appropriate measures to remedy it, for instance to the Economic Security Council, should such a council be set up. It should be composed of independent experts selected by the UN General Assembly. It could use indices such as the Human Development Index as the basis on which to judge whether divergence had increased. It could dispose of funds raised by international taxation to finance measures against poverty. These measures would have to be planned and carried out by UN agencies or other suitable organisations. Regarding Africa, where neoliberalism has at least contributed to the breakdown of statehood, a special action of Marshall Plan dimensions for the continent – as once proposed by Bruno Kreisky (1980 and 1981) – appears necessary to stop further divergence and marginalisation. This – or a similar – body could also serve to monitor the implementation of UN summit meetings, such as Copenhagen with its 20:20 target or the commitment to reduce extreme poverty and malnutrition by one-half by the year 2015.

Another task emerging from the analysis above would be to draw attention to violations of legal obligations against SCs, especially of the statutes of international actors such as the Bretton Woods twins or the WTO. Additionally, it should immediately publicise incidents when pressure is put on SCs not to exercise their membership rights, and condemn such behaviour. It would thus contribute to safeguarding the rights of the poor. Past record unfortunately shows how necessary this task is.

One might discuss whether this panel should also monitor consistency and comparability of aid statistics, as it would certainly observe to what extent the famous 0.7 per cent target of ODA is reached by those countries that bound themselves voluntarily to reach it. Raffer (1998) proposed independent auditing of aid statistics by a group of independent experts from both donor and recipient countries to improve their quality, consistency and comparability. This new form of reviewing should replace present peer reviews of OECD donors. It would not imply large additional costs since it would replace present peer reviews. These also cost money that could be used to cover the expenses of independent auditing instead (ibid.). These aid experts might report to this UN body. Independent auditing would secure a minimum of statistical correctness, but it cannot be expected to correct all the numerous faults of present ODA. As this would make what the OECD diplomatically calls 'broadening' of ODA impossible, donors are unlikely to accept this form of performance monitoring. Presumably, they are no more likely to agree to a body helping to safeguard contractual rights of SCs in the immediate future.

REFERENCES

Blokker, Niels (1989), *International Regulation of World Trade in Textiles: Lessons for Practice, A Contribution to Theory*, Dordrecht: Martinus Nijhoff.

Caufield, Catherine (1998), *Masters of Illusion: The World Bank and the Poverty of Nations*, London: Pan.

Fischer, Stanley (1997), 'Capital account liberalization and the role of the IMF', IMF Seminar 'Asia and the IMF', Hong Kong, 19 September, http://www.imf.org/external/np/apd/asia/FISCHER.HTM

Heckscher, Eli (1950), 'The effect of foreign trade on the distribution of income', in H. Ellis and L. Metzler (eds), *Readings in the Theory of International Trade*, London: Allen & Unwin, pp. 272ff. (slightly abbreviated version of the original published in *Ekonomisk Tidskrift*, **XXI**, 1919, pp. 497ff.).

International Bank for Reconstruction and Development (IBRD) (1992), *World Debt Tables 1992–93*, vol. 1, Washington, DC: IBRD.

International Bank for Reconstruction and Development (IBRD) (1999), *1998 Annual Review of Development Effectiveness*, Operations Evaluation Department, Task Manager: Robert Buckley, Washington, DC: IBRD.

Kreisky, Bruno (1980), 'Massive transfer of resources and the development of infrastructure', Occasional Paper 80/1, Vienna Institute for Development.

Kreisky, Bruno (1981), 'The McDougall Memorial Lecture 1983', Occasional Paper 81/3, Vienna Institute for Development.

List, Friedrich (1920), *Das nationale System der politischen Ökonomie* (The national system of political economy), Fischer: Jena.

Ohlin, Bertil (1967), *Interregional and International Trade*, Cambridge, MA: Harvard University Press.

Organization for Economic Cooperation and Development (OECD) (1985), *Twenty-Five Years of Development Co-operation: A Review, 1985 Report*, Paris: OECD.

Raffer, Kunibert (1990), 'Applying Chapter 9 insolvency to international debts: an economically efficient solution with a human face', *World Development*, **18** (2), 301ff.

Raffer, Kunibert (1993), 'International financial institutions and accountability: the need for drastic change', in S.M. Murshed and K. Raffer (eds), *Trade, Transfers and Development, Problems and Prospects for the Twenty-first Century*, Aldershot: Edward Elgar, pp.151ff.

Raffer, Kunibert (1995), 'The Impact of the Uruguay Round on developing countries', in Fritz Breuss (ed.), *The World Economy after the Uruguay Round*, Vienna: Service Fachverlag, pp. 169ff. (reprinted: *Asian Journal of Economics and Social Studies*, **13** (3), 187ff.).

Raffer, Kunibert (1997), 'Helping Southern net food importers after the Uruguay Round: a proposal', *World Development*, **25** (11), Special Section: 'In Honor of Hans Singer', pp. 1901ff.

Raffer, Kunibert (1998), 'Looking a gift Horse in the mouth: analysing donors' aid statistics', *Zagreb International Review of Economics and Business*, **1** (2), 1ff.

Raffer, Kunibert and H.W. Singer (1996), *The Foreign Aid Business: Economic Assistance and Development Co-operation*, Cheltenham, UK and Brookfield, VT, USA: Edward Elgar.

Raffer, Kunibert and H.W. Singer (2001), *The Economic North–South Divide: Six Decades of Unequal Development*, Cheltenham, UK and Northampton, MA, USA: Edward Elgar.

Stiglitz, Joseph (2000), 'What I learned at the world economic crisis: the insider', *The New Republic*, 17 April, copy received by e-mail from CoC_Bretton_Expand @egroups.com.

Wade, Robert (1998), 'From miracle to meltdown: vulnerabilities, moral hazard, panic and debt deflation in the Asian crisis'. Paper presented at a seminar at the Institute of Development Studies, Sussex University, http://www.ids.ac.uk/ids/research/wade.pdf.

World Trade Organization (WTO) (1996), *WTO Focus*, no. 14, December.

World Trade Organization (WTO) (2000), *Annual Report 2000*, Geneva: WTO.

6. Globalization, North–South uneven development and international institutions

Amitava Krishna Dutt*

---

1 INTRODUCTION

It is now generally agreed that inequality across nations has been growing. Sala-i-Martin (1996) uses purchasing power parity-adjusted data from the Penn World Tables from 1960 to 1990 for 110 countries (for which data is available for all the years between 1960 and 1990) to find that the dispersion of GDP per capita, measured by the standard deviation of the log of per capita income levels of countries, increased steadily from 0.89 in 1960 to 1.12 in 1980, showing increasing inequality in the world economy as represented by what has come to be called sigma-divergence. Stocker (1994) finds that the Lorenz curve for international income distribution for 89 countries for which data are available from the Penn World Tables has shifted outward between 1960 and 1990 and that the Theil index increased from 0.46 in 1960 to 0.51 in 1990. If one uses Penn data to plot the log of GDP per capita for the year 1960 (the first year for which the Penn data on GDP are available for 110 countries) on the horizontal axis and the growth rate of per capita GDP on the vertical axis, one does not obtain a very good fit, since the points are all over the quadrant. However, Sala-i-Martin (1996) shows that the regression equation actually has a positive slope, implying what has been called beta-divergence. Baumol et al. (1989) run quadratic equation regressing growth rates of per capita income on the initial level of per capita income and its square to find an inverse-U-shaped relationship, suggesting a positive relationship between starting income level and per capita growth for most of the sample, and a negative one for a small group of high-income countries. Quah (1993) estimates a 5×5 Markov chain transition matrix in which each country's per capita income relative to the world average is the basic data to show that they imply distributions which show a thinning middle and an accumulation at both low and high tails, or what has come to be called the twin-peakedness of world income distribution. Some countries do seem to be converging at the top, but others are converging to a different, low-income level. Moreover, there is little mobility between country groups.

In contrast to these trends, inequality between regions within many countries has been on the decline. For the US, Barro and Sala-i-Martin (1995) report that the cross-sectional standard deviation of the log of per capita personal income net of transfers for states and territories declined between 1880 and 1992, although there were periods of reverse movements in the 1920s and for a part of the 1980s. They also report that when the annual growth rate of states during the period from 1880 to 1990 is regressed on initial per capita personal income in 1880, one obtains a negative coefficient. Hence there has been both sigma- and beta-convergence in the US. They also report that one observes both types of convergence across Japanese prefectures during the 1930–90 period, although there was sigma-divergence during the 1930s when military spending was at a high level. Finally, they report convergence within European countries between 1950 and 1990, especially in countries such as Italy and Spain, which had high initial inequality. Moreover, if one thinks of the European Union as a single political region, there has been convergence within that region as well, with the exceptions of Greece and Italy's southern half, the Mezzogiorno.

Myrdal (1957) drew attention to these trends many years before this evidence was examined rigorously, and explained them in terms of what he called backwash and spread effects. Myrdal (1957: 39–40) argues that rich countries, such as those of Western Europe, 'have in recent generations been approaching the "welfare state". In these countries state policies which are directed toward greater regional equality have been initiated: the market forces which result in backwash effects have been offset, while those resulting in spread effects have been supported'. Myrdal argues that if economically advanced countries

> demonstrate an approach to harmony of individual interests – as indeed, they definitely do – this is not the old harmony of natural law, utilitarianism and economic equilibrium theory, brought about by natural forces in the market. It is to a large extent a 'created harmony', created through policy interferences by organized society with the operation of market forces which, if left to themselves, would have led to disharmony. And the approach to harmony of interests is narrowly restricted to the nation. The welfare state is nationalistic. (ibid.: 48–9)

Myrdal did not argue that government policies equalized income within all countries, or that *only* government policies were responsible for equalization in countries within which such equalization occurred. He pointed out that while equalization occurred within advanced countries, the same was not necessarily true for less-developed countries (LDCs). This is partly because poor countries have what he called weaker spread effects than backwash effects due to market forces, while for richer countries spread effects are strengthened by better systems of education, transport and communications and the like. Moreover, the more limited resources of LDCs and greater existing inequalities make it less likely that governments in them can produce the kinds of created harmony possible in richer countries. Studies of regional development within LDCs such as India and Brazil appear to confirm Myrdal's thesis (see Raman 1996–97, for instance). There can, of course, be other forces at work within countries that are absent in the world economy. For instance, unskilled labor is free to flow within regions of a country, but not so between the North and the South. However, Barro and Sala-i-Martin (1995) find that migration within countries does not do much to explain convergence within the US, Japan and Europe in terms of affecting the speed of convergence. Barro and Sala-i-Martin also point out that the differences in legal, cultural, linguistic and institutional barriers to the mobility of capital and other factors is arguably smaller between regions than between countries. Moreover, greater homogeneity regarding these factors within countries can also explain why different regions in the country will eventually grow at the same rate for reasons internal to each region.

Nevertheless, there is some evidence that government policies may have a role to play in reducing inequality within countries. For example, in the US the declining trend of inequality, which was reversed during the arguably less egalitarian policies of the Reagan administration in the 1980s, suggests this to be the case. Moreover, in the US transfers tend to reduce interstate inequality, although they are not the main source of decline of inequality (ibid.: 393). For Japan, the focus on military buildup by the government, when egalitarian policies were de-emphasized, explains increasing inequality during the 1930s, in contrast to a generally decreasing trend after the Second World War.

Myrdal's main conclusion was that in the absence of a world state a created harmony could not be established in the global economy, so that the unequalizing forces at work between rich and poor nations were not mitigated even to the extent possible even within poor countries. He wrote in the mid-1950s, a few years after the formation of the United Nations and specialized agencies such as the International Bank of Reconstruction and Development, that 'we have hardly more than the faintest beginnings of something like an international authority which could perform for the world as a whole the task of the national state in an individual country' (Myrdal 1957: 63).

Almost half a century later, international institutions have gained considerably in size, scope and influence. The United Nations Organization has grown, as have the International Monetary Fund (IMF) and the World Bank. The World Trade Organization (WTO) has recently come into existence, with most trading countries of the world becoming its members. The growth in influence of international non-governmental organizations (NGOs) and their coordination at international conferences has led some observers to see in them the seeds of a global parliament. The implication of these developments for global inequality and North–South uneven development is therefore a subject of great importance and interest.

The purpose of this chapter is examine the implications of these international institutions for the question of North–South uneven development in a globalizing world. To do so, the next section examines some of the main mechanisms of divergence and convergence between rich and poor countries, as stressed in the theoretical literature on North–South models, and in the light of real world experiences. Section 3 then examines how these mechanisms have been affected by the international organizations, discussing in turn the Bretton Woods institutions, the WTO, and other international institutions including civil society institutions. Section 4 makes some concluding comments about the future of North–South development patterns in light of the discussion in these two sections.

2   THE MECHANISMS OF DIVERGENCE AND CONVERGENCE

Differences in the rates of growth of rich and poor countries, which are related to whether there is divergence or convergence, may in part be caused by factors entirely internal to them, having nothing to do with how they interact with each other. For instance, assume that we have two regions, a rich one called the North and a poor one called the South, which do not interact with each other in any way. We may even assume that they are on different planets and that their residents do not know of each other's existence. For this case of no interdependence, different growth theories have different implications for the question of convergence. The Solow model implies that if the regions have identical structures (that is, production functions, saving rates and population and labor supply growth rates), the poorer region with a lower per capita output would grow faster than the richer region, implying convergence. This is because the latter, by having a higher capital–labor ratio, has experienced a larger decline in the marginal and average productivity of the reproducible factor, capital, and is closer to its steady-state capital–labor ratio. Of course, with different structures – for instance with the North having a higher saving rate or a more productive technology – it is possible for there to be divergence with the North growing relatively faster. New growth theory models which depart from the assumption of diminishing returns to capital imply non-convergence (as in the simple AK model which implies identical growth rates for rich and poor regions with similar structures) or even divergence, if we have increasing returns to capital. Neo-Keynesian models can imply higher growth rates for rich regions if greater uncertainty in poor regions implies weaker 'animal spirits' and makes their desired investment function lower than that in rich countries. Finally, neo-Marxian models with higher real wages (due to tighter labor markets) in the North than in the South, uncompensated by productivity differentials, result in convergence.

Although convergence and divergence can be explained by factors internal to the North and the South along these lines, it is more relevant to look at forces of convergence and divergence due to the interaction between rich and poor regions, particularly in an increasingly integrated world economy. Myrdal's spread and backwash effects also invoke forces which relate to interactions between rich and poor regions. We therefore turn to mechanisms of divergence and convergence based on different types of interaction, discussing, in turn, interaction involving trade, capital flows, labor flows, technology transfers, and a portmanteau category of 'all other' interactions. The literature on these issues is enormous. We concentrate on a few major factors emphasized in the burgeoning literature on North–South models.

North–South models are models of the global economy in which there are two regions, the North and the South, which interact with each other through trade or other means. There are two major varieties of North–South models. One type assumes that there are major structural differences between the two regions that create some sort of asymmetry in the interaction between them. This may be reflected in differences in the macroeconomic conditions in the two regions, which results in differences in the major determinants of growth in the two regions. Some pioneering models of North–South interaction characterize the North differently: Findlay (1980) assumes a neoclassical structure with full employment of labor that is determined by labor supply growth; Taylor (1983) assumes that excess capacity and unemployed labor exists and that growth is determined by effective demand in a Keynes–Kalecki fashion; Molana and Vines (1989), in a Kaldorian manner, assume that there is unemployed labor and a given real wage. All these contributions assume that the South has surplus labor at a given real wage and that Southern growth is saving determined, a unanimity perhaps reflecting more W. Arthur Lewis's influence on the literature than agreement on the South's true structure. Other models assume neoclassical full employment conditions in both the North and the South, but characterize the North as the leader in innovation where new technology is developed, and the South as the follower where this technology is transferred, as in the models of Grossman and Helpman (1991). These models can obviously shed light on what the implications of interaction between the two regions are for their development patterns, especially given changes in global economic conditions – for instance, those resulting in increases in North–South trade, capital flows, or technology transfers. A second type of model – for instance, that of Krugman (1981) –

deliberately assumes away differences between the two regions in order to show how slight differences in conditions can result in big differences in development patterns between them. This type of model examines how the relative development of the two regions depends on whether or not they interact with each other, and how differences in the current levels of development may have come about based on past events.

International Trade

The neoclassical theory of international trade emphasizes the fact that countries can and do gain by trading with each other. According to textbook Ricardian or Heckscher–Ohlin–Samuelson theories of trade and comparative advantage, if the North and the South trade with each other, they gain by exporting goods in which they have relatively better technology, or which use their abundant factor intensively. Although this approach does not have clear implications for convergence and divergence, the fact that both regions benefit from trade has generally been taken to imply a process of convergence (as implied by the factor price equalization theorem with identical technology). Of course, in the presence of distortions of one kind or another (such as production externalities and factor market imperfections), it is not difficult to think of situations in which regions will not gain from trade and can in fact be better off by restricting trade. Mainstream economists usually believe that the distortions are more interesting as intellectual curiosa than as empirically important features of the real world. However, North–South models often have different implications.

One mechanism of divergence which has been highlighted in this literature focusses on learning by doing and argues that some sectors lead to more learning by doing than others. In Krugman's (1981) model, mentioned earlier, each region can produce two goods, a manufactured good and an agricultural good, where the manufactured good experiences increasing returns (which can be interpreted as learning by doing) and the agricultural good does not. Assuming that both goods require labor for production, and the manufactured good only requires capital, it is possible to trace the time path of each region if they do not trade, where they accumulate capital (as a constant fraction of profits in manufacturing), produce more manufactured goods, and experience greater productivity growth due to learning in manufacturing. If the two regions are identical except for the fact that the North has a higher initial stock of capital, and they are allowed to trade with each other, the North will export the manufactured good and the South will import it (by virtue of the fact that the North has initially more capital and hence higher productivity in that sector due to greater learning). Consequently, while the North will experience more learning by doing and expand its capital stock faster, the South will experience less of it as it specializes increasingly in agricultural production. Even though both regions will gain initially by opening up trade, in the long run there will be divergence. Broadly similar results can be obtained from other models which allow for sector-specific scale economies or learning, such as those of Ethier (1982) and Boldrin and Schienkman (1988), and the more recent models of agglomeration in the 'new economic geography' literature (see Ottaviano and Puga 1998, for a survey).[1] The basic idea behind this explanation is that North–South trade leads to a pattern of trade specialization in which the North exports goods which result in greater technological change or scale economies than the goods which the South exports.

This idea can be challenged in a number of ways. First, it can be argued that although the manufacturing–agriculture pattern of trade may have existed in an earlier phase of history, many LDCs have now become manufacturing export-ers, and are therefore not denied learning by doing due to their pattern of specialization *vis-à-vis* rich countries. It can be countered that the mechanism discussed above does not require the South to export agricultural goods but, rather, that the North specializes in export goods that lead to more technologi-cal change than those in which the South specializes. This condition may be satisfied if the North specializes in goods requiring more sophisticated process-ing. Second, rising wages in the North can reverse the forces of uneven development; while this is certainly a possibility, the outcome depends on the strength of this tendency in relation to the rate of productivity increase. Third, it can be argued that the North is increasingly becoming de-industrialized, and increasingly becoming specialized in the production of services which argu-ably experience slower productivity growth. It can be countered, however, that all services do not involve low rates of productivity growth, especially what may be called high-tech services and, moreover, many poor countries have also experienced significant increases in the share of services. Fourth, it can be argued that even if there is more rapid technological change and capital accu-mulation in the North, this does not imply that the South will be worse off, because it will experience improvements in its terms of trade over time. It can be countered, however, that the pattern of demand for Northern and Southern products may be such that the terms of trade will not shift in favor of the South, an issue to which we now turn.

North–South trade can lead to divergence not just because the pattern of trade results in more rapid technological change in the North compared to that in the South, but also because the South produces goods with lower income elasticity of demand than does the North. If this is indeed the case, the Northern income elasticity of Southern exports will be lower than the Southern income elasticity of Southern imports, as in Thirlwall's (1979) model of balance-of-payments-constrained growth. Dutt (2003) shows that under conditions of balanced trade and no international capital flows, the global world economy will converge to a long-run equilibrium with a constant terms of trade, but in which the South grows at a slower rate than the North in terms of total output. Given the empirically observed higher rate of population growth in the South this implies that in terms of per capita income, there is divergence. The reason for this result is straightforward: for the South to balance its trade, it must grow more slowly than the North to balance the fact that identical rates of growth would imply that its imports would rise faster than its exports. Allowing for capital flows does not change this result if one assumes that there are upper limits to the South's international borrowing or international debt as a ratio of its total production or exports, as discussed in Dutt (ibid.).

The question then arises whether Southern exports are less income elastic than Northern exports. The earlier conjecture on this was based on the fact that Southern exports were in large part primary products with low income elasticity of demand while Northern exports were manufactures with higher income elasticity. However, the composition of exports of many LDCs has since changed, with manufactured products receiving a higher weight. Such changes, however, need not have changed the income elasticity differences, with the South producing simpler manufactured goods than the North. Empirical work which estimates the Southern income elasticity of Southern imports and the Northern income elasticity of Southern exports seems to confirm this (see ibid.).

What these models imply is that given the nature of North–South trade, that is Northern specialization in goods that have strong technological spinoff effects or that have high income elasticity, and Southern specialization in other goods, uneven development is a likely result. The implication for the South is then to attempt to change the pattern of specialization to favor the production of more technology improving and income elastic goods. The experience of late industrializers in the past, such as the US, Germany and Japan, and more recent success stories, such as South Korea and Taiwan, certainly bear this out as well. This implies that Southern economies need to pursue trade and industrial policies that can change their structures in a short span of time, which requires the use of import restrictions and subsidies to particular sectors.

The response of most mainstream economists to this is that even if the composition of trade does matter, it is not clear that government intervention in trade can solve the problem. Since the 'distortions' which arise due to technological factors are production distortions, the appropriate response is to intervene with domestic production subsidies, not with trade restrictions. Moreover, they argue against all kinds of interventions, in trade or in the domestic economy, because they arguably breed inefficiency, directly unproductive activity and government corruption. A discussion of the debate on the relative merits of the market and the state is well beyond the scope of this chapter. Here we can do no more than agree that while government intervention has bred inefficiencies in certain Southern countries, it has also played a positive developmental role not only in many successful LDCs (see Amsden 2001), but also in the currently-developed countries in the past, including Britain, the US, and Japan.

International Capital Flows

A major part of the neoclassical story by which the South is expected to develop and catch up with the North is through North–South capital flows. In this story, the developed North is capital abundant because of high levels of saving and investment in the past, while the South is capital scarce and labor abundant. Due to diminishing returns to capital, the return on capital is therefore lower in the North than in the South. Capital owners will thus send their capital from the North to the South, which will lead to faster capital accumulation in the South, which will result in convergence.

There are numerous reasons why, however, this denouement may not take place in the real world. Even neoclassical models with scale economies imply that capital does not move from the North to the South. Moreover, some models of North–South interaction have examined how capital mobility can result in divergence, rather than convergence. For instance, Burgstaller and Saavedra-Rivano (1984) have extended Findlay's (1980) model to allow for capital mobility, following his assumptions of a neoclassical North with full employment and a classical South with surplus labor, with each region producing a single good. In this model, the capital owned by Northern and Southern capitalists is given at a point in time, due to past saving. However, with the Southern profit rate assumed to be greater than the Northern one with all Northern capital staying in the North, Northern capitalists are allowed to move their capital instantaneously to the South, so that profit rates are equalized interregionally. It is shown that a steady-state equilibrium, with some of the capital stock located in the South being owned by Northern capitalists, exists and is stable given certain plausible conditions. The analysis shows that with capital mobility, since the Northern profit rate rises, the lower wage–rental ratio will imply a lower capital–labor ratio in Northern production, but a higher per capita capital ownership (in steady state) due to capital exports. With capital proportional to income, this implies that per capita income in the North rises with capital mobility. Since per worker output is the same, but the South has to pay out profits for the use of capital, per worker income falls due to capital mobility. It is also shown that relative Southern employment will fall if the Northern propensity to spend on the

Southern good is less than that out of Southern profits, due to a reduction in the demand of the Southern good caused by the redistribution of income due to capital mobility.

Blecker (1996) develops an alternative model in which the two regions are completely specialized in the production of a single good, and the Northern capital owners own a portion of the capital stock in the South, as in the model just discussed. The Southern economy has a fixed real wage and surplus labor. The North is assumed to be demand constrained in the sense that growth depends on desired accumulation rather than on the rate of growth of labor supply as in the Taylor model, but the price of the Northern good is flexible and production fully utilizes capital. Excess demand for the Northern good changes the rate of profit in the North by changing the price of the Northern good. Investment by Northern capital owners in the North and the South responds to differences in profit rates in the two regions, and domestic Southern investment in the South is saving determined. In steady state, when the capital stocks of the North, the foreign capital in the South, and the domestic capital in the South grow at the same rate, then the rate of profit in the South times a constant discount factor (less than one, reflecting barriers to capital mobility) is equal to the Northern rate of profit. A reduction in the discount factor (implying greater capital mobility) reducing the long-run equilibrium ratio of the Southern to Northern capital stock, implies uneven development. This is explained by the fact that capital flows to the North due to a lower discount factor (due to lower risk or policy changes) turn the terms of trade against the South, which expands the demand for Northern goods and increases Northern growth faster than that of the South.

The uneven development patterns in these models are related both to adverse movements in the terms of trade caused by capital flows, a mechanism which was stressed in the early writings of Hans Singer and Raul Prebisch, and to profit repatriation, also stressed in the earlier literature on dependency. It is argued in some quarters, however, that the nature of international capital flows has changed in recent years. Foreign direct investment (FDI) flows, for instance, reflect a deep form of integration where capital goes wherever it needs to find the lowest cost of production so that different components are produced in different places. It is therefore no longer appropriate to think of capital flows as increasing Southern production and turning the terms of trade against the South. In many parts of the world capital headed for the South can in fact displace Northern production and employment. A model which depicts this form of integration is developed in Dutt (1998a) where the North is modeled as having excess capacity along Kaleckian lines and the South with surplus labor and a fixed real wage, as in Taylor (1983). When Northern capital goes to the South, in response to higher rates of profit than can be obtained in the North, it takes with it the technological capability of producing the Northern good in the South. This model implies that if the ratio of foreign capital to capital installed in the North rises over time there will be more even development. On the other hand, if the global economy finds itself on a path in which foreign capital flows fall, there will be uneven North–South development. If the South is able to attract more foreign investment by changing its policies or by other means, it is more likely that uneven development patterns can turn into more even ones.

What this model suggests is that FDI can help Southern development, but only if it can attract such FDI and only if it can do so into the right sectors. On this question, the experience of successful Asian countries suggests that FDI is not necessarily attracted by liberal policies regarding FDI, but to economies that have already developed and achieved higher rates of growth, to exploit domestic markets, and to exploit a relatively cheap but disciplined and educated workforce. In fact, many of the successful Asian countries experience growth and capital inflows with relatively illiberal regimes in which the state had a strong role to play in the economy and in managing markets and competition to generate growth. Moreover, these countries even followed illiberal policies towards transnational corporations (TNCs), imposing sectoral restrictions, domestic input and export performance requirements (see Dutt 1998b). In contrast, large parts of the South have been unable to attract more than a trickle of FDI, despite following liberal FDI policies. While the total stock of FDI increased almost seven times between 1980 and 1997, increasing from 4 to 12 per cent of world GDP, little has gone to the poorest countries. Scott (2001) points out that about 70 per cent of FDI flows was within the group of rich countries, eight LDCs received another 20 per cent, and the rest was divided among the more than 100 remaining poor countries, with the truly poor countries receiving less than 7 per cent of all FDI flows to LDCs in the 1992–98 period.

Another aspect of international capital flows is that all of it cannot be depicted as FDI which increases the stock of productive capital, and a large part, indeed the largest part, is often in the form of short-term flows of portfolio capital or bank borrowing. (Indeed, even the statistics on FDI can be misleading, since some of it is more appropriately thought of as portfolio investment and mergers and acquisitions.) These inflows can be very large at times, and lead to speculative bubbles and, after the bubbles burst, lead to huge outflows and thence to balance of payments crises. Even relatively advanced parts of the South, such as South Korea, have not been spared such problems, as demonstrated by the Asian financial crisis of 1997.[2] An early model of North–South capital flows developed in Taylor (1986) to analyze the debt crisis of the 1980s can also yield useful lessons about financial fragility in more recent crises, since it models asset markets explicitly within the North–South structure developed in Taylor (1983) to model how confidence affects the supply of loans from the North, and how endogenization of the confidence variable can lead to financial instability in the global economy.

Labor Migration

A simple neoclassical framework with diminishing returns to labor suggests that labor migration can be an important source of convergence between regions. A region with a higher wage attracts workers from a region with a lower wage. The consequent increase in labor supply in the high-wage region reduces the wage (and per capita income) in that region and the reduction in labor supply in the low-wage region increases the wage and per capita income, leading to convergence in per capita incomes.

International migration, however, appears to be the absentee in the globalization process. While trade and FDI flows have increased at a faster rate than world production in the last two decades or so, migration flows have exhibited little change if one excludes the temporary surge after the change in political regimes in Eastern Europe (see Faini et al. 1999). The share of foreigners in the population changed very little over the 1980s in most advanced countries. While there has generally been a liberalization of restrictions on international trade and capital flows, the same cannot be said of labor flows, with most advanced countries severely restricting immigration. In 1997 the US allowed 737 000 immigrants from LDCs and Europe 665 000 which, taken together, amount to only 0.04 per cent of all potential immigrants from these countries (Scott 2001).

Moreover, the migration that does take place is largely that of skilled workers from poor countries (apart from family members and political asylum seekers and illegal immigration) who are allowed entry into rich countries to overcome specific types of shortages. Concerns have recently been expressed in rich countries about such migration, and there is a long tradition of analyzing the consequences of such migration for poor countries due to the so-called brain drain.[3] Skilled labor has played an increasingly important role in discussions of inequality and even in the context of North–South trade. Wood (1994), for instance, has replaced the traditional two factors of labor and capital in the traditional trade theory model with the two factors skilled and unskilled labor, to examine the effects of trade on the relative wages of skilled and unskilled workers.

A North–South model of the migration of skilled workers is developed in Dutt (2000a), drawing on endogenous growth models of economies of scale and increasing product variety. In this model, skilled and unskilled labor are two different factors of production which have qualitatively different roles in the production process. Unskilled workers and intermediate services are used in the production of the final good under conditions of constant returns to scale and perfect competition. Intermediate services are differentiated products, each produced by a monopolistic competitor under conditions of increasing returns, with skilled labor as the only factor of production. The given supply of skilled labor determines the number of intermediate services produced in the economy, and an increase in the number of such services increases productivity in the final good-producing sector given a Dixit–Spence production function.[4] Two economies – the North and the South – are considered, both producing the final good and non-traded services and fully employing both kinds of labor. Assuming that the wage of skilled workers is higher in the North than in the South, if migration of skilled labor is allowed, it will move from the South to the North. This implies that in the North there is a fall in the wage of skilled labor, a rise in the wage of unskilled labor and a rise in per capita income, and in the South a rise in the wage of skilled labor, a fall in the wage of unskilled labor and a fall in per capita income. There is therefore uneven development in the sense of a divergence in per capita income and in the sense of income distributional changes. The model also implies that the migration of unskilled labor from the South to the North will have exactly the opposite result, of causing convergence in per capita income levels, and of improving the distribution of income in the South (while worsening it in the North).

Technology Transfers

The main mechanism by which North–South convergence is expected to take place by those who argue that globalization will lead to greater worldwide equality is the mechanism of technology transfer. First, it is discussed in the literature on post-Second World War convergence within advanced countries. Baumol (1986) stresses the public good nature of productivity-enhancing innovations in advanced countries, which can ultimately be shared by others. Abramovitz (1986) argues that while the leading country's rate of technological progress is limited by the actual rate of innovation, the laggard can adopt the leader's practices in the organization of production and management, and thereby experience much more rapid technological change. These ideas, indeed, hark back to some of the themes discussed in the earlier work of Veblen (1915) on the advantages of being a latecomer to industrialization and of Gershchenkron (1952) on relative backwardness. Second, it is stressed in recent empirical predictions of global inequality. In Lucas's (2000, p. 164) model, convergence is due to the fact that late developers are assumed to grow at a rate faster than that of the leader, by a factor proportional to its income gap from the leader. He argues that convergence is the result of the fact that 'knowledge produced anywhere benefits producers everywhere', although he states also that there could also be other factors at work, such as '[g]overnments in unsuccessful economies can adopt the institutions and policies of the successful ones', and '[h]igh wages in the successful economies lead to capital flows to the unsuccessful economies, increasing their income levels'. Third, it is stressed in the theoretical literature on convergence and unequal growth. The convergence result, which is obtained in many endogenous growth models such as those of Grossman and Helpman (1991), Segerstrom et al. (1990) and Rivera-Batiz and Romer (1991), is due to the crucial assumption that knowledge is diffused internationally. Such diffusion of knowledge is also the mechanism by which divergence eventually leads to convergence in the Baldwin et al. (2001) model.

It is straightforward to show in a model in which the two regions each produce one good with labor alone, under conditions of full employment, and in which Northern productivity grows exogenously and Southern technology grows at a rate which depends on the productivity gap between the North and the South, that if the North has an initially higher productivity of labor, the rate of growth of output per capita will eventually become equal. There will therefore be a convergence of growth rates over time, and the South may even experience faster growth than the North (if the initial productivity gap is greater than the productivity gap in steady state) so that there is sigma-convergence. In steady-state equilibrium, however, the gap between incomes per capita will persist since the North will always be the technological leader and the South can never overtake it. The model also implies that the steady-state relative per capita income in the two regions will move to favor the South if the rate of transfer of technology increases.

Models of this type can be used to examine the effects of changes in a number of factors that affect North–South interaction. One issue that has been stressed is the role of the protection of intellectual property rights. It can be argued that stricter protection of property rights on Northern innovations will lead to a slower rate of technology transfer from the North to the South, and thereby result in a wider gap between steady-state per capita income levels of the two regions. Against this, however, it has been claimed that the loose property rights protection will actually reduce the returns to innovations and therefore reduce the flow of new innovations in the North. Since this flow is what determines the steady-state rate of world growth, the result will be to slow down growth in both the North and in the South. While this is clearly a possibility, it is not the only possible outcome. For instance, Grossman and Helpman's (1991) model implies that more rapid technology transfer with the looser protection of property rights may actually increase the rate of Northern innovation. This occurs because Northern goods producers face more competition from Southern producers who benefit from technology transfers, which reduces Northern employment and wages in production and make it more lucrative for labor to enter the research and development (R&D) sector, which results in an increase in the rate of innovation. Although this mechanism can only be expected to operate in the long run, and requires more training and education to make the transfer of labor in the North possible than Grossman and Helpman seem to think, it does show that there is no necessary inverse relation between easier technology transfer and the rate of innovation in the world economy. Another issue that has been stressed in the literature is the role of TNCs and FDI in technology transfer. It is an important vehicle of technology transfer stressed in Findlay's (1978) early model of FDI. In this approach, the major development impact of FDI is through technology transfers rather than through capital flows.

All of this analysis, however, assumes that as long as the North has a higher productivity than the South, the South can transfer technology from the North at a rate that depends on the gap in technology: the greater the gap the faster the rate of transfer of technology. Reality, as even the analysts of technology transfer and convergence have noted, may well be different. The technology gap between North and South can determine the potential for technology transfer, but actual rate of technology transfer will depend on many other factors. Abramovitz (1986), for instance, argues that transfers are not automatic but that they depend on a plethora of conditions in the recipient country, which he calls 'social capability'. This can be somewhat narrowly defined as technical competence, measured by years of education, or more broadly understood to include a country's political, commercial, industrial and financial institutions, as well as other aspects of economic systems, including openness to competition and the establishment of new firms, and 'obstacles to change raised by vested interests, established positions and customary relations among firms and between employers and employees' (ibid.: 389). Moreover, such capability is not given, but evolves over time. If we limit ourselves to the narrow notion of social capability to focus on technological factors, we may draw on the recent approach to technological change. This argues that the distinction between the two processes of 'innovation' and 'diffusion' is a false one, since successful diffusion actually involves continuing and incremental technical change to modify borrowed technology to suit local conditions and to attain higher standards of production (Bell and Pavitt 1993). This approach makes a distinction between production capacity and technological capability, where the former 'incorporates the resources used to produce industrial goods at given levels of efficiency and given input combinations', while the latter 'incorporates the additional and distinct resources needed to generate and manage technical change, including skills, knowledge and experience, and institutional structures and linkages' (ibid.: 260–61). Baumol (1986) also expresses some doubts regarding the ability of LDCs to participate in the process of innovation sharing. He argues that such sharing will mostly take place among countries producing similar products. As one country experiences technological innovation in an industry, other countries that produce the product of that industry or close substitutes will feel under competitive pressures to obtain access to that innovation.

> Industrialized countries, whose product lines overlap substantially and which sell a good deal in markets where foreign producers of similar items are also present, will find themselves constantly running in this Schumpeterian race, while those LDCs which supply few products competing with those of the industrialized economies will not participate to the same degree. (ibid.: 1077)

These ideas have a number of implications for the analysis of technology transfer. First, the growth of technological capability can be expected to increase the ability of a poor country to effectively assimilate foreign technology: not only can it do so at a faster rate, but it can be expected to do so with increasingly more sophisticated types of technology. This implies that the rate of technology transfer will be affected by the gap between the technological capability of the leading and lagging countries. Given a wide gap, much of the technology used in the leading countries will be beyond the grasp of producers and engineers in the lagging country, so the rate of transfer will be low. As the gap narrows, the poor country will be able to assimilate a larger portion of the technology used in the rich country, so the rate of transfer will be high. Combined with the idea that the potential for technology transfer depends positively on the actual productivity gap between the rich and poor countries, it can be shown that there is an inverse-U-shaped relation between technology transfers and the productivity gap (Dutt 2000b; Verspagen 1991). There need not, therefore, be a unique steady-state equilibrium value of the ratio of Southern to Northern productivity, but rather, there may be multiple equilibria. The upper one will be similar to the one discussed earlier, which will be stable in the sense that if the ratio of Southern to Northern productivity is lower than it, technology transfer will take place and there will be catching up. But this equilibrium will be at high levels of the productivity ratio. At lower levels, however, this catching up will not occur as the South will have lower technological capability, so if the technology gap is below that level, there will be divergence.

Second, changes in the degree of intellectual property rights protection will change the speed of technology transfers, as discussed earlier. In terms of this modified analysis, this implies not only that if the South is beyond the low level equilibrium it will converge to a position with a higher technological gap between the North and the South, but also that the position of the lower equilibrium will be changed so that initial levels of technological gap which earlier led to convergence may now lead to divergence.

Finally, the distinction between technical change and technological learning leads us to the determinants of technological capability. The effect of technology transfer and consequent technical change on technological capability may not be a positive one. It has been pointed out that technology transfers, especially by TNCs, can adversely affect the development of indigenous technological capability in the South,[5] which in fact may reduce the ability of the host country to properly assimilate the foreign technology (see also Helleiner 1989: 1469–70). Moreover, changes in the pattern of product composition due to trade liberalization can also have deleterious effects on technological capability, as discussed in our analysis of the effects of trade and learning by doing.

Other Types of Interaction

Beyond these major forms of interaction, which receive the greatest attention in the economics literature, the North and South interact in a number of other ways. Without entering into an exhaustive discussion of all possible types of interaction, we confine our comments to two additional types of interactions that can have an important bearing on the relative performance of the North and the South.

One type of interaction refers to the ability of the North to force the South to pursue certain kinds of policies. In the past this was achieved through colonization. Alam (1994) has shown that colonized countries had lower rates of growth than countries which were not colonized or which were decolonized up to 1950. He has argued that this has had much to do with the pursuit of independent growth-promoting policies by the latter group of countries, policies which were not available to colonized countries, which were forced to adopt policies supporting the economic interests of the colonizing countries. After general decolonization, however, this type of open intervention was no longer possible. However, pressure on Southern governments – both those which are corrupt, or those whose policy options are severely constrained – can be imposed by the North in more subtle and not-so-subtle ways, by gunboat diplomacy of various kinds threating cuts in foreign aid and restriction of market access, and by pressure from TNCs which often have much greater economic clout than host countries, and as we shall discuss later, through the influence of international institutions. All this is a far cry from the ideas of Lucas (2000) and others that convergence will occur because the countries of the South will learn appropriate policies from countries of the successful North. Aside from debates on what exactly the right policies are (and how these may change with changes in the structure of the global economy), the ability of Southern countries to choose appropriate policies unilaterally is open to serious doubt.

A second type of interaction is through what can be called 'cultural' influence, which affects preferences and aspirations of consumers in the South, inducing them to follow consumption patterns in the North through international demonstration effects, and also by affecting their aspirations. Although these influences are partly related to trade in goods, capital flows (involving TNCs) and labor migration, they can also be independent of them, for instance, through travel and tourism, and through communications media, such as television and the internet. International demonstration effects can imply changes in Southern consumption patterns which favor Northern goods due to perceived greater status and brand names and can reduce saving propensities there, all of which can exacerbate the forces of uneven development (see Dutt 1990, ch. 9). Beyond these effects, these types of interactions bring the world closer together and enlarge the geographical scope of reasons for which happiness depends more on consumption and income relative to that of others than on their absolute levels (see, for instance, Lichtenberg 1998). Thus, even if greater North–South interaction in this form has no effect on relative income levels, it may have important implications for reducing the level of well-being in the South as, for instance, the Southern consumer obtains more information on Northern consumption patterns from the television screen.

3 INTERNATIONAL INSTITUTIONS

We now turn to the question of how the forces of convergence and divergence discussed so far are affected by the activities of international institutions.

The international institution that comes closest to being a world government is, of course, the United Nations. Although its main goal is to maintain world peace, from its inception the UN has taken the view that international peace and economic progress are linked and has committed itself to social progress and development and to higher standards of living, especially in the developing world. In the 1990s about 80 per cent of the financial and staff work were devoted to economic and social programs in developing LDCs (Patterson 1995). To focus its commitment to help the developing world the General Assembly of the UN has proclaimed successive development decades. The second of these, adopted in 1970 and called the International Development Strategy, had the explicit goal of closing the gap between rich and poor nations and aimed to create a just world order by encouraging cooperation between the North and the South in all spheres of economic and social life. The plan called for rich countries to transfer to LDCs annually one per cent of their GNP, mostly in the form of long-term, low-interest loans for development purposes. The UN also recognized the rights of countries to control their natural resources and regulate foreign investment within their borders, and even to nationalize foreign-owned property after paying compensation. In the 1990s, however, this emphasis on development has been broadened and arguably diluted, by focussing more on so-called social aspects such as poverty, hunger and living conditions, rather than on development strategies for regions as a whole.

The UN undertakes numerous development projects in LDCs, most of them coordinated and administered by the United Nations Development Programme (UNDP) established in 1965. These projects are wide-ranging in nature, ranging from agriculture and manufacturing, transportation and communications, to health, social welfare, environmental protection and community development. The UNDP's focus, like that of the UN as a whole, has shifted towards human development, attempting to increase its partnership with NGOs, advance the role of women and encourage free enterprise and political freedom, and even helping with holding free elections. There are also numerous specialized agencies of the UN that deal with specific sectors or issues. They include: the World Health Organization; the Food and Agriculture Organization which promotes rural development and provides food security; the International Labour Organization which tries to help member countries with vocational training, employment and management policies and occupational health and safety policies; the United Nations Educational, Scientific and Cultural Organization (UNESCO) which supports international cooperation in education, science, culture and communications, trains teachers and administrations, and finances school construction projects; the United Nations Industrial Development Organization (UNIDO) which promotes industrial development through investment and training programs, and fosters technology transfer to and between LDCs; the United Nations Conference on Trade and Development (UNCTAD) which provides a forum for North–South negotiations of development policies and formulates policy principles on international trade and related development issues; and, of course, the World Bank and the IMF.

Although the UN has a huge bureaucracy and is involved with a large number of projects, the role of most of the UN agencies in affecting overall development patterns is arguably quite limited. Their work is aimed at individual projects increasingly to promote human development objectives. On broader development policy issues, especially concerning North–South economic relations, they merely conduct research, provide advice, formulate policy principles and announce goals. They are also often resource constrained and have little power to affect policy making in countries, especially in advanced countries. However, one should also take into account the possible growth and development impact of the projects funded by the UN agencies. The full impact of such flows of resources, as well as those that are made bilaterally by countries, may be taken as a measure of their role in the global economy. This is measured by official development assistance, which includes disbursements of loans (net of repayments of principal) and grants made on concessional terms by official agencies of the members of the Development Assistance Committee (DAC), by multistate institutions, and by certain Arab countries to countries listed by DAC as developing. Loans having a grant element of more that 25 per cent and technical cooperation and assistance are included in the figures. As a percentage of their GDP, the total development assistance of low-income countries according to the World Bank classification fell from 2.1 per cent in 1985 to 1.3 per cent in 1998. For middle-income countries it fell steadily from 0.9 to 0.4 per cent, while for the subset of these countries classified as lower-middle-income countries it fell from 2.0 to 1.0 per cent. We therefore find that development assistance as a whole, to low- and middle-income countries, has been declining in importance.[6] (See Table 6.1.)

Table 6.1   Official development assistance as a percentage of GDP of recipient regions

	1985	1990	1998
Low-income countries	2.1	2.6	1.3
Middle-income countries	0.9	0.7	0.4
Lower-middle-income countries	2.0	1.2	1.0

Source: World Bank, *World Development Report*, various issues.

The two agencies which have the largest impact on economic policies and development are certainly the World Bank and the IMF, which originated at Bretton Woods in 1944. The World Bank is the world's largest lending body and the largest source of development aid, while the IMF seeks to help countries with balance of payments problems by lending to member nations. We now turn to these institutions, before discussing the World Trade Organization and other international institutions.

The Bretton Woods Institutions

Although the precise nature of the policy advice given by the two powerful Bretton Woods institutions, the World Bank and the IMF, to developing (and now post-socialist) countries may have changed over the years, the basic principles governing it are neo-liberal in nature, and known as the 'Washington consensus'.[7] The goal of the institutions at their inception towards the closing years of the Second World War, following Keynes's vision, was to have a well-ordered international economic system with national governments playing a major role in regulating national economies and the international economic system. The subsequent neo-liberal stance was arguably shaped by the dissatisfaction, especially after the 1970s, with earlier development experience which was dirigiste in nature, and the pressures imposed by TNCs, international financial market interests, and the US Treasury, which wanted greater access to global markets.[8] We will not discuss all the elements of the policy advice given by these institutions (but see Pieper and Taylor 1998, for a useful review) but focus on some major issues that affect overall growth and international economic relations.

The primary purpose of the advice given by the IMF is to stabilize the economy in order to reduce trade deficits and especially imports and sometimes to control inflation by fiscal and monetary austerity, and devaluing domestic currency. The World Bank's advice is more broad ranging, since it involves structural adjustment. This requires that countries depart from their earlier import-substituting industrial policies which, the Bank argues, have distorted the economy and led to various kinds of inefficiencies. Standard recommendations include: removal of non-tariff barriers and reduction of imports tariffs; reduction of capital controls, including those on foreign exchange transactions and profit remittances; financial liberalization, which generally results in higher interest rates; rationalization of domestic tax systems, generally by reducing taxes on the rich; and reducing domestic subsidies, including those on production. In recent times the IMF has become involved in promoting more comprehensive reforms beyond stabilization in a narrow sense, pushing, for instance, capital market liberalization and wholesale industrial restructuring (see Stiglitz 2002).

Although what these institutions provide are 'recommendations', they are obeyed for a number of reasons. First, the institutions are backed by the United States and other economic powers which have a disproportionate say in these institutions since votes are according to financial contributions. Second, their representatives provide hard currency. The IMF supplies this in the form of loans, for instance, under its 'standby arrangements', or gives signals that the countries are following the 'right' policies which restores the confidence of private lenders to lend to them. The IMF imposes various 'conditionalities' which embody the policies it advocates, the violation of which results in the withdrawal of assistance. The World Bank funnels funds for development projects after raising them from primarily private sources. Third, countries which normally approach these institutions for advice, particularly the IMF, are in dire straits and have few options other than to accept the recommendations to manage their external payments positions.

Implementation of these policies often exacerbates the forces of uneven development. IMF-guided stabilization is contractionary, and leads to lower rates of growth. Of course, the countries initially had problems, but sometimes the medicine can be worse than the disease, slowing down growth further by reducing investment demand as a result of high interest rates (to attract foreign capital), and by reducing government spending. Moreover, the World Bank, by pushing up interest rates in the name of financial deregulation also reduces investment. Lower rates of growth, if they persist for a long time, arguably have the result of slowing down technological change and also making the countries less attractive to FDI (in addition to worsening the plight of the poor who typically receive little or no government protection).

In terms of trade links, reduced trade protection is likely to exacerbate the problems of uneven development due to a greater dependence on goods in which the South has a static comparative advantage, which tend to have low income elasticities and which generate less technological change. Quick trade liberalization has the result of reducing output of manufactured goods and reducing employment, which have further contractionary effects on the growth process, not to speak of the worsening of the problem of poverty.

In terms of their effects on capital flows, exchange rate devaluation can make it cheaper to acquire domestic assets, and therefore encourage capital flows. However, it can also lead to capital losses on assets already held, and thereby reduce confidence. Fears of further devaluation can prevent capital inflows as well. Slower growth means that the debt/GDP ratio increases, which can signal lower creditworthiness and also scare off foreign investors. Contractions can lead to unrest and political instability, which can reduce the confidence of foreign investors further. The removal of capital controls due to structural adjustment leads to greater volatility of capital flows. Such capital inflows lead to speculative booms which can cause exchange appreciation which can erode competitiveness to some degree, and which can then fuel capital outflows which can cause a crisis, as shown by the experience of many LDCs, including some relatively more developed ones, such as South Korea.

In sum, the policies pressed on LDCs by the Bretton Woods institutions have arguably severely restricted the ability of these countries to follow the kinds of policies, such as industrial and trade policies, which could promote national development, and made these countries often follow contractionary policies which are directly detrimental to growth. What is more, the countries which have performed more poorly and for whom assistance from these institutions becomes more important, are subjected to these kinds of restrictions even more, implying that countries which do poorly continue with their poor performance. Rich countries, on the other hand, have greater economic leverage and are much less likely to acquiesce to the 'advice' of these institutions.

The World Trade Organization

The WTO oversees the more important international agreements in four main areas: trade in goods; trade in services with the General Agreement on Trade in Services (GATS); intellectual property rights with the Agreement on Trade-related Aspects of Intellectual Property Rights (TRIPs Agreement); and foreign direct investment with the Trade-related Investment Measures (TRIMs). The agreement regarding trade in goods is based on the General Agreement on Tariffs and Trade (GATT) system, which was established in 1948 as an intergovernmental organization affiliated with the UN, and agreements on the three remaining were added on during the Uruguay Round negotiations (1986–94).

The plan in 1948 had been to establish the International Trade Organization (ITO) as the third organization along with the World Bank and the IMF, to create a system which would oversee the liberalization of world trade. Although several countries ratified it, the institution never got off the ground, in large part due to US opposition. Instead, the GATT came into place, with the objective of slowly liberalizing world trade (although much less comprehensively than what was proposed in the ITO system) by removing import quotas and export subsidies and gradually reducing tariffs using the principles of reciprocity, non-discrimination and transparency, through periodic rounds of multilateral negotiation. However, from its inception GATT had many kinds of loopholes which allowed signatory countries to impose various kinds of trade restrictions. By the beginning of the 1980s it seemed that the GATT system was a failure and that protectionism was on the rise through various kinds of measures such as subsidies, tax rebates, and voluntary export restraints such as the 1974 'Multi-fibre Agreement' under which the US and the European Community were forced to limit the level and growth of exports to the LDCs. Many countries were following some form of industrial policy. The US, although it did not have an official industrial policy, heavily subsidized its defense and high-tech sectors.

With the rising influence of exporting interests in the US and other countries and the increasing spread of TNCs which wanted external market access, and the rise of conservative governments in the US, the UK and elsewhere, the tide began to change, however. The Uruguay Round of negotiations was started in 1986 and signed in 1994. In 1995 the GATT system was replaced by the WTO. We briefly turn to the main planks of the WTO system.

On the liberalization of trade in goods, textiles, clothing and agriculture were fully integrated into the GATT, it was agreed that voluntary export restrictions and other non-tariff barriers were eliminated, tariffs were to be significantly reduced, and safeguards allowing temporary tariffs due to balance of payments difficulties were to be narrowed down. Production subsidies which significantly affected trade were to be removed in some cases and severely restricted in others.

Services was covered for the first time, under GATS, covering all commercial services. Government regulatory capacity, including the right to limit foreign investment, was curtailed in many sectors. Provisions were made to allow LDCs more time to satisfy the agreements, and even more time to the least-developed countries, but it is clear that they have to follow the path to increasing liberalization.

The TRIMs Agreement requires member countries to phase out performance requirements imposed by host countries on TNCs, especially those related to trade. TRIMs are of two types: positive ones such as tax concessions to attract FDI, and negative ones which place restrictions on FDI, such as local content requirements, limitations on the use of imported components, export requirements, local R&D requirements, and requirements to match the use of foreign exchange to foreign exchange generated. The actual TRIMs argument was a compromise which prohibits only those TRIMs which are inconsistent with other articles of the GATT94 agreements, such as those involving national treatment and elimination of quantitative restrictions on imports. An 'illustrative list' prohibits TRIMs such as local content requirements, export linkages, trade or foreign exchange balancing measures and limitations on imported inputs, although it is suggested that export performance and technology transfer requirements are not necessarily inconsistent with the agreement. It has been claimed that the agreement is biassed towards TNCs since positive TRIMs are not covered by the agreement while negative ones are. Though there are temporary exemptions to help LDCs, the agreement rules out several measures used by successful TNC hosts to promote growth, and the agreements provide an impetus for greater import liberalization in the future (Dunkley 2000: 68).

The TRIPs Agreement is a comprehensive multilateral agreement which establishes obligations on all WTO members' intellectual property rights policies where the standards are comparable to those of the major industrial countries, and stipulates how the enforcement of these obligations is to be carried out. The forms of intellectual property rights which are protected by the agreement include copyright, computer programs, trademarks, geographical indications, industrial designs, patents, undisclosed information (or trade secrets) and the layout designs of integrated circuits. Patents are for twenty years, longer than currently offered by most countries, and cover almost all product and process inventions. Disputes are handled through the WTO and retaliatory action can be in terms of departures from other provisions of the agreement, such as market access, which is contrary to other types of retaliatory actions which are intraissue.

Decisions in the WTO are made by a voting system in which each country has one vote. However, the advanced countries, and especially the US, have been able to have their way on many issues. During the negotiation process there was opposition to the provisions of the services and intellectual property rights agreements from several LDCs, but despite such resistance, they were included in the final agreement. The TRIPs provisions were incorporated on the insistence of the US which threatened to pull out of the negotiations if they were not included. This occurred as a result of pressure on the US government by organized business interests, including pharmaceutical manufacturers pushing for patents, and publishing, motion picture and software designing interests for copyrights. Countries, including the least-developed ones, could become members of WTO only if they signed all of the provisions of the Uruguay Round, in contrast to previous rounds of the GATT in which countries could decline membership in new accords such as the Anti-Dumping Code. If countries did not accept the new TRIPs and other provisions, they would have to give up all of the cumulative market access rights as negotiated in earlier GATT rounds. Countries not accepting the TRIPs provisions, therefore would have to enter into bilateral negotiations with countries like the US for continued access to their markets, without having any rights and security guaranteed by the multilateral system and its dispute resolution system (Stegemann 2000).

The analysis of the role of the WTO suggests that, despite some concessions shown to them in terms of speed of adoption, LDCs have been put in a position such that they cannot follow trade and industrial policies to attempt to change their pattern of specialization in trade, even using many kinds of domestic production subsidies. At the same time, countries in the North have persisted in the use of protectionist measures which discriminate against the imports of LDCs (see Raffer and Singer 2001; Stiglitz 2002). The bargaining position of countries in the South against TNCs has been seriously impaired, and they will no longer be able to impose those kinds of restrictions on TNCs that have proved advantageous to host countries in the past. They have also had to open up their service sectors to trade and investment, which were heavily restricted, especially for balance of payments reasons and for channeling it to sectors where greater technological learning could be expected, by successful developers such as South Korea. Opening up their service sectors to foreign competition in areas such as television will undoubtedly increase cultural interactions and exacerbate international demonstration effects. At the same time, the liberalization of services in semi-skilled sectors, in which LDCs have a comparative advantage, has been blocked (Raffer and Singer 2001: 208). The TRIPs provisions will increase the cost to the South of technology transfer, while at the same time creating favorable conditions for TNCs which assert intellectual property rights on traditional processes used in LDCs in the areas of foodstuffs, agricultural products, traditional medicine, and the like. All this can be expected to have an unfavorable effect on the South not only for technology transfers but also for balance of payments reasons due to increasing royalty flows (Dunkley 2000: 189–90). The dispute settlement process in the WTO, moreover, is heavily biassed against LDCs given the high costs of litigation, and the structure of punishments according to which only the country which has won the complaint can take retaliatory action against the perpetrator (clearly less of a concern to rich countries like the US than to smaller LDCs). Finally, recent moves towards greater cooperation between the WTO and the Bretton Woods institutions, ostensibly for achieving 'greater coherence in global policy making', is likely to further weaken the position of the South *vis-à-vis* the North in dealing with trade policy issues (Raffer and Singer 2001: 216–17).

Other Institutions

Although the UN, and especially the Bretton Woods institutions and the WTO are the major international institutions which affect the global economy, there are other groups which have begun to play an increasingly important role. Some of this has taken the form of street demonstrations and protests against globalization, such as those at official meetings in Seattle and Prague. Partly perhaps in response to them, the US government, the secretary-general of the UN, the director-general of the WTO, the managing director of the IMF, and the president of the World Bank have called for greater citizen participation in the world order.

Civil society, comprising non-profit organizations and voluntary associations dedicated to civic, humanitarian, economic and social causes, now plays an increasing role in the global arena. During the 1990s these forces have promoted treaties to limit global warming, defeated a multilateral investment agreement and mounted a campaign to cancel the international debts of the world's poorest countries. A millennium NGO forum held at the UN in May 2000, to which the UN secretary-general invited 1400 representatives of international civil society groups to present views on global issues, and which agreed to establish a permanent assembly of civil society organizations, has been argued by Falk and Strauss (2001) to represent an initial step toward creating a global parliament.

In addition to civil society groups, Falk and Strauss point out that the participation of business elites in the international economic system is becoming institutionalized. The World Economic Forum, at Davos, Switzerland, has emerged as a forum in which many of the world's most powerful business leaders meet with many of the world's senior policy makers over roundtables and presentations, making recommendations on shaping global policy. The Forum also conducts and disseminates its research, and has consistently been supportive of neoliberal policies. The UN is frequently represented at these meetings. The Forum, and other overlapping networks of corporate leaders have also received the supportive collaboration of most governments, especially those of rich countries. But these institutions have arguably increased the bargaining power of corporate interests in the global economy, and strengthened their influence on governments and the major international institutions.

Obviously, the power and resources of corporate and banking communities cannot be matched by those of global civil society. But Falk and Strauss argue that only when these two interests work together within an overarching representative body can they achieve responses to policy which can be viewed widely as legitimate, and offer democratic oversight to international institutions like the IMF, the World Bank and the WTO. They argue that the assembly should not be composed of states, unlike the UN, but have its authority directly from the global citizenry, so as not to be bound by the laws to which they give consent. The delegates would be elected directly by the citizenry and therefore need not vote along national lines. The assembly would play an important role in providing a legitimate forum in which alternative policies could be debated, weakening the destructive forces of ultranationalists and opportunists from the left and right who seek to dismantle the global system. They argue that progress in the direction of creating a global parliament may be achieved through what they call the new diplomacy which makes room for flexible coalitions between civil society and receptive states (rather than just relations between states), and through the 'single negotiating text method' in which an organizing committee would consult with sympathetic groups from civil society, business, and national governments and establish an assembly with a proposed treaty. The process could start with a small number of states, which would then persuade other countries and groups to become involved.

Whatever the likelihood of the formation of such a body, the formulation of the concept underlines what is absent in the international arena. We do not have anything like a legitimate world parliament which can mediate policy disputes between different parts of the world, and which can act anything remotely like a national government in trying to promote worldwide development.

4   CONCLUSIONS

This chapter has tried to analyze the role of international institutions in the determination of North–South development patterns. It has noted that there is evidence of divergence and uneven development patterns in the global economy which appear to be widening the development gap between rich and poor countries, and inquires whether international institutions can help to mitigate this tendency. There is some presumption that they may be able to do so. There appears to have been convergence within countries such as the US and Japan, and within Europe, where there are governments which affect the development process. Although there is no world government to oversee the international development process, it could be hoped that international institutions will play the role of an international government which can bring about convergence.

To analyze this question we have reviewed the theory of North–South models and some evidence on actual North–South interactions to examine the forces of convergence and uneven development. We have argued that although there are forces for convergence, there is enough theory and empirical evidence to suggest that there are strong forces of uneven development in the international economy, due to international trade, international factor movements, technology transfers and other mechanisms. Moreover, international institutions, including the World Bank, the IMF, and the WTO, have done little to stem these forces, and by promoting the liberalization of trade and capital flows, and by protecting intellectual property rights, and by not promoting the greater mobility of labor, they may well have exacerbated the forces of global uneven development. As the forces and effects of globalization spread there is every reason to be wary of its implications for North–South uneven development.

If this analysis is found acceptable at least to some degree, what are its implications for the possibilities of the reversal of uneven development and for Southern development in the future? The answer to this question can be discussed by speculating in turn on the possibilities of national policies by countries in the South, and of alternations in the nature of the global economic system to strengthen spread effects and weaken backwash effects.

On the first point, it is possible for countries of the South to give greater thought to what kinds of policies they can pursue to strategically delink themselves from the global economy, thereby following industrial policies in a way that will eventually enable them to reap the benefits of international economic linkages (see Singh 1992, for instance). Obvious examples of appropriate policies include capital controls that can be used without violating existing international agreements (as done by Malaysia, for instance), and trade and industrial policies which may require withdrawal from the WTO. This cannot be interpreted as complete autarky, for the dangers of economic isolation in promoting inefficient and antiquated industrial systems without exposing themselves to foreign competition and the possibility of drawing on foreign technology are well known. Even if larger Southern countries can achieve some gains with these methods, it may be impossible for smaller ones, given the small size of their markets and for them the importance of cooperation with other Southern countries, cannot be overstated. But it is an open question whether the internal politics of the countries in the South will enable them to adopt such policies in a way that will lead to growth rather than to more cronyism and efficiency, and whether it will be feasible to de-link strategically in a world in which globalization gathers steam.

On the second point, one can speculate on whether it is possible that the global economy will change in a way that will allow more even global development. Given the focus of this chapter, we can ask whether international institutions can be expected to become more like national governments that have been able to promote the forces of even development within their countries, by allowing individual countries to pursue policies that can promote development, by transferring resources from the rich to the poor countries, or by strengthening international spread effects. If current trends are any guide, despite recent strides made in terms of the influence of international civil society, the development of anything remotely resembling national governments which are able to promote balanced development seems like a utopian dream. After all, such governments do not arise and operate in a vacuum. There has to be some sense of a shared history and destiny of people in a country, buttressed by internal migration, to develop enough sympathy for people in backward areas of their country to support policies of balanced economic development. Such feelings are largely absent in a world divided by cultural, linguistic and geographical barriers in which international migration is severely restricted. Moreover, it is helped by threats of separatist movements in backward areas which can destroy national unity, something that is impossible in the context of a possible global government monopoly. Indeed, something like a more competitive world political system existed during the Cold War, when competition between the two superpowers was severe enough for the superpowers to help economic development efforts at least in their strategically important client states (see Johnson 1998), a system that has now disappeared following the demise of the Soviet bloc. Furthermore, it is helped by appropriate government institutions which ensure a reasonably level playing field. Powerful international organizations, like the Bretton Woods institutions, do not even protect the weak even in the sense that democratic governments with one-person–one-vote do. Even the WTO, in which every country has one vote, reveals clearly how the deck is stacked against the South.

However, the very forces of globalization, which have strengthened some of the backwash effects as discussed above, have the potential – albeit one that is likely only to bear fruit, if at all, in the distant future – to increase understanding and promote solidarity among world citizenry. At the same time that Southern consumers learn of and copy the consumption patterns of those in the North, Northern citizens can be exposed to the problems facing their Southern counterparts. Although some may be deterred from supporting a global system more conducive to Southern development by focussing on corrupt and autocratic Southern regimes, others may be persuaded by a better understanding of the functioning of the global economic system and of feelings of sympathy for human beings everywhere, and support moves by their own national governments to push for international institutions which will genuinely strive for equitable global development, rather than promote the narrow national interests of their governments and private businesses based in their own countries.

NOTES

*   An earlier version of this paper was presented at the CSI Symposium 'The Role of International Institutions in Globalisation' held at the University of Innsbruck, Austria, 14–16 November 2001. I am grateful to Dr Peter Egger and to other participants of the conference for comments and discussions.
1. The last type of model introduces transports costs which constitute a barrier to trade. When transport costs are reduced exogenously, these models imply divergence due to the enjoyment of scale economies in the differentiated product exported by the North. In some of these models convergence eventually occurs because factor prices rise in the North.
2. See Stiglitz (2002: ch. 4) for an excellent discussion.
3. See Bhagwati (1979), for instance.
4. This production function implies higher productivity when the number of inputs is increased given the total amount of resources used to produce them.
5. See Jenkins (1987: ch. 4) and Casson and Pearce (1987: 96–107) for good reviews of the issues involved and the conflicting evidence.
6. See Raffer and Singer (2001: chs 5 and 6), for a fuller discussion, and an analysis of the possible causes of the decline in aid.
7. See, for instance, Pieper and Taylor (1998) and Stiglitz (2002).
8. On this, see especially the view of Stiglitz (2002) who, after serving as Chief Economist at the World Bank, comes down particularly heavily on the IMF.

REFERENCES

Abramovitz, Moses (1986), 'Catching up, forging ahead, and falling behind', *Journal of Economic History*, **46** (2), 385–406.

Alam, M.S. (1994), 'Colonialism, decolonisation and growth rates: theory and empirical evidence', *Cambridge Journal of Economics*, **18** (3), June, 235–57.

Amsden, Alice H. (2001), *The Rise of 'the Rest'. Challenges to the West from Late-industrializing Countries*, Oxford: Oxford University Press.

Baldwin, Richard E., Philippe Martin and Gianmarco I.P. Ottaviano (2001), 'Global income divergence, trade and industrialization: the geography of growth take-offs', *Journal of Economic Growth*, **6**, March, 5–37.

Barro, Robert J. and Xavier Sala-i-Martin (1995), *Economic Growth*, New York: McGraw-Hill.

Baumol, William J. (1986), 'Productivity growth, convergence, and welfare: what the long-run data show', *American Economic Review*, **76** (5), 1072–85.

Baumol, William J., Sue Ann Batey Blackman and Edward N. Wolff (1989), *Productivity and Leadership: The Long View*, Cambridge, MA: MIT Press.

Bell, Martin and Keith Pavitt (1993), 'Accumulating technological capability in developing countries', Proceedings of the World Bank Annual Conference on Development Economics 1992, Washington, DC: World Bank.

Bhagwati, Jagdish (1979), 'Economic migration of the highly skilled: economics, ethics and taxes', *Third World Quarterly*, **1** (3), 17–30.

Blecker, Robert (1996), 'The new economic integration: structuralist models of North–South trade and investment liberalization', *Structural Change and Economic Dynamics*, **7**, 321–45.

Boldrin, M. and J.A. Scheinkman (1988), 'Learning by doing, international trade and growth: a note', in P.W. Anderson, K.J. Arrow and D. Pines (eds), *The Economy as an Evolving Competitive System*, Redwood City, CA: Addison-Wesley, pp. 285–300.

Burgstaller, Andre and Neantro Saavedra-Rivano (1984), 'Capital mobility and growth in a North–South model', *Journal of Development Economics*, **15** (1–3), May–August, 213–37.

Casson, Mark and Robert D. Pearce (1987), 'Multinational enterprises in LDCs', in N. Gemmell (ed.), *Surveys in Development Economics*, Oxford: Blackwell, pp. 90–132.

Dunkley, Graham (2000), *The Free Trade Adventure: The WTO, Uruguay Round and Globalization – A Critique*, London and New York: Zed Books.

Dutt, Amitava K. (1990), *Growth, Distribution and Uneven Development*, Cambridge: Cambridge University Press.

Dutt, Amitava K. (1998a), 'Transnational corporations, direct foreign investment, and growth', in Richard Kozul-Wright and Robert E. Rowthorn (eds), *Transnational Corporations and the Global Economy*, Basingstoke: Macmillan and New York: St. Martin's Press, pp. 164–91.

Dutt, Amitava K. (1998b), 'Globalization, foreign direct investment and Southern growth: evidence from selected Asian countries', in J.R. Chen (ed.), *Economic Effects of Globalization*, Aldershot: Avebury, pp. 45–96.

Dutt, Amitava K. (2000a) 'Globalization, South–North migration and uneven development', unpublished paper, Department of Economics, University of Notre Dame, IN, USA.

Dutt, Amitava K. (2000b), 'North–South technology transfers, convergence, and uneven development', *Decision*, **27** (1), January–June, 59–86.

Dutt, Amitava K. (2003), 'Income elasticity of imports, North–South trade and uneven development', in A.K. Dutt and J. Ros (eds), *Development Economics and Structuralist Macroeconomics*, Cheltenham, UK and Northampton, MA, USA: Edward Elgar, pp. 307–35.

Ethier, W.J. (1982), 'Decreasing costs in international trade and Frank Graham's argument for protection', *Econometrica*, 50, 1243–68.

Faini, Riccardo, Jaime de Melo and Klaus Zimmerman (1999), 'Trade and migration: an introduction', in Riccardo Faini, Jaime de Melo and Klaus Zimmerman (eds), *Migration: The Controversies and the Evidence*, Cambridge: Cambridge University Press, pp. 1–20.

Falk, Richard and Andrew Strauss (2001), 'Toward global parliament', *Foreign Affairs*, January/February, **80** (1), 212–20.

Findlay, Ronald (1978), 'Relative backwardness, direct foreign investment, and the transfer of technology: a simple dynamic model', *Quarterly Journal of Economics*, **92** (1), February, 1–16.

Findlay, Ronald (1980), 'The terms of trade and equilibrium growth in the world economy', *American Economic Review*, June, 291–9.

Gerschenkron, Alexander (1952), 'Economic backwardness in historical perspective', in Bert F. Hoselitz (ed.), *The Progress of Underdeveloped Areas*, Chicago: University of Chicago Press. Reprinted in A. Gershchenkron, *Economic Backwardness in Historical Perspective*, New York: Frederick A. Praeger, 1962.

Grossman, Gene and Elhanan Helpman (1991), *Innovation and Growth in the World Economy*, Cambridge, MA: MIT Press.

Helleiner, Gerald K. (1989), 'Transnational corporations and direct foreign investment', in H. Chenery and T.N. Srinivasan (eds), *Handbook of Development Economics*, Vol. 2, Amsterdam: North-Holland, pp. 1441–90.

Jenkins, Rhys (1987), *Transnational Corporations and Uneven Development*, London: Methuen.

Johnson, Chalmers (1998), 'Economic crisis in East Asia: the clash of capitalisms', *Cambridge Journal of Economics*, **22**, 653–61.

Krugman, Paul (1981), 'Trade, accumulation, and uneven development', *Journal of Development Economics*, **8**, 149–61.

Lichtenberg, Judith (1998), 'Consumption because others consume', in David C. Crocker and Toby Linden (eds), *Ethics of Consumption. The Good Life, Justice and Global Stewardship*, Lanham: Rowman & Littlefield, pp. 155–75.

Lucas, Robert E. (2000), 'Some macroeconomics for the 21st century', *Journal of Economic Perspectives*, **14** (1), Winter, 159–68.

Molana, H. and David Vines (1989), 'North–south growth and the terms of trade: a model on Kaldorian lines', *Economic Journal*, **99** (396), June, 443–53.

Myrdal, Gunnar (1957), *Rich Lands and Poor Lands*, New York: Harper & Brothers.

Ottaviano, Gianmacro I.P. and Diego Puga (1998), 'Agglomeration in the global economy: a survey of the "new economic geography"', *The World Economy*, **21**, 707–31.

Patterson, Charles (1995), *The Oxford 50th Anniversary Book of the United Nations*, New York: Oxford University Press.

Pieper, Ute and Lance Taylor (1998), 'The revival of the liberal creed: the IMF, World Bank, and inequality in a globalized world economy', in Dean Baker, Gerald Epstein and Robert Pollin (eds), *Globalization and Progressive Economic Policy*, Cambridge: Cambridge University Press, pp. 37–63.

Quah, Danny T. (1993), 'Empirical cross-section dynamics in economic growth', *European Economic Review*, **37** (2–3), April, 426–34.

Raffer, Kunibert and Hans Singer (2001), *The Economic North–South Divide: Six Decades of Unequal Development*, Cheltenham, UK and Northampton, MA, USA: Edward Elgar.

Raman, Jaishankar (1996–97), 'Convergence or uneven development: a note on regional development in India', *Indian Economic Journal*, **44** (4), 135–43.

Rivera-Batiz, Luis A. and Paul M. Romer (1991), 'Economic integration and endogenous growth', *Quarterly Journal of Economics*, **106** (2), 531–56.

Sala-i-Martin, Xavier (1996), 'The classical approach to convergence analysis', *Economic Journal*, **106**, 1019–36.

Scott, Bruce R. (2001), 'The great divide in the global village', *Foreign Affairs*, January/February, **80** (1), 212–20.

Segerstrom, Paul S., T.C.A. Anant and Elias Dinopoulos (1990), 'A Schumpeterian model of the product life cycle', *American Economic Review*, **80** (5), 1077–91.

Singh, Ajit (1992), 'The actual crisis of economic development in the 1980s: an alternative policy perspective for the future', in A.K. Dutt and K.P. Jameson (eds), *New Directions in Development Economics*, Aldershot: Edward Elgar.

Stegemann, Klaus (2000), 'The integration of intellectual property rights into the WTO system', *The World Economy*, **23** (9), September, 1237–67.

Stiglitz, Joseph E. (2002), *Globalization and Its Discontents*, New York: W.W. Norton.

Stocker, Herbert (1994), 'A world falling apart? Trends in the international distribution of income', Department of Economics, University of Innsbruck, unpublished.

Taylor, Lance (1983), *Structuralist Macroeconomics*, New York: Basic Books.

Taylor, Lance (1986), 'Debt crisis: north–south, north–north and in between', in M.P. Claudon (ed.), *World Debt Crisis: International Lending on Trial*, Cambridge, MA: Ballinger.

Thirlwall, Anthony P. (1979), 'The balance of payments constraint as an explanation of international growth rate differences', *Banca Nazionale del Lavoro Quarterly Review*, March, No. 128, 45–53.

Veblen, Thorstein (1915), *Imperial Germany and the Industrial Revolution*, New York: Macmillan.

Verspagen, Bart (1991), 'A new empirical approach to catching up or falling behind', *Structural Change and Economic Dynamics*, **2** (2), 359–80.

Wood, Adrian (1994), *North–South Trade, Employment and Inequality*, Oxford: Oxford University Press.

7. Comment on 'Globalization, North–South uneven development and international institutions' (A.K. Dutt)

Peter Egger

1 INTRODUCTION

The question of which forces drive international factor price convergence and the international distribution of income has attracted a lot of interest in the last decade. In particular, the question of the development of the poor (the South) as compared to the rich (the North), that is, of convergence versus divergence, is an important issue. The chapter by Dutt is a useful survey of the literature on the sources of international income development and distribution. Moreover, it develops a fruitful presentation of the interaction of these sources with the activities of the major international institutions.

My comment focusses on two determinants of national and international factor income distribution, which deserve some additional attention: international outsourcing and vertical versus horizontal multinational enterprises (MNEs) and their effects on national/international income distribution. In this context I also briefly refer to the role of the World Trade Organization (WTO).

2 INTERNATIONAL OUTSOURCING AS A SPECIFIC FORM OF TRADE

The traditional models of North–South trade and development consider mostly the final goods trade. However, if the traditional goods trade is a driving force behind the development of (national and) international income distribution through gains from specialization, this scope should even be increased if international fragmentation[1] of the value-added chain were allowed for. Baier and Bergstrand (2000) derive simulation results from a stylized computable general equilibrium model. Using reasonable parameter estimates, they find that outsourcing might account for about one-sixth of the growth of world trade between 1960 and 1990. However, this is not enough to know which form of trade (that is, final or intermediate goods trade) is responsible for the effects on income in general and wages in particular.

Kohler (2003a) provides a rigorous analysis of how fragmentation affects national income distribution. He illustrates that the effect of fragmentation on the domestic factor price and income distribution depends on the factor intensities of the fragments, which remain at home and are not sourced abroad. Assume that in the North, the relatively labor-intensive industries face the strongest incentive to outsource fragments to the South (for example, because of the relatively small Ricardian difference of the South therein, or their high intensity in unskilled labor, which is abundant in the South and so on). Then, the induced effective price increases are largest in these industries. Furthermore, assume that the remaining fragments in the North are relatively skilled-labor intensive (as compared to the North's skilled- to unskilled-labor endowment ratio). Then, the North's skilled- to unskilled-labor ratio will increase, hence income distribution will get more skewed (which seems likely to be the case). In contrast, if the remaining fragments of the large-scale outsourcing industries in the North are unskilled-labor intensive, the gap between skilled and unskilled workers' wages in the North will close (this seems not quite realistic). On the other hand, there will be scope for income convergence within the South, if the latter outsources predominantly skilled-labor-intensive industries to the North, and the remaining fragments in the South are unskilled-labor intensive (as compared to the South's skilled- to unskilled-labor endowment ratio). Therefore and regarding anecdotal evidence, national income divergence *within* the North and national income convergence *within* the South seems to be a likely outcome. However, this finds striking empirical evidence in both the US and Europe: Feenstra and Hanson (1996), Greenaway et al. (1999), Egger and Egger (2003) and others identify a clear positive impact on the skilled- to unskilled-wage and/or employment ratio. Egger and Stehrer (2003) estimate a pronounced negative effect of fragmentation in the Central and Eastern European countries on the skilled- to unskilled-wage bill ratio.

However, Kohler's (2003a) model does not easily allow for any conclusions about the effects of outsourcing on the international distribution of incomes. Deardorff (2001a) focusses on the role of fragmentation for the national *and* international development of incomes. He concludes that if there are some impediments to factor price equalization (for example, transportation costs, tariff or non-tariff barriers to trade and so on), fragmentation may drive factor price equalization to 'the extent that factor prices are not equalized internationally without fragmentation' (p. 135).

The theoretical evidence is that outsourcing may be seen as a means of national income convergence *within* the South and of international income convergence *between* the North and the South. Hence, all political measures that reduce the costs of outsourcing, support income convergence. Accordingly, the role of the WTO becomes not only essential for final and intermediate goods tariff reductions but also for the development of rules of origins and cumulation in the tariff systems. So far, cumulation is only at a bilateral level (for example, Pan-European rules of origin between the EU and the Central and Eastern European countries; compare also Kohler 2003b), which runs the risk of generating substantial trade-diverting effects.

3   VERTICAL VERSUS HORIZONTAL MNEs

The now standard and mostly static models of trade and multinational enterprises[2] basically lead to two important conclusions. First, similar to trade in homogeneous products, vertically oriented MNEs exploit factor cost differences and, accordingly, are motivated by differences in *relative* factor endowments. Second, horizontal MNEs, such as trade in differentiated goods, are mainly driven by market size and *absolute* factor endowments. The latter is due to the local-market-oriented strategy of affiliate sales. In contrast to horizontal MNEs, the vertical ones engage in the final goods trade (they do research in the North, produce in the South and sell in the whole world). This leads to what is known as complementarity of vertical multinational activity and trade and substitution of horizontal MNE activity and trade (see Caves 1996, for an overview). Consequently, any trade impediment reducing strategy *ceteris paribus* fosters vertical MNE activity. Assume two sectors (research and differentiated goods production), three factors (physical capital, skilled and unskilled labor: K, S, U), two countries and vertical MNEs that can establish in only the skilled-labor-abundant country.[3] Let the typical Northern vertical MNE's *production* be low-skilled labor intensive, while research be high-skilled labor intensive.[4] Then, trade liberalization between the North and the South has two consequences: (i) a widening of the skilled- to unskilled-labor wage gap (w_S^N/w_U^N) in the North (being well endowed with high-skilled labor: $S^N/U^N > S^S/U^S$) and a closure of this gap in the South (note the obvious analogy to the fragmentation case); (ii) a potential closure of the gap in international factor incomes.[5] In fact, the latter essentially depends on how weighted prices for research output and goods between the two countries develop.

This is different from the typical outcome of a horizontal MNE model, where *all* multinationals *produce* in both countries. Consequently, they can exploit gains from specialization to only a minor extent as compared to vertical MNEs. Accordingly, there is less scope for national and international income convergence as compared to the vertical model.

Due to the implications of the two models (large countries should host more horizontal MNEs; 'poor' – that is, unskilled-labor-rich Southern countries – should host more vertical MNEs) we can draw two conclusions regarding trade liberalization activities: (i) trade liberalization fosters both traditional exports *and* vertical MNE activity between the North and the South, and (ii) this effect should be relatively weaker in large Southern economies, where horizontal MNEs should play a relatively more important role. In other words, there is more scope for national and international convergence between the average OECD economy and countries like Malaysia than there is for China. Empirically, this results in the claim for a relaxation of the pooling assumption in the convergence parameter. This could be tackled by (i) interacting the convergence parameter with country size and/or GDP per capita or (ii) allowing the convergence parameter to differ across an arbitrary number of country groups, where the group definition depends on size and/or GDP per capita.

Through a multilateral agreement on investment, the WTO would be able to reduce the fixed costs of setting up plants in foreign economies (however, even the OECD has so far not managed to establish such an agreement). If such an agreement were to take place between the North and the South, this should shift the variable trade costs to fixed investment costs ratio, favoring multinational production as compared to trade, and foster international income convergence (direct effect). Moreover, this should induce a shift in the relative importance between horizontal and vertical MNEs in favor of the former. This might result in a relative increase in the activity of MNEs in large rather than in small economies in the South. In turn, this would potentially shift the *relative* pace of the international convergence of incomes in favor of the large countries. This result is obtained from the above argument that vertical MNE activity uses the gains from specialization more rigorously than does horizontal activity. Hence, the international income equalization effect is somewhat reduced in the small countries, since the horizontal to vertical MNE ratio is small there and increased through the reduction in fixed plant set-up costs (indirect effect).

NOTES

1. This term is from Jones and Kierzkowski (1990), but the phenomenon is also labeled as disintegration of production, outsourcing, slicing up the value-added chain, super-specialization, intra-product specialization, multi-stage production or subcontracting. Compare Deardorff (2001b) for the references and Kohler (2001) for a brief survey of the literature.

2. Helpman (1984), Markusen and Venables (1998, 2000), and Markusen and Maskus (2002) all give surveys.
3. This set-up differs from the previous literature in terms of the factor space (see Egger and Pfaffermayr 2003). It makes the trade-off between proximity to the market and concentration of production facilities less trivial and obtains a coexistence of MNE and export activities for large areas in the factor and parameter space.
4. Of course, assumptions have to be made on the fixed costs at both the corporate and the plant level. I omit this for the sake of brevity.
5. There is some early empirical evidence that outward foreign direct investment of the US indeed might have reduced US income distribution (Frank and Freeman 1978).

REFERENCES

Baier, Scott and Jeffrey H. Bergstrand (2000), 'The growth of world trade and outsourcing', unpublished manuscript, University of Notre Dame, IN.
Caves, Richard E. (1996), *Multinational Enterprise and Economic Analysis*, (2nd edition), Cambridge: Cambridge University Press.
Deardorff, Alan V. (2001a), 'Fragmentation in simple trade models', *North American Journal of Economics and Finance*, 12 (2), 121–37.
Deardorff, Alan V. (2001b), 'International provision of trade services, trade, and fragmentation', *Review of International Economics*, 9 (2), 233–48.
Egger, Hartmut and Peter Egger (2003), *Outsourcing and Skill-specific Employment in a Small Economy: Austria and the Fall of the Iron Curtain*, Oxford Economic Papers, forthcoming.
Egger, Peter and Michael Pfaffermayr (2003), 'Trade, multinational sales and FDI in a three-factors model', *Review of International Economics*, forthcoming.
Egger, Peter and Robert Stehrer (2003), 'International outsourcing and the skill-specific wage bill in Eastern Europe', *The World Economy*, 26 (1), 61–72.
Feenstra, Robert C. and Gordon H. Hanson (1996), 'Globalization, outsourcing and wage inequality', *American Economic Review*, 86, 240–45.
Frank, R.H. and R.T. Freeman (1978), *Distributional Consequences of Direct Foreign Investment*, New York: Academic Press.
Greenaway, David, Robert Hine and Peter Wright (1999), 'An empirical assessment of the impact of trade on employment in the United Kingdom', *European Journal of Political Economy*, 15, 485–500.
Helpman, Elhanan (1984), 'A simple theory of international trade with multinational corporations', *Journal of Political Economy*, 92, 451–71.
Jones, Ronald W. and Henryk Kierzkowski (1990), 'The role of services in production and international trade: a theoretical framework', in Ronald W. Jones and Anne O. Krueger (eds), *The Political Economy of International Trade: Essays in Honor of Robert E. Baldwin*, Cambridge, MA: Blackwell, pp. 31–48.
Kohler, Wilhelm (2001), 'A specific-factors view on outsourcing', *North American Journal of Economics and Finance*, 12 (1), 31–53.
Kohler, Wilhelm (2003a), 'The distributional effects of international fragmentation', JKU Linz, Department of Economics, working paper No. 0201, April 2002. Revised version published in *German Economic Review*, 40, 89–120.
Kohler, Wilhelm (2003b), 'International fragmentation: a policy perspective', in S. Arndt, H. Handler and D. Salvatore (eds), *Eastern Enlargement: the Sooner, the*

Better?, Vienna: Austrian Federal Ministry for Economic Affairs and Labor, 2000, pp. 227–47. Revised version to appear in *Journal of Policy Modeling*, forthcoming.

Markusen, James R. and Anthony Venables (1998), 'Multinational firms and the new trade theory', *Journal of International Economics*, **46**, 183–203.

Markusen, James R. and Anthony Venables (2000), 'The theory of endowment, intra-industry and multinational trade', *Journal of International Economics*, **52**, 209–34.

Markusen, James R. and Keith E. Maskus (2002), 'Discriminating among alternative theories of the multinational enterprise', *Review of International Economics*, **10** (4), 694–707.

8. The Bank for International Settlements: which activities can be justified from a normative economic perspective?

Peter Bernholz*

1 NORMATIVE ECONOMIC PRINCIPLES CONCERNING THE SPHERE OF GOVERNMENT

Economics as a positive science does not pass value judgments. Still, some principles have been developed to judge whether and which government activities are warranted, provided that certain value postulates are accepted. The normative postulates presuppose the validity of three positive propositions:

1. Competitive markets are more efficient – except for the existence of public goods or externalities (see below) – and innovative than political or bureaucratic decision-making processes if safe property rights and an adequate legal framework are provided. Thus they are superior in supplying goods and services to the population.
2. In contrast to political decision processes there are no outvoted minorities in markets. Everybody can buy what he or she wants, even if a majority would prefer that they should spend their money on other goods.
3. Free market regimes provide more freedom to individuals.

Thus if an optimal provision of goods and services to the population and maximal individual freedom are accepted as postulates, markets should be as extended as possible and political and bureaucratic decision making as limited as possible. It follows that government activity has to be justified in each case by what economists call 'market failures'. The same is true for international and supranational organizations, including financial organizations like the International Monetary Fund (IMF), the World Bank and the Bank for International Settlements (BIS), which have been founded by and are more or less dominated by governments.

But what are market failures? Apart from insufficient competition, econo-mists have identified two such failures:

1. There are external economies which are not taken into account by market participants when they take decisions. Negative externalities are present, for example, when a firm pollutes a river or cars pollute the air. Positive externalities are present when, for example, the production of honey has the side-effect that fruit trees are fertilized and bear more fruit. Educa-tion may be another example. In all these cases the negative or positive side-effects do not enter the calculation of firms or consumers. Thus an overextension (underextension) of the production or consumption of goods or services for negative (positive) externalities takes place. An inefficient use of resources is the consequence.
2. Public goods are produced in an insufficient amount or not at all if their provision is left to markets. In the jargon of the economist, public goods are goods which can be consumed or used by everybody at the same time. Whereas a piece of meat or bread can be consumed by only one individual, a television broadcast can be seen by everybody at the same time without loss of quality. Another example of a public good is a legal system. Because everybody can use public goods freely, once they are demanded by some individuals having the strongest preferences for them, others are motivated not to pay for them. Thus an underprovision of public goods results if there are no means available to exclude (at sufficiently low costs) individuals who are not paying.

The existence of externalities and (or) of such public goods, from whose use non-paying individuals cannot be excluded, is thus a *necessary* condition for government activities. In the case that this condition is fulfilled, govern-ment could help to prevent negative externalities, to provide an adequate amount of public goods and to see to it that no underprovision of goods and services related to positive externalities results. However, the existence of such market failures is not a *sufficient* condition for government activity for two reasons. First, as shown by public choice theory there are also 'govern-ment failures' such as bureaucratic inefficiency and overextension, political favors to interest groups, and outvoting of minorities resulting in neglect of their wishes. Second, in some cases private organizations and (or) activities may develop spontaneously to compensate for market failures, especially if the possibility of government failure is taken into account. One example is the financing of television by advertisements, another the development of arbitration of business conflicts by private courts.

Many economists would argue that there is a third reason for government intervention, namely income redistribution in favor of the poor and needy.

Since the BIS does not and should not undertake such redistributive activities, we need not develop this point further.

In the following sections we have to ask ourselves which BIS activities can be justified because they are preventing negative or providing positive externalities or public goods.

2   ACTIVITIES OF THE BIS

The BIS was founded 'under the Hague Agreements of January 1930 ... whose main purpose was to facilitate the German reparations after World War I' (BIS 1999, pp. 1–2). But from the very beginning the further expansion of its tasks was facilitated by Article 3 of the original statutes, 'to promote the cooperation of central banks and to provide additional facilities for international financial operations'. From the perspective of public choice theory and the theory of bureaucratic organizations the history of the BIS can be interpreted as an effort to safeguard its further existence and to extend its activities by adopting ever new tasks. It succeeded in doing so after its original mandate of facilitating German reparations had largely been realized, and even after its liquidation had been agreed at the Bretton Woods Conference in 1944. A surge of new activities and an extension of the old ones can again be observed after the creation of the European Monetary Union (EMU), which put an end to several of the existing tasks of the BIS.

It is not the aim of this chapter to examine and to explain the historical development or the present tasks of the BIS from this public choice and bureaucratic theory perspective (see Vaubel 1991a and 1991b for such an approach, mainly directed at the IMF). Moreover, even if one is convinced (as is the present author) that such a perspective is fruitful, this does not preclude that the BIS provides public goods and (or) positive externalities, or prevents negative externalities, so its existence may be justified from this point of view. In examining the activities and the possible tasks of the BIS from this different perspective, four categories have to be considered, that is, the BIS operating as:

- a banker to central banks;
- a forum for international monetary and financial cooperation;
- a center for monetary and economic research;
- a participant in international crisis management.

It is obvious that these categories overlap somewhat. Nevertheless, it is convenient to examine them separately in the following sections.

3   THE BIS AS A BANKER TO CENTRAL BANKS

The balance sheet of the BIS stood at US$131 billion, and its own funds (capital and reserves) at US$5.7 billion on 31 March 1999 (BIS 1999). An amount of US$112 billion was placed by about 120 central banks as currency deposits with the BIS, representing about 7 per cent of the foreign exchange reserves of the world. Since these deposits have to be available at short notice, they are mainly reinvested with short-term maturity by the BIS with top-quality commercial banks or in short-term government securities. Besides these banking operations, the BIS conducts a much more limited range of foreign exchange and gold operations on behalf of its customers. In recent years the investment services offered to central banks also include instruments of up to five years and tailor-made portfolio management schemes. The BIS is not allowed to make advances to governments or to open current accounts for them (Article 24 of the Statutes). Its operations have to be in conformity with the monetary policy of the central banks of the countries concerned (Article 19).

There can be no doubt that these banking services could also be provided by private banks. It seems, however, that central banks prefer to deposit some of their reserves with the BIS for the following reasons:

1.   Confidentiality: the counterparts to transactions with the BIS do not know which central bank invests or withdraws its (foreign exchange) reserves.
2.   Greater security is provided by the strong reserve position of the BIS and its more cautious investment policies. It has 20 per cent Tier 1 reserves compared to the average 4 per cent for private banks. On the other hand, the return paid on deposits by the BIS is somewhat lower.
3.   US authorities prefer to place deposits through the BIS rather than through US banks so as not to be accused of discriminating among them, which might prove harmful politically.

These advantages of the BIS as perceived by central banks constitute an obstacle to a placement of the corresponding tasks with private financial institutions. This obstacle might, however, be overcome by agreeing on adequate institutional arrangements with the latter. Certainly, they scarcely have the character of public goods; nor are they connected with positive externalities. On the other hand, it is obvious that they make the BIS independent of financing by governments (apart from the initial capital provided minus dividend payments received) and allow it to finance the services it provides out of its own resources. For the fiscal year ending 31 March 1999 the profits of the bank amounted to about US$598 million, of which US$113 million were disbursed as dividends (BIS 1999, pp. 172–3).

4 ACTIVITIES OF THE BIS IN PROVIDING A FORUM FOR INTERNATIONAL MONETARY AND FINANCIAL COOPERATION

One of the main tasks of the BIS is to act as a host for, to participate in and to provide secretarial support for international committees and groups working to promote monetary and financial stability (compare BIS 1999 and White 1998, 1999). At the moment there are at least nine committees or groups of this kind (see the appendix for a more detailed list). First, there are the committees resulting from the collaboration of the Group of Ten (G10) (including Switzerland as an eleventh member):

1. Committee of Governors of the central banks of the G10 countries, which presently meets seven times a year. Here the future representation is in flux because of the founding of EMU and the European Central Bank. A reduction of the number of meetings is envisaged.
2. Basle Committee on Banking Supervision, which meets four times a year (G10).
3. Committee on the Global Financial System, which meets four times a year. It is composed of representatives from the central banks of the G10 countries and of systematically significant emerging market countries (G10 'plus').
4. Committee on Payment and Settlement Systems (G10), which meets three times a year.
5. Committee on Gold and Foreign Exchange (G10), which meets seven times a year.

The last four committees mentioned work under the auspices of the G10 governors and comprise about twenty standing and ad hoc subgroups or working groups.

Second, there are committees and groupings whose secretariats are located at the BIS:

6. Financial Stability Forum (G7 plus and international financial institutions) with four subgroups and ad hoc working groups, which meet twice a year.
7. Secretariat of the Group of Ten Ministers and governors, which meets twice a year.
8. International Association of Insurance Supervisors, which meets four times a year.
9. Joint Year 2000 Council, which meets twice a year. This council is formed jointly by the Basle Committee on Banking Supervision, and the Committee on Payment and Settlement Systems.

There are also other meetings of central bank governors:

10. Meetings of governors of the G10 and of systematically significant emerging market economies (G10 plus).
11. Meetings of the governors of the BIS shareholding central banks.
12. Regular meetings of central bank experts. There are 13 groups of experts of different composition (for example, G10 plus, G10 plus EU central banks, G10 and CEEC/CIS Central and Eastern European Countries and Commonwealth of Independent States central banks), the International Organization of Securities Commission (IOSCO) and the International Association of Insurance Advisors (IAIS).

Besides these activities the BIS, partly in collaboration with other central banks and international institutions, also organizes seminars and training courses to disseminate knowledge. Beginning in 1999 the Financial Stability Institute, founded as a joint initiative of the BIS and the Basle Committee on Banking Supervision, commenced its activities. It should also be mentioned that the BIS has recently opened an office in Hong Kong, has strongly extended its membership of central banks after the formation of EMU, and now also organizes meetings outside of Basle.

5 TAKING A CLOSER LOOK AT SOME OF THE SERVICE ACTIVITIES RELATED TO THE BIS

We shall now analyze whether the activities undertaken and the services supplied by the committees provide public goods or positive externalities, or prevent negative externalities from arising. How could this be the case? It should be clear that well-functioning market economies need a sound institutional framework. This is also true for stable money, financial institutions and financial markets. As recent banking, currency and financial crises like those in South East Asia and Latin America have again demonstrated, instability of financial institutions including banks as well as instability and overreactions of financial and foreign exchange markets can still pose a threat for and damage the workings of the real economy. They also showed that such crises have a tendency to spread internationally because of the openness and the interrelations of financial markets all over the world. Even if one shares the view that such crises arise mainly as a consequence of mistaken fiscal and monetary policies and of weaknesses of the institutional structure of domestic banks and of domestic financial markets of the countries concerned, there may be possibilities for beneficial outside influence and intervention.

Central bankers and banking supervisors may be trained, regulations to improve the behavior of banks may be invented, developed, disseminated and (or) coordinated, information about international indebtedness may be spread and bookkeeping standards may be harmonized. Central bankers may regularly meet behind closed doors and critically discuss the policies of their colleagues and thus contribute to better monetary policies, supported by the reputation at stake and the social pressure present in primary groups.

It follows from the definitions in Section 1 that through such activities public goods may be provided and positive externalities created or negative externalities prevented (for a more comprehensive discussion of public goods or bads or negative externalities related to financial markets, see Wyplosz 1999). For example, the supply of needed information about domestic and international indebtedness in domestic and foreign currencies provides a public good. For knowledge is not lost to those supplying it and can also be used to prevent risky investments by those receiving it. The invention and introduction of beneficial regulations and standards for sound banking practices leads to positive external effects for other members of the international community. Such regulations and standards can be considered to be a supply of public goods. The training of central bankers leads to positive externalities as far as it allows better monetary policies to be pursued. The standardization of good bookkeeping practices of banks offers better possibilities of monitoring the soundness of their financial position and preventing negative externalities.

In looking at the work of these committees (compare BIS 1999 and White 1998, 1999), it is obvious that, because of lack of space, we have to concentrate on the more important aspects of the work done in the 'BIS committees' and by the BIS itself. In doing so we propose to look at their contributions mainly from the perspective of promoting financial stability. After the description of activities an evaluation will follow.

Activities of the Basle Committee on Banking Supervision

We begin by describing the efforts undertaken to develop and to introduce institutional frameworks which may contribute to the stability of the international financial system and consider first the Basle Committee on Banking Supervision. Established in 1974, this committee first sought to ensure that all internationally active banks were adequately supervised. The Basle Concordat of 1975 established the principle that no foreign banking establishment should escape supervision and that the home supervisors of the country in which the parent banks resided should supervise them on a consolidated basis. In the Minimum Standards paper of 1992, four standards were accepted to ensure that home supervisors practiced effective supervision and that they obtain adequate information about cross-border activities of banks. If the first requirement is not fulfilled, the host country of the branch can refuse a banking license. If the second requirement is not followed, the home supervisor can refuse to allow the continuation of the foreign business. However, since legal impediments to a free flow of information still remained, delegates from 150 countries at the International Conference of Banking Supervisors in Stockholm in 1996 endorsed a report prepared by a joint working group of the Basle Committee and the Offshore Group of Banking Supervisors. It proposed procedures for the conduct of cross-border inspections by home authorities monitoring their own banks and for closing potential supervisory gaps depending on certain corporate structures.

The committee sought (like other committees mentioned below) the cooperation of representatives of major banks, mainly to get information on the possible consequences of the regulations considered. The committee has also worked closely with non-G10 supervisors, the IMF and the World Bank in the Basle Committee's Core Principles Liaison Group to strengthen the financial systems of emerging market economies by promoting the Core Principles for Effective Banking Supervision that were finalized in September 1997. A main task is now to promote and to monitor the implementation of the core principles. The Liaison Group is currently trying to establish criteria for assessing implementation of these principles in different countries. The dissemination of the Core Principles has also been a big step in the sense that it served as a model for the creation of core principles for other areas. To better ensure the implementation of the Core Principles, another code has been prepared by the IMF together with the BIS and relevant international committees of regulators, namely a Code of Good Practices on Transparency in Monetary and Financial Practices. It suggests that there should be transparency with respect to the supervisors' mandate, the effectiveness of their powers, and their democratic accountability to other bodies. The Code will be monitored by the IMF.

The efforts undertaken to secure worldwide banking supervision may conflict with ideas about national sovereignty supported by special interest groups. Thus France and Singapore still do not allow inspection by foreign home country supervisors. Others like the United States are afraid that information given to foreign supervisory agencies may find its way into the public domain, given the laws of the respective country. It is thus a policy of the BIS related committees to involve national authorities from the very beginning and to try to reach unanimous agreement.

Because of the breakdown of sectoral barriers and the growth of international financial conglomerates, the attention of the Basle Committee has now also been directed to the supervising problems related to the securities and insurance industries. In doing so it has established close contacts with the

International Organization of Securities Commissions (IOSCO)[1] and the International Association of Insurance Advisors (IAIS).[2] The secretariat of the latter moved to Basle in 1998. All three groups now meet regularly in the Joint Forum on Financial Conglomerates.

A second task of the Basle Committee has been to develop and to promulgate minimum capital adequacy requirements in tune with the risks banks are running. In 1988 the Basle Capital Accord was published, and by September 1993, all banks of the G10 countries with significant international operations were meeting these minimum requirements. In recent years the committee has devoted increasing attention not only to credit risk but also to market risk and the risk connected with the growing use of credit derivatives. It is also now prepared to use the results generated by the firm's own internal models for its calculation of exposure to market risk, albeit under certain restrictions. Here again, a collaboration with representatives of major private banks has taken place. Some problems, like the treatment of short-term capital flows to emerging markets via domestic banks, have still to be solved by the committee.

A third task concerns the complications posed by different accounting practices in the G10 countries. The implied problems between the Accounting subgroup of the Basle supervisors and the International Accounting Standards Committee have been discussed, with the intention of solving them.

We turn now to the normative evaluation of the Basle Committee. The efforts to ensure international supervision of all banks together with the design of supervising standards and to come to an agreement on who should supervise, if successful, clearly provide positive externalities or prevent negative externalities. Banks and other financial institutions presumably become more stable, so the probability of financial crises and of their contagion effect decreases. The development of effective and superior supervising standards (of Core Principles) can be considered to be the creation of new public goods, since they are available to all countries and can be applied by all of them at the same time. The same is true for the design and spreading of identical accounting standards, provided that they are good standards. The efforts to include more and more countries, especially emerging market economies, also have positive externalities in the sense that the beneficial consequences are the more pronounced the more countries are applying the same standards. Furthermore, both emerging market economies and underdeveloped countries are usually those lagging in the application of good banking supervision and bookkeeping standards. The sanctions agreed on for the case of ineffective supervision and of providing inadequate information concerning cross-border supervision of foreign branches of the banks supervised can be seen as measures to spread the use of the public goods.

According to information from a major private bank, the processes initiated by the Basle Committee have become a catalyst for improving the internal risk management of banks. Before, major banks had looked at their risk management as one part of their potential competitive advantage. Consequently no sharing of information and no codification of best practice took place. This has changed with the activities of the committee, since major banks now realize that they may themselves be hurt by liquidity problems or the failure of other important banking institutions. The Basle Committee is seen as an honest broker. Furthermore, the banks believe that they have great influence in the process since they are able to transmit the nature of their concerns.

The design of minimal capital requirements can also be described as the provision of a new public good. With the further development of financial instruments and the breakdown of dividing lines between banks and other financial institutes, the extension of the activities of the Basle Committee to market and derivatives risks and to standards for the insurance and securities industries may create similar positive externalities and public goods. The major banks, however, seem to be somewhat critical of the nature of the minimal capital requirements. They agree that the committee has provided a valuable service. This insofar as it has removed the discussion of how to best meet credit risks, from the barriers to a free flow of information stemming from the conception that better risk management is again mainly an aspect of competitive advantage. But it is argued that these minimal capital regulations look at the problem from an outdated perspective, namely that capital has the function of being a safeguard against possible losses. Now, however, it is said that only current post-tax revenues are used as a buffer for current losses. This is so since the importance of commercial lending has substantially decreased and since banks are mainly using credit instruments in whose valuation the expected risk exposure is already included. As a consequence, only the risks implied by market volatility have to be covered, which is done by using revenue. According to this view, building minimum capital requirements on the own capital of financial institutions is distorting market behavior, since many decisions are now taken with a view to how the capital considered by regulations is affected.

There are some other possible problems. Whereas the collaboration with the IMF and the World Bank in the Principles Liaison Group and in developing the Code of Transparency may be helpful for implementing standards, it may also create an unwanted and unnecessary overlap with these institutions. Whether it is preferable for the IMF and the World Bank to monitor the implementation of the Code (and possibly of other codes developed by other Basle committees), given their main tasks, is an open question. Also, though the international application of identical effective standards certainly has positive externalities, one should not overlook the fact that it may hinder the development of even better standards: the competition among different actors to invent and to apply new standards is reduced, since this task is then left solely to the Basle Committee and its collaborators. The same may be said about the collaboration with IOSCO and IAIS in the Joint Forum on Financial Conglomerates. Whereas this collaboration allows, through the exchange of information and ideas, standards to be developed and gaps in the supervision of the securities and insurance industries to be closed, it again may mitigate innovative competition. Depending on the nature of the agencies with which the Basle Committee combines forces there may also be a danger that the interests of pressure groups can enter into the proposals and agreements.

Finally, we have to point to the potential danger of systemic risk which may arise from a simultaneous introduction of supervising and bookkeeping standards, and especially of minimal capital requirements in several countries. For whereas these standards and minimal requirements are beneficial in the sense indicated, once they have been introduced, the introduction itself may lead to a deterioration of the existing situation or even to a crisis. For instance, the introduction of minimal capital requirements in many countries at the same time may lead to restrictive behavior by banks in extending credit and thus to a credit crunch, especially in times of tight conditions or of unstable expectations. The art in introducing new standards and regulations at the right time and (or) successively is thus itself an attempt to prevent negative externalities.

Activities of the Committee on the Global Financial System

The name of the former Euro-currency Standing Committee was changed by the G10 governors in February 1999 and its mandate extended to monitor developments in financial markets and national economies and to examine the relationship between monetary and financial stability. It was originally established to look into the expansion of international bank lending, and was mainly preoccupied in the 1980s with the debt crisis of the less-developed countries. The committee gave a mandate to the BIS to coordinate the collection and dissemination of international banking data to better enable official and private sectors to monitor risk in this field. These banking statistics have greatly expanded both in content and geographically in recent years.

The BIS also maintains an extensive database on international securities markets and has strongly expanded its reporting on derivatives markets. This analysis tries to highlight strains in the international financial system. Recent examples since 1996 have included comments on the heavy exposure of Korean and Thai banks to short-term foreign currency financing, and the strong reduction of risk premia concerning both credit and market risks associated with risky investments worldwide.

The committee also oversees the improvement of the BIS international banking and derivatives statistics and the promotion of greater dissemination about official reserve positions. The improvement in the timeliness, quality and coverage of the BIS consolidated banking statistics is a further task. In March 1999 the BIS, the IMF, the World Bank and the Organization for Economic Cooperation and Development (OECD) jointly published for the first time a set of creditor-based measures of countries' external debt. In addition, the committee is working on the possible enhancement of disclosure practices by financial institutions in relation to market and credit risks resulting from their trading activities, including those involving off-balance sheet instruments.

Whereas this work of the committee relates to improvements in transparency, another concern after the Asian crisis has been the promotion of deep and liquid markets. Three reports were completed on these issues in 1998/99. One report prepared by a joint study group with the Committee on Payment and Settlement Systems (CPSS) reviewed settlement procedures and risk-management practices in over-the-counter derivatives markets and identified measures which could be taken to mitigate risk. A second report studied the functioning of repo markets and outlined preconditions for a proper working of them.

The committee has also focussed its attention during the last decade on the implications of financial innovations, especially the rapid growth of derivative markets, for the functioning and stability of financial markets. Though they concluded that derivatives enhance market efficiency, they also think that these innovations led to a diminution of transparency, so that it became more difficult for market participants to evaluate the creditworthiness of counterparties. The committee has thus in association with the supervisors taken steps to encourage market participants to improve their public disclosure practices by drawing on information generated by their internal risk-management systems. The semi-annual statistics on derivatives markets, which the BIS began to collect in mid-1998, should also help in this evaluation.

We turn now to normative evaluation. The committee, together with the BIS, takes responsibility for the timely gathering and transmission of information to banks, other financial institutions, regulating agencies and central banks. Such provision and transmission of information is a public good, since many agents can use this information without reducing the quality or amount of its use by others. Also, information, for example, about international indebtedness of banks, foreign exchange exposure and the volume of derivative obligations, may have the positive external effect of preventing financial crises, since market participants may behave more cautiously given the better information.

Since the Commission has given the mandate to the BIS to collect and disseminate data on international banking and more recently on international securities and derivative markets, the BIS is in this case directly involved in the provision of public goods and positive externalities. The efforts to increase the quality, coverage and timeliness thus have to be judged positively, too. By highlighting the tensions in its reports, the BIS further tries to help to prevent negative externalities arising from financial markets because of contagion and their effects on the real economy. However, whether the recent collaboration of the BIS with the IMF, the World Bank and the OECD in providing the first publication of creditor-based measures of countries' external debt is warranted, can be questioned. Whereas such collaboration may make the collection of data easier, it again presents an overlapping of the tasks of international institutions. The second task taken up by the committee has been the promotion of deep and liquid markets. As far as its proposals are accepted and implemented this would also help to prevent or at least to mitigate crises and their contagion effects, and thus remove negative externalities.

The Committee on Payment and Settlement Systems

Besides financial institutions and financial markets, the payment and settlement system has been called the third pillar of the international financial system. With the huge increase in the gross volume of transactions in recent years, a misfunctioning of the payment and settlement system could easily lead to liquidity problems for financial institutions which might spread to other market participants. The same could happen if payments are not settled in time. While the focus of the committee has been on the timely settlement of large-value transfers, issues relating to retail payment systems, especially to innovations and to the implications of electronic money, have also begun to receive attention.

One of the committee's first projects was a detailed review of the development of payment systems in the G10 countries, the results of which were published in a 'Red Book' in 1985. Since then, similar studies have been carried out on the payment systems of other countries and considerable efforts have been made to explore and evaluate different cross-border and multi-currency interbank netting schemes. Reports which have been agreed on by the G10 central banks, have established minimum standards for private sector systems. Recently the committee focussed on banks' real-time gross settlement systems. The report is the first of its kind and not only provides an overview of principal concepts and main design features, but also looks into the risks associated with such systems and policy implications.

During recent years the committee has extended its interest to settlement systems for securities and foreign exchange, with efforts focussing on a disclosure framework for systems operators that will allow participants to better evaluate the risks they are running. Here the committee has been engaged in an ongoing dialogue with private sector groups. It established that settlement exposures in foreign exchange markets are much greater than previously thought (Report of July 1998). Thus a report published in 1997 indicated how to reduce such risks. The report also strongly suggested that participants should take such measures to avoid punitive response from public authorities. Another report published in 1997 provided a comprehensive review of clearing arrangements for exchange-traded derivative instruments, identified weaknesses and made proposals for remedying them.

In cooperation with IOSCO, the committee is continuing to promote greater transparency in securities settlement arrangements through the implementation of the Disclosure Framework for Securities Settlement Systems, published in February 1997. A great number of such systems have now made information publicly available. A joint working group with IOSCO has also analyzed how securities lending influences transactions on securities clearance and settlement systems, and what implications this has for securities regulators and central banks. The working group consists of representatives of central banks and securities regulators from G10 and emerging market countries. Ongoing efforts are directed to defining 'Core Principles' for the design and operation of payment systems. The Task Force developing these principles comprises G10 central banks, an equal number of other central banks, the European Central Bank, the IMF and the World Bank.

When looking at the work of the committee from a normative economic perspective we first have to agree that deficiencies in settlement systems can lead to financial crises or make them more probable because of the domino effect. And this would imply, as already stated, negative externalities for market participants and the real economy. The development and implementation of minimum standards for settlement systems thus provides a public good which helps market participants to avoid these negative externalities. Proposals to limit settlement exposures in foreign exchange markets serve a similar purpose, since financial crises can also originate or be strengthened in exchange markets. The extension of the work of the committee to securities settlement systems has a similar effect, since problems in securities markets may easily spread to other markets. The effort to develop and implement disclosure frameworks for settlement systems again has a positive external effect, since the better evaluation of exposure risks may help market participants to limit such risks, so that the probability of financial crises originating in settlement systems is reduced.

Thus the attempt to develop Core Principles should also have a positive effect. But it is open to question whether the collaboration in the Task Force with the IMF and the World Bank creates another unwanted overlap rather than a clear division of responsibilities. Moreover, the collaboration with IOSCO may prevent competition in the development of new and better solutions for payment systems.

Committee on the Global Financial System, other Working Groups and the Financial Stability Forum

The committee and its groups (see appendix) are working on problems connected with the global financial system, the reasons for the recent financial crises in Asia, Eastern Europe and South America and possible remedies. A Working Group on Transparency and Accountability studied how transparency and accountability could contribute to better economic performance, and the information needed for this purpose. Another Working Group on Strengthening Financial Systems tried to reach a consensus on principles and policies that would help the development of a stable and efficient financial system. It also set out options for an enhanced cooperation and coordination among national and international authorities concerned with financial stability. A third Working Group on International Financial Crises developed principles and examined policies that could prevent or facilitate the orderly solution of future financial crises. These three groups comprised representatives from central banks and finance ministries of industrial countries and emerging market economies. Their recommendations were endorsed by the finance ministers and central bank governors of 26 countries during the 1998 annual meetings of the IMF and the World Bank.

Since the release of the reports of the three working groups, and following the initiative of the G7 countries, senior officials from 33 countries have met in Bonn and Washington to discuss topics ranging from the maintenance of sustainable exchange rate regimes to proposals for strengthening the IMF and the World Bank and policies to minimize the social impact of crises. As is well known, one result of these discussions has been the creation of a Financial Stability Forum to improve international cooperation with respect to actions to strengthen financial systems. The BIS and other international financial institutions and organizations participate in the meetings of the Forum. In addition, the general manager of the BIS serves, in a personal capacity, as its chairman, and its secretariat (currently comprising five personnel) is located at the BIS. In a sense, the Forum extends the work of the Basle committees, now including governments. It is hoped by members of the BIS that the Forum will be able to set priorities, coordinate activities and locate gaps in the often overlapping and compartmentalized efforts to find ways of increasing the stability of the international financial system.

The BIS and the Basle Committee took a joint initiative in 1997 to create the Financial Stability Institute, whose first chairman took up his position on 1 February 1999. The Institute will also focus on strengthening financial systems and institutions, starting with banking and gradually adding securities dealers and insurance.

Finally, secretariats of the G10 Ministers and Governors, the International Association of Insurance Supervisors and the Joint Year 2000 Council are also located at the BIS. The Joint Year 2000 Council comprises the Basle Committee on Banking Supervision, the Committee on Payment and Settlement Systems, IOSCO and the IAIS. It investigated the year 2000 computer problems, their solution and their possible consequences.

From a normative point of view, the activities of the three working groups may have provided a positive externality if they had contributed in their recommendations valuable new ideas on strengthening the international financial system. It has to be said, however, that it is not clear whether they have merely replicated the work done by the committees discussed above. The same may happen with the newly created Financial Stability Forum, of which the BIS is a member, together with other international financial institutions (IFIs) and organizations. On the one hand, the Forum may just be an example of 'symbolic action' versus real benefit, but on the other, if the Forum should succeed in setting priorities, and locating and closing gaps, it could be a useful supplement to the public goods contributing to international financial stability. Moreover, since the ministers of finance are also behind this effort, it may be easier to implement the recommended steps. However, the possible introduction of politics into the deliberations (quite unlike the other committees) may have negative consequences for the recommendations and their implementation. This, together with the participation of many international institutions and organizations, may lead to dubious compromises. It may also again imply an overlapping of activities.

A Monetary Policy Forum for Central Bankers

According to personal communications by participants, an important service has been provided by the BIS in serving as a regular meeting place for the G10 governors (currently seven times a year). It allows the governors to exchange confidential information, and to have critical discussions about and sometimes to coordinate actions concerning monetary policies away from the attention of the mass media. Peer group pressure in favor of stable monetary policies should also not be underestimated. Personal acquaintance allowed the building of mutual confidence so important in times of crises. In recent years efforts have been made to include the governors of emerging market economies in this process. Thus the governors of the G10 are now also meeting seven times a year with governors of emerging market economies. Moreover, the deputy governors of emerging market economies, too, are now meeting at the BIS. As can be seen from the appendix, these meetings are supplemented by regular meetings of different groups of central bank experts, for example, the groups of central bank economists and statisticians concerned with domestic monetary policy and monitoring emerging markets.

From a normative perspective the regular meetings of the governors seem to have been very useful, as confirmed by private communication by participants. The frank and critical discussions behind closed doors together with peer group pressure seem to have had a positive effect on the dissemination of sound and stable monetary policies. They thus had a positive external effect. Related to these meetings, the regular meetings of the specialists of the central bank in different fields should be conducive to the better implementation of such stable monetary policies. In this sense they also contributed to the positive external effects.

Training Services Provided

The BIS, sometimes in cooperation with other financial institutions, is organizing regular workshops and seminars. For example, the Committee on Payment and Settlement Systems has supported an increasing number of payment system workshops and seminars, which were jointly organized with regional central bank groups.

The training needs of countries in transition were addressed within the framework of the Joint Vienna Institute, which is sponsored by the BIS, the European Bank for Reconstruction and Development (EBRD), the International Bank for Reconstruction and Development (IBRD), the IMF, the OECD and recently the World Trade Organization (WTO), and was established in late 1992. More than 10 000 officials had attended courses and seminars by 1999.

The Financial Stability Institute also intends to hold seminars in which heads of supervision from emerging markets will interact with those from industrialized countries and experienced financial sector participants. Moreover, training programs for middle-level senior supervisors are planned with seminars in Basle and each of the major regions of the world. Cooperation with the World Bank, the IMF and central banks is envisaged.

From a normative perspective, the training of central bank employees, banking supervisors and so on, especially from emerging market economies and from underdeveloped countries, is a necessary, but not sufficient condition for the implementation of sound monetary policies and banking practices.

Training spreads knowledge and the knowhow to acquire and to use information without taking it away from others. It therefore creates positive externalities not only for the individuals concerned but also for the countries where participants apply what they have learned. Again, however, it has to be asked whether the collaboration of the BIS and other IFIs and international organizations allows economies of scale in education, or whether an unnecessary overlap is created.

General Evaluation of the BIS Services from a Normative Economic Perspective

We have concluded in the subsections above that the activities of the different committees and groups located at the BIS provide public goods and (or) positive externalities in many cases. They do so in helping to prevent or mitigate future financial crises by developing good standards of supervision, sensible minimal capital requirements (though there remain some doubts here), standards for well-functioning settlement systems, by providing training for central bank officials and regulators and by encouraging the spread of good monetary policies with the help of mutual information, critical discussions and peer pressure. Thus a rather positive picture emerges from a normative economic viewpoint, even though there was some possible overlap with the activities of other financial institutions, a possible limitation of competition for the development of institutional innovation and, in some cases, the danger of political and interest group influence.

This positive evaluation, however, does not necessarily imply a positive evaluation of the activities of the BIS. For except in the few cases mentioned, the BIS is not itself an active member of these committees and groups. Their members are usually national experts, whereas the staff of the BIS, especially those providing secretarial help to the committees and to prepare the sessions, have as their primary function the support of the cooperation of others. This approach makes the BIS quite different from all other IFIs. The BIS also provides the localities for the meetings and secretariats at its own expense. Apart from the exceptions of direct participation in committees, the provision of training and the gathering and dissemination of information concerning international financial data, the BIS thus only indirectly provides public goods and positive externalities by serving these committees and groups. But these supportive services do not necessarily themselves constitute public goods or provide positive externalities.

As a consequence, the question has to be asked whether these services could not be provided by other organizations. What then, are the comparative advantages of the supply of these services by the BIS? It seems that the BIS has in fact developed a trustworthy and confidential atmosphere and a specific knowledge of efficiently organizing such meetings. It has created a crystallization point allowing different committees to be formed[3] and permitting them and their members to come together to discuss critical and new issues away from the attention of the mass media, to exchange information and to get stimulation for new developments. This hypothesis is clearly supported by the observation that more and more central banks and other actors obviously prefer to act within the framework provided by the BIS. It is also supported by the fact that the general manager of the BIS has been elected to serve as chairman of the Financial Stability Forum, and that the previous general manager served as a member and another BIS official as the secretary of the Delors Committee, which had the task of preparing the proposal on EMU. In a way, the BIS is creating, besides a confidential and stimulating atmosphere, economies of scope for the different committees and groups. It allows them to cross-fertilize each other with ideas, to innovate and to produce public goods or positive externalities at less cost. The fact that the BIS usually bears the cost of providing the secretarial help and the location may help, but it is certainly not the decisive factor why so many committees and working groups have been connected with the BIS.

A second question which may be asked is whether the activities and innovations undertaken by the different committees and groups could not be left to private organizations. For as explained in Section 1, the provision of public goods or positive externalities is only a necessary but not a sufficient reason for the activity of international organizations. And indeed, we have examples of related private activities. The credit ratings of firms provided by Moody's or by Standard and Poor's are examples, as, more recently, are the indexes of economic freedom calculated by the Fraser Institute in Vancouver and the Heritage Foundation in Washington. Thus it could even be that the 'unfair' competition by the public committees and groups meeting at the BIS prevents further private activities in the development of international bookkeeping and monitoring standards. It seems, however, that this is not the case. It is doubtful whether enough of a private demand for such standards would exist, given that they are public goods. The risk for private firms to devise and try to sell such standards is and would thus probably be too high to motivate them to make the necessary investments. This should be even more true for regulations and minimal capital requirements concerning banks and financial institutions. And the implementation of such public goods by market pressure alone would probably also not be sufficient, so an involvement of the different national authorities appears to be necessary. We thus conclude that, at least for the time being, most of the activities undertaken by the committees and groups located at the BIS fulfill a useful function in providing public goods and positive externalities.

6 FUNCTIONS OF THE BIS AS A TRUSTEE

The BIS continues to act as a Trustee for the Dawes and Young loans, into which German reparations were consolidated in the 1920s. It also acts in the capacity of collateral agent to hold and invest collateral for the benefit of the holders of certain long-term US dollar denominated Brazilian, Peruvian and Côte d'Ivoire (here also of French franc) bonds under agreements signed in 1994, 1997 and 1998, respectively. Concerning these tasks, no public goods or positive externalities seem to be provided. For apart perhaps from the special trust which participants have in the BIS, such a function could certainly be fulfilled by private banks.

7 FINANCIAL ASSISTANCE TO CENTRAL BANKS

For decades, the BIS has also been involved in providing short-term bridging loans to central banks during financial crises. Since the BIS has been able to act much more quickly and without conditions, that is, overnight, than other financial institutions, especially the IMF, it has sometimes played an important role in this field. It has usually granted short-term financial assistance until replaced by IMF or other credits. The BIS credits were always guaranteed by the participating central banks. They could be given without conditionality or political pressure. The BIS broke with this tradition to give only bridging loans with its participation in the international financial support program for Brazil in late 1998. In this case it made funds available without a commitment that they would soon be replaced by other credits, though they were again for the most part backed or guaranteed by the 19 participating central banks. For most of this credit facility of up to US$13.28 billion in favor of the Banco Central do Brasil the BIS thus coordinated the assistance of the 19 central banks. Since 19 bilateral agreements with Brazil would have been difficult to negotiate in a short time, economies of scale resulted because the BIS acted quickly as an intermediary in providing the facility.

One can argue that by preventing the spread of a financial crisis with the help of financial assistance positive externalities are provided to other financial institutions and, if the crisis is prone to have negative consequences for the real economy, even to producers, workers and consumers. This would also hold for the BIS as long as the other IFIs are not able to help quickly and perhaps as long as it is not influenced itself by political pressures. Positive externalities strengthened by economies of scale would also be present if the BIS is better at quickly coordinating needed financial help by a number of central banks. On the other hand, there seems to be an unnecessary overlap with the activities of other IFIs, especially the IMF. The argument that the

BIS could act more quickly is, however, no longer valid since the creation of the Supplemental Reserve Facility of the IMF at the end of 1997. Also, it is doubtful whether the political independence of the BIS can be maintained if the financial assistance should no longer consist only of short-term bridging loans. But if this is true, then only the important function of coordinating the help granted by several central banks would remain. And here some people might ask whether this task is really better served by the BIS than by the IMF.

8   CONCLUSION

By studying the different activities of the BIS, the following conclusions can be drawn. The main contribution of the BIS in supplying international public goods and positive externalities consists in the services it provides to the many committees and groups which are located at the BIS and (or) whose meetings are organized by it and whose secretariats it provides. The public goods and positive externalities are mainly created and implemented by these committees, which develop new standards, regulations and so on that increase international financial stability. The BIS seems to be an efficient provider of support which allows economies of scope, a congenial and confidential atmosphere and cross-fertilization among different committees and groups, and which furthers the provision of new international public goods at low cost. The BIS itself supplies such goods directly by gathering and disseminating financial information concerning an increasing number of countries, financial markets and institutes. It participates itself as a member in some of the committees and provides positive externalities by organizing and sponsoring training programs for international financial specialists.

However, the recently increasing collaboration with other IFIs like the IMF, the World Bank and even organizations like the OECD, is not without problems. For though it may be helpful to gather information and to better implement internationally certain innovations, it creates more and more overlapping activities. The influence of politics and perhaps even of certain interest groups may increase, and the bottom-up approach followed by the BIS may come into conflict with the top-down approach of the IMF and the World Bank. Also coordination, though clearly helpful in setting common standards and regulations, may sometimes restrict the competition to develop even better public goods. However, it is not the task of this chapter to judge whether the participation of the IMF and the World Bank in the tasks usually followed by the 'BIS committees' is warranted, given their own main tasks.

Whereas the service activities of the BIS contribute directly or indirectly to the creation and implementation of international public goods and (or) positive externalities, this cannot be said in the same way of its other activities, for example, concerning its function either as a trustee or as a lender to central banks during crises. The argument in favor of the former activity is the reputation of trustfulness and competence enjoyed by the BIS. That of the latter, namely the ability to arrange short-term bridging loans promptly and without conditionality to help to overcome financial crises, is no longer valid since the introduction of the Supplemental Reserve Facility by the IMF in 1997. However, the economies of scale achieved by the competent and speedy arrangement of multilateral financial agreements with countries needing support may be helpful.

The banking activities of the BIS as a banker to central banks scarcely serve to produce public goods or positive externalities, though they are valued by central banks because of their confidentiality and safety. One could argue that the confidentiality allows the creation of a positive externality since it prevents private banks from observing the investment or withdrawal of foreign exchange reserves of central banks in financial markets. Such withdrawals could be seen as a sign of a need to expend funds on foreign exchange market interventions, thus leaving insufficient reserves. This itself might engender capital flight and thus contribute to financial instability. However, apart from this argument, profits from its banking operations do make the BIS financially independent and allow it to finance its service activities, besides distributing an annual dividend.

NOTES

*   This chapter was originally written as a paper for the International Finance Institution Advisory Commission of the US Congress, the so-called Meltzer Commission.

     I am grateful to Andrew Crocket (BIS), Guenther Schleiminger (formerly BIS) and William R. White (BIS) for providing valuable material and information. I also have to thank the chairmen of IOSCO, IAIS and the Offshore Group of Banking Supervisors, Peter Clark, Knut Hohlfeld and Colin Powell for providing information about their organizations. Tim Shepheard-Walwyn, Managing Director of UBS gave valuable information concerning the collaboration of leading private banks with the BIS committees.

1.   'IOSCO is a private, not for profit, international organization that was created in 1983 by amending the by-laws of a previously regional interamerican association of securities regulators to transform it into an international body. All the voting members of IOSCO are agencies having securities regulatory responsibilities. A number of self-regulatory organizations (such as major stock exchanges) and international organizations having a mission related to either the regulation or the development of securities markets (such as the IBRD), have the status of affiliate members. Individuals cannot become IOSCO members ... IOSCO is financed by a yearly contribution from its members' (Peter Clark, Secretary General of IOSCO in a fax to the author, 8 September 1999).

2.   'The IAIS ... is a public organization and legally speaking an association under Swiss law (Verein). ... The members of the IAIS are insurance supervisory or regulatory bodies i.e., public organizations. ... The IAIS activities are financed by its member fees. The Swiss Government supported the establishment of the IAIS Secretariat in Basle by a subsidy that was paid from 1997 till 1999. The BIS supports the IAIS Secretariat by providing office

space and equipment free of charge and also administrative support. There exist no special arrangements regarding the co-operation with the different BIS committees' (Knut Hohlfeld, Secretary General of IAIS in a letter to the author, 14 September 1999).

3.   An interesting example is the formation of the Offshore Group of Banking Supervisors. According to a fax message received from its chairman, Colin Powell OBE, on 8 September 1999, 'in 1979 the Basle Committee on Banking Supervision decided that there would be virtue in initiating a meeting of Banking Supervisors representing offshore centres. ... [It] was concerned that the banks for which its member countries were responsible were at risk because it was thought their subsidiaries or branches in offshore centres, through which loans were being booked, were not subject to a sufficiently high standard of supervision'. Consequently it was on the initiative of the Basle Committee that the first meeting of Offshore Banking Supervisors was held in Basle at the BIS in 1980. By 1999, 18 offshore financial centers were members of the group, which only admits new members who guarantee effective banking supervision according to the rules promulgated by the Basle Committee and make a commitment against money laundering.

REFERENCES

Bank for International Settlements (1999), *69th Annual Report*, 1 April 1998–31 March 1999, Basle, June 7.

Vaubel, Roland (1991a), 'A public choice view of international organization', in Roland Vaubel and Thomas D. Willett (eds), *The Political Economy of International Organizations*, Boulder, CO, San Francisco and Oxford: Westview Press, pp. 27–45.

Vaubel, Roland (1991b), 'The political economy of the International Monetary Fund: a public choice analysis', in Roland Vaubel and Thomas D. Willett (eds), *The Political Economy of International Organizations*, Boulder, CO, San Francisco and Oxford: Westview Press, pp. 204–44.

White, William R. (1998), 'Promoting international financial stability: the role of the BIS', unpublished paper presented at the conference 'Coping with financial crises in developing and transition countries: regulatory and supervisory challenges in a new era of global finance', organized by the Forum on Debt and Development and held at De Nederlandsche Bank, Amsterdam, March 16–18.

White, William R. (1999), 'The Asian crisis and the Bank for International Settlements', unpublished paper presented at the conference 'Asia and the future of the world economic systems', organized by the Royal Institute of International Affairs and held in London, March 17–18.

Wyplosz, Charles (1999), 'International financial instability', in Inge Kaul, Isabelle Grunberg and Marc A. Stern (eds), *Global Public Goods: International Cooperation in the 21st Century*, Oxford: Oxford University Press, pp. 154–91.

APPENDIX   COMMITTEES AND GROUPS MEETING AT THE BIS

1.   Meetings in the Context of the G10 Central Banks

Committee of governors of the central banks of G10 countries (7 meetings per year)
Committees working under the G10 governors' auspices:

- Basle Committee on Banking Supervision
- Committee on the Global Financial System
- Committee on Payment and Settlement Systems
- Committee on Gold and Foreign Exchange

Basle Committee on Banking Supervision (G10) (4 meetings per year)
Standing subgroups:

- Capital Group
- Research Task Force
- Models Task Force
- Core Principles Group: (a) Core Principles Coordinating Group; and (b) Core Principles Liaison Group
- Risk Management Group
- Joint Forum Group on Financial Conglomerates (with IOSCO and IAIS)

Ad hoc subgroups:

- Y2K Task Force
- Working Group on highly leveraged institutions
- Working Group on core principles methodology
- Working Group on cross-border banking
- Task force on commercial real estate

Committee on the Global Financial System (G10 'plus') (4 meetings per year)

- Working Group on financial market events in Autumn 1998
- Working Group on lender of last resort
- Working Group on enhanced transparency regarding aggregate positions
- Working Group on macro-stress testing
- Multidisciplinary Working Group on enhanced transparency

Committee on Payment and Settlement Systems (G10) (3 meetings per year)

- Task Force on payment system principles and practices (G10 'plus')
- Working Group on retail payment systems
- Subgroup on foreign exchange settlement risk
- Joint Working Group on securities lending

Committee on Gold and Foreign Exchange (G10) (7 meetings per year)

2.   Other Meetings of Central Bank Representatives Organized by the BIS

Other meetings of central bank governors (7 meetings per year)

- Governors of the G10 and of significant emerging market economie (G10 'plus')
- Governors of BIS shareholding central banks
- Deputy governors of emerging market economies

Regular meetings of central bank experts

- Central bank economists (G10 'plus')
- Working party on domestic monetary policy (G10 plus EU central banks)
- Central bank statisticians (G10 'plus')
- Group of experts on monetary and economic data bank questions (G10 'plus')
- Central bank econometricians/model builders
- Emerging Markets Monitoring Group (G10 'plus')
- Coordinators of technical assistance and training of G10 and CEEC/ CIS central banks
- Special Study Group (SSG-2) (bank note printers)
- Computer Experts Group
- Working party on information technology security issues
- Central bank security managers
- Group of central bank heads of internal audit
- Central bank legal experts

3. Committees or Groupings Whose Secretariats Are Located at the BIS

Financial Stability Forum (G7 'plus', IFIs) (2 meetings per year)
Standing chairman's subgroup
Ad hoc working groups:

- HLIs (Highly Leveraged Institutions)/Leverage
- Short-term capital flows
- Offshore centers

Secretariat of the G10 Ministers and Governors (2 meetings per year)

- Standing G10 Deputies

International Association of Insurance Supervisors (IAIS) (4 meetings per year)

Joint Year 2000 Committee (2 meetings per year)

- formed jointly by the Basle Committee on Banking Supervision, the Committee on Payment and Settlement Systems, IOSCO and IAIS

9. Basle II: quantitative impact study on small and medium-sized enterprises in Austria

Walter S.A. Schwaiger

1 OVERVIEW

In this chapter the capital charges according to the new credit risk based requirements of Basle II are calculated for a bank that holds a banking book consisting of small and medium-sized enterprises (SMEs) in Austria. The calculations are based on the Foundation Approach of the Internal Rating Based (IRB) framework. For this the risk of default of Austrian enterprises is calculated by using the database from Creditreform (Austria) consisting of 11 610 Austrian enterprises with revenues between 1 and 50 million euros. The other credit risk factors of Basle II are taken from the standardized supervisory rules for unsecured, senior exposures. For the calculations the same methodology is used as in Schwaiger (2002), that is, the same rating system is calibrated, with 12 non-default classes and one default class. But the results are new because according to the Quantitative Impact Study 3 (QIS3) we use the new formulae that were announced by the Basle Committee on Banking Supervision in Hong Kong on 10 July 2002 and published on 1 October 2002. Consequently this chapter can be seen as the first QIS3 study giving detailed insights into the capital requirements for Austrian SMEs as a whole as well as for different industries and regions.

The chapter is organized as follows. In Section 2, three different rating systems and differences in the construction methodology are presented. In Section 3 the rating system calibrated with the Creditreform database is used to quantify the credit risk capital requirement for the loan portfolio consisting of all Austrian SMEs in the database. In Section 4 these requirements are calculated for different industries and Austrian regions, and in the final section the chapter is summarized and concluded.

2 DIFFERENT RATING SYSTEMS AND THEIR CONSTRUCTIONS

Rating systems are composed of different rating classes into which the different enterprises (borrowers) are grouped. The main purpose of such rating systems is the differentiation of the credit quality and its quantification in corresponding probabilities of default (PDs), where the credit quality and the PDs are conversely related, that is, the better the credit quality the lower the PD and vice versa.

Depending on the institution that classifies the different enterprises (borrowers), three different kinds of rating systems can be distinguished: the rating system of external rating agencies (for example, Moody's, Standard and Poor's, Fitch); the bank internal rating systems; and the rating systems of external credit agencies. The different information used is indicated in Figure 9.1. The external rating agency and the internal bank rating systems are the main actors in the Basle II framework. The specialty of both lies in the inclusion of specific (private) information that both institutions have access to. The external rating agencies are consulted by the borrowers, giving them the opportunity to conduct an in-depth investigation. The banks on the other hand are the (potential) money providers, which gives them private insights. Beyond this, banks can often discover further details about the borrowers' financial situation and their past financial behavior from the borrowers' bank account.

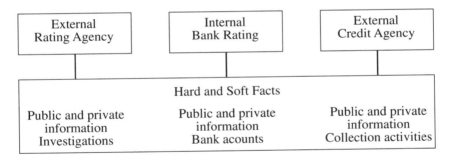

Figure 9.1   Different kinds of ratings

The third rating provider, that is, the external credit agencies, is generally less well known. They mainly provide information of the enterprises' (borrowers') credit qualities in the form of score values rather than rating information. But as will be shown in this chapter, the score values can easily be transformed into rating classes. Furthermore it will be argued that such a transformation is central to any 'flexible' and thus 'stable' rating system. The corresponding construction mechanism should therefore be relevant for each such rating system including that of external rating agencies and banks. Beyond giving insight into the construction principles, the rating system derived for an external credit agency provides the information needed to calculate concrete consequences of the new capital requirements in Basle II. In contrast to the rarely available rating information of external rating agencies and the not publicly available bank internal ratings, the ratings of external credit agencies are available and cover a huge number of enterprises in different industries and regions.

Rating systems are constructed by mapping the enterprises' credit quality into a score value that gets transformed into a rating class by partitioning the score value range in distinct, that is, non-overlapping intervals. Traditionally the interval boundaries are fixed over time. This fixing is indicated in Figure 9.2 by the straight line describing the mapping of the score value into the rating class. At first glance this procedure seems to be the obvious way to construct rating systems.

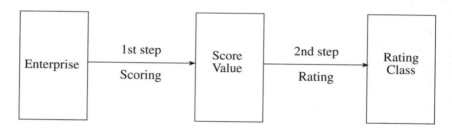

Figure 9.2   Mapping enterprises into ratings: the traditional approach

Due to the fixed score value ranges for the different rating classes, the credit quality migrations and defaults of the enterprises over time reflect in exact correspondence the stochastic development of the economy over the business cycle. As a consequence, both the migration probabilities and the PDs that are derived out of such a rating system will fluctuate stochastically over time. In contrast to this 'natural' fact of stochastic PD structures over time, is the 'natural' desire of more or less stable structures. In this sense a rating system should be constructed such that the PDs for the different rating classes stay the same over time as well as over different industries and regions. Both 'natural' aspects can be reconciled by making the mapping of the score values into the rating classes flexible. Such a flexible mapping is indicated in Figure 9.3 by the spring between the fields containing the score value and the rating class.

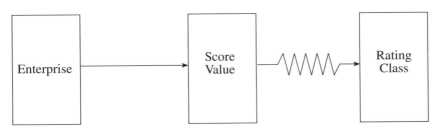

Figure 9.3   Mapping enterprises into ratings: the flexible approach

The flexible approach consists of flexible score value intervals for the different rating classes, thereby including additional degrees of freedom so that the PDs can be stabilized over time and over industries. This stabilization occurs because the PDs are relative numbers quoted as percentages. It becomes possible by dynamically changing the score value intervals so that the stochastic business cycle effects are absorbed in the distribution of the enterprises as well as the distribution of defaults over the different rating classes. The absolute default numbers of course still depend on the business cycle and move stochastically with it over time.

The flexible approach is used to transform the 'Bonitätsindex' from Creditreform (Austria) into a rating system. According to the requirements of Basle II, the construction is performed in such a way that the PDs increase as the quality of the rating classes decrease and no more than 30 per cent of the enterprises are in a single rating class.[1]

Figure 9.4 contains the power curve for all Austrian SMEs in the database for the beginning of the year 2000. This curve shows the distribution of the defaults that occur over the year relative to the enterprises ranked at the beginning of the year, where the ranking[2] is according to the Bonitätsindex

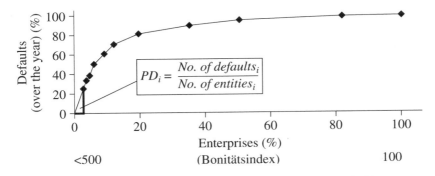

Figure 9.4   Power curve for Austrian SMEs (as at 1 January 2000)

from Creditreform. The quality of this rating system is quite good.[3] This can be seen by looking at 20 per cent of the lowest ranked enterprises that comprise 80 per cent of the defaults so that the 20/80 per cent rule, well known from the insurance industry, is satisfied.

The PDs for the different rating classes correspond to the different slopes of the power curve between adjacent points for the different rating classes. The PD of the lowest rating class is the slope from the origin to the first point on the power curve. It is calculated by dividing the number of defaults by the number of enterprises in this rating class. Furthermore it can be seen from Figure 9.4 that the slopes decrease as the ratings improve, showing the required decreasing PD structure. The PDs for the different rating classes are given in the second column of Table 9.1.

Table 9.1   PD curve for the rating classes of Austrian SMEs

Rating class	PD (%)	Enterprises (%)
01	0.03	0.04
02	0.17	10.17
03	0.30	23.64
04	0.44	23.74
05	1.21	14.48
06	1.98	9.73
07	3.62	4.85
08	3.76	5.37
09	9.47	2.50
10	10.20	0.86
11	11.32	1.39
12	14.09	3.24

In order to calculate the capital requirements for the Austrian SMEs not only the PDs but also the loan exposures of the enterprises in the different rating classes are needed. This information is not available in the Creditreform database, but it can be quite closely approximated using enterprises' revenues. In Figure 9.5 it can be seen that the distribution of revenues has more (less) mass in the higher (lower) rating classes than the distribution of enterprises. These differences show the necessity of taking heterogeneous exposure sizes into account for calculating the capital requirements under Basle II. Furthermore the consequences of using the revenue approximated exposure sizes are obvious: they reduce the capital requirements due to the mass transformation into the positive direction of better rating classes.

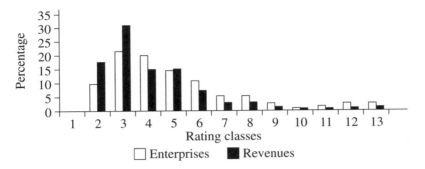

Figure 9.5 Distribution of enterprises and revenues over rating classes (as at 1 January 2000)

3   CAPITAL REQUIREMENTS FOR AUSTRIAN SMEs

The capital requirements according to Basle II are calculated by using the formulae that were published by the Basle Committee on Banking Supervision in October 2002 (Basle 2002) when QIS3 was launched. The relevant formulae for the SMEs are the following:

$$
\begin{aligned}
K &= LGD \times N\left[\frac{1}{\sqrt{1-R_{SME}}} \times G(PD) + \sqrt{\frac{R_{SME}}{1-R_{SME}}} \times G(0.999)\right] \\
&\quad \times M_{Corp.} \\
&= LGD \times N[b(PD) \times G(PD) + a(PD)] \times M_{Corp.} \\
&= LGD \times PD^* \times M_{Corp.} \\
&= Unexpected\ Loss\ \times M_{Corp.}
\end{aligned}
\tag{9.1}
$$

$$
\begin{aligned}
R_{SME} &= 0.12 \times \frac{1-\exp(-50 \times PD)}{1-\exp(-50)} + 0.24 \\
&\quad \times \frac{1-[1-\exp(-50 \times PD)]}{1-\exp(-50)} - 0.04 \times \left(1-\frac{S-5}{45}\right)
\end{aligned}
\tag{9.2}
$$

$$
M_{Corp.} = \frac{1+(M-2.5)\times[0.08451-0.05898\times\ln(PD)]^2}{1-1.5\times[0.08451-0.05898\times\ln(PD)]^2}
\tag{9.3}
$$

where:

K = Capital requirement
LGD = Loss given default
M_{Corp} = Maturity factor (for corporates)
M = Maturity: 2.5 years for SMEs
PD = Probability of default
R_{SME} = Correlation modified for SMEs
S = Sales (revenues)
$N(.)$ = Normal distribution
$G(.)$ = Inverse of normal distribution.

In formula (9.1) three additional lines were included to demonstrate that the capital requirements banks have to hold for unsecured, senior, that is, not subordinated, loan exposures to SMEs according to the Foundation Internal Rating Based Approach (Foundation IRB Approach) depend essentially on three components:

- the loss given default (LGD),
- the modified probability of default (PD^*) and
- the maturity factor ($M_{Corp.}$).

As can be seen in the third line, the original PD gets transformed into a modified PD (PD^*) via a non-linear transformation of the empirically estimated PD with coefficients also depending on the PDs and by using the normal distribution function $N(.)$ and its inverse $G(.)$. This procedure is shown in Figure 9.6: starting from the PD the percentile value is calculated in

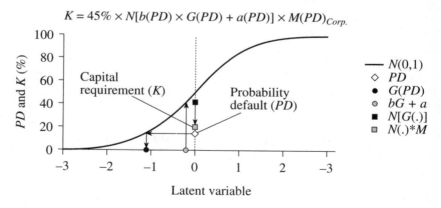

$$K = 45\% \times N[b(PD) \times G(PD) + a(PD)] \times M(PD)_{Corp.}$$

Figure 9.6   Basle II credit risk model

the first step via the inverse of the normal distribution. In the second step the resulting value becomes elongated, and in the third step the result is transformed back into the modified PD (PD*) by the normal distribution function. In the final step the modified PD is multiplied by the maturity factor and the loss given default percentage of 45 per cent for senior, unsecured loan exposures to receive the capital requirement (K) according to the Foundation IRB Approach of Basle II for SMEs. The connection to SMEs is given by the correlation factor in formula (9.2) where an SME reduction term is included that itself depends on SME sales (S) measured in millions of euros.

Behind the formulae of Basle II there is a theoretical model which is actually quite simple. In it the modified probability corresponds to the credit value at risk, that is, the percentile of the loss distribution of a portfolio consisting of infinitely fine-grained loan exposures. To make this transparent, equation (9.4) is introduced. There the *PD* modification in equation (9.1) results by equating the (observed) *PD* with the latent variable z and the systematic factor x then evaluating the equation at the 0.999 percentile value of the systematic factor and finally solving it for the (implied) latent variable that gives the percentile of the portfolio loss distribution.[4]

$$G(PD) = \sqrt{1 - R_{SME}} \times z - \sqrt{R_{SME}} \times Percentile_{0.999}(x)$$
$$G(PD) = \sqrt{1 - R_{SME}} \times z - \sqrt{R_{SME}} \times G(0.999)$$
$$\frac{1}{\sqrt{1 - R_{SME}}} \times G(PD) + \frac{\sqrt{R_{SME}}}{\sqrt{1 - R_{SME}}} \times G(0.999) = z \qquad (9.4)$$
$$\frac{1}{\sqrt{1 - R_{SME}}} \times G(PD) + \sqrt{\frac{R_{SME}}{1 - R_{SME}}} \times G(0.999) = z.$$

The capital requirements according to Basle II for the Austrian SMEs in the database are calculated in Table 9.2. The table contains all the ingredients that are needed for the calculation as well as the results. The (marginal) capital requirements K for the SMEs are given in column 6. They are called 'marginal' requirements as they relate to the individual *PD* of each rating class. The overall requirement is calculated by multiplying the marginal requirements by the revenue percentages in each rating class and summing them up successively, that is, cumulatively from the first to the twelfth rating class. The result[5] of 5.40 per cent is shown in bold in the table.

The interpretation of this result is as follows: a bank that holds a portfolio with loans given to the 11 610 Austrian SMEs in relation to their revenues has to hold ('equity') capital according to Basle II of 5.40 per cent of its overall loan exposure when it uses the Foundation IRB Approach and the loans are unsecured and senior. The 5.40 per cent contrasts with the current

Table 9.2 Capital requirements for Austrian SMEs (percentages)

Rating class	PD	R_{SME}	$M_{Corp.}$	Revenues	marg.K_{SME}	weight.K_{SME}	cumul.K_{SME}
01	0.03	20.92	190.60	0.09	1.00	0.00	0.00
02	0.17	19.59	146.44	18.24	2.72	0.50	0.50
03	0.30	18.36	137.83	31.93	3.54	1.13	1.63
04	0.44	17.99	132.44	15.52	4.44	0.69	2.32
05	1.21	14.59	121.71	15.83	6.72	1.06	3.38
06	1.98	12.47	117.59	7.77	7.98	0.62	4.00
07	3.62	9.97	113.36	2.88	9.86	0.28	4.29
08	3.76	9.83	113.12	3.15	10.01	0.32	4.60
09	9.47	8.11	108.10	1.62	15.86	0.26	4.86
10	10.20	8.15	107.76	0.83	16.63	0.14	5.00
11	11.32	8.04	107.30	0.98	17.58	0.17	5.17
12	14.09	8.01	106.39	1.15	19.95	0.23	**5.40**

'Basle I' requirement whereby the banks have to hold 8 per cent capital for corporate loans independent of their individual credit risks (PDs). The calculated difference between 5.40 and 8 per cent is one of the main results of this chapter. It shows that Basle II reduces – with the proposed QIS3 formulae – the capital requirements for Austrian SMEs quite substantially on average. Although there is an overall reduction in capital requirements for the bank holding the Austrian SMEs, this bank has to hold different marginal capital requirements for the SMEs in the different rating classes. These requirements are seen in column 6 of Table 9.2. For the best six rating classes the bank, according to Basle II has to hold less capital than in the case of Basle I and for the remaining rating classes the requirements are higher. It can be expected that this differentiation of the capital requirements due to the credit quality measured by the PDs will be the main qualitative consequence for the banking industry resulting from Basle II.

4   CAPITAL REQUIREMENTS BY INDUSTRIES AND REGIONS

In this section, the overall capital requirements are calculated for different Austrian regions and different industries. In Figure 9.7, the requirements according to Basle II are given for the production, construction, retail, wholesale and tourism industries. The results for the construction, retail and tourism industries are above and those for the production and wholesale industries are below the overall requirements for all Austrian SMEs.

The reasons for the differences among industries can be seen by the distribution of the enterprises and their revenues over the 12 rating classes. In

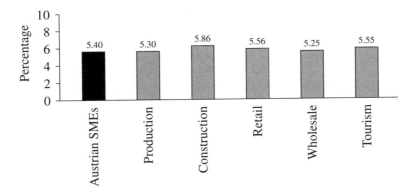

Figure 9.7   Capital requirements for Austrian SMEs, by industry

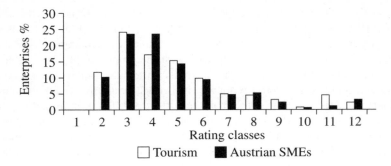

Figure 9.8   Capital requirements for Austrian SMEs in the tourism industry

Figure 9.8, the distribution of the enterprises in the tourism industry is given and compared to the distribution of all Austrian SMEs. The higher capital requirement for the tourism industry is largely due to rating class 11, where considerably more tourism enterprises are located compared to all Austrian SMEs. On the other hand in the best rating classes the tourism industry hosts even more enterprises than in the corresponding classes of the Austrian SMEs. This investigation shows that the Basle II framework can yield profound insights into the 'microstructure' of industries (as well as regions). It is worthwhile noting that the tourism industry is actually better than it appears to be. Because of its low equity capital the industry does not look very 'healthy'. But when the PDs are taken into account it can be seen that other aspects in addition to the amount of equity capital are relevant in determining the health or otherwise of an enterprise (borrower) and consequently of the whole industry/region.

The capital requirements calculated so far were based on enterprises that were not in default at the beginning of the year. In addition to such borrowers there are also enterprises that are already in default. Since the standard definition of default proposed in Basle II is quite loose, there will be even more defaults in the future than there would be under Basle I. To get an impression of the impact the defaulted enterprises have on the capital requirements the default class (number 13) is included in the analysis.

The results are shown in Figure 9.9, where it can be seen that the capital requirement for all Austrian SMEs rises from 5.40 to 6.10 per cent. Furthermore, the inclusion of the default class leads to different effects in the different industries. The range extends from the wholesale and tourism industries where the additional capital charges are relatively small, to the construction industry where the additional charge is quite large. The differences in the additional capital charges clearly indicate that among the industries there are various 'skeletons in the closet'.

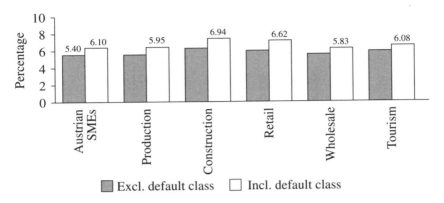

Figure 9.9 *Capital requirements for Austrian SMEs, by industry, including the default class*

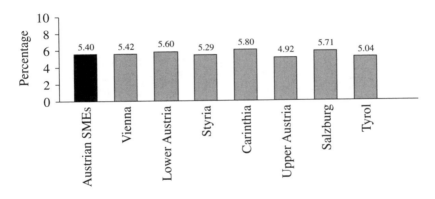

Figure 9.10 *Capital requirements for Austrian SMEs, by region*

The capital requirement calculations of Basle II can also be used to analyse differences in the credit quality of Austrian regions. Figure 9.10 contains the overall capital charges for Vienna, Lower and Upper Austria, Styria, Carinthia, Salzburg and Tyrol. Vienna is quite close to the Austrian SME average, whereas Upper Austria, Tyrol and Styria are below and Lower Austria, Salzburg and Carinthia are above. Somewhat surprising is the poor ranking of Salzburg. The reason is made transparent in Figure 9.11, where it can be seen that Salzburg has higher revenues in all lower rating classes and therefore higher weightings compared to the revenues of all Austrian SMEs. These 'overloadings' overcompensate the positive effects of the higher weightings in the better rating classes, leading to the relatively high overall capital requirement for Salzburg.

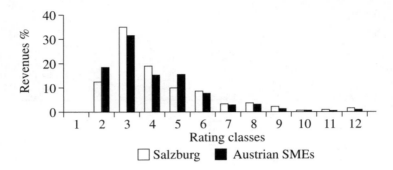

Figure 9.11   Capital requirements for Austrian SMEs in Salzburg

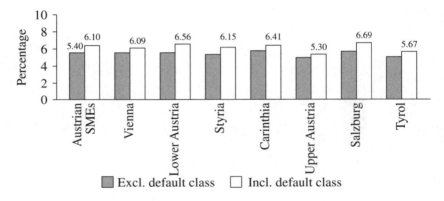

Figure 9.12   Capital requirements for Austrian SMEs, by region, including the default class

Figure 9.12 shows the additional capital charges for the regions that arise when the default class is included. As for industries, it can be seen that this inclusion raises all requirements but with different magnitudes. In Upper Austria and Carinthia, for example, they are substantially lower than in Lower Austria and Salzburg. These different increases mean that Salzburg, for example, even falls behind Carinthia in terms of capital requirements.

5   SUMMARY AND CONCLUSIONS

In this chapter the Creditreform database (Austria), consisting of 11 610 Austrian enterprises with revenues between 1 and 50 million euros was used to investigate the consequences of Basle II on Austrian SMEs. The main result of this quantitative impact study (QIS3) is that there must be an overall capital requirement of 5.40 per cent for a portfolio of unsecured and senior loans to be given to non-defaulted Austrian SMEs according to the Foundation IRB Approach. This percentage shows a reduction of the capital requirements compared to the current Basle I requirement of 8 per cent. When interpreting the reduction induced by Basle II, three important aspects have to be taken into account:

1. the presence of risk mitigation facilities reduces the requirement of 5.40 per cent even further;
2. the inclusion of the defaulted enterprises ('skeletons in the closet') increases the requirements; and
3. the requirement of 5.40 per cent is to cover the credit risk inherent in the SME loan portfolio. But beyond this, for the first time, Basle II also requires that capital be held to cover the operating risk inherent in the bank's business activities. This additional charge must be added to the credit risk requirements to make the comparison with the current requirement of 8 per cent meaningful. As the operating risk charge is expected to be less than 1 per cent its inclusion does not seem to prevent an overall reduction of the capital requirements according to Basle II.

Further minor but still important results were derived by investigating the credit risk related capital requirements for different regions and industries. It was shown where the overall requirement for all Austrian SMEs was overperformed and where it was underperformed. Further, the reasons for this performance were shown for the tourism industry and for Salzburg by showing the specific microstructures in the distribution of enterprises and revenues over the different rating classes. These insights into the microstructure of portfolios show that Basle II offers a comprehensive framework for analyzing and measuring the credit risk of loan portfolios: it consists of the segmentation of the entire portfolio into different 'risk buckets' according to the classes of the rating system. This probably new perspective is the main qualitative change that Basle II will bring to the banking industry, and the future will show how different banks will/can handle this fundamental change.

NOTES

1. The last criteria is no longer an official requirement of Basle II for individual banks. It is included in the study under investigation as the database of Creditreform covers a very broad range of Austrian SMEs and for such a 'macroeconomic' perspective it is of course still meaningful.
2. The best-ranked enterprises have a Bonitätsindex of 100. The ranking goes down as the

Bonitätsindex increases. The lowest non-defaulted ranking is reached when the Bonitätsindex is just less than 500. A Bonitätsindex of 500 and 600, respectively, corresponds quite closely to the standard definition of default given in Basle II.

3. For further information on that point, see, for example, Moody's (1999) and Eller et al. (2002).

4. The interpretation of the latent variable as a portfolio loss percentile rests on the statistical law of large numbers. Essentially it states that by enhancing the sample (portfolio) size, the loss distribution converges to its mean value. This fundamental property allows the percentiles of the loss distribution to be calculated from the expected losses and under additional restrictions even from the quantiles of the (systematic) risk factor. Besides minor technical restrictions, two assumptions, especially, are of economic importance: there is only one risk factor and the homogeneous portfolio is infinitely fine grained. For more details on all the conditions and statistical steps the interested reader is referred to Gordy (2001) who comments on this point: 'Although unlikely to pose a near-term obstacle to Basle reform, dependence on this assumption may limit the long-term viability of risk-bucket rules for regulatory capital'.

5. This result is derived under the assumption that the loan exposures of the enterprises are proportional to their revenues. To get a feeling for the consequence of this assumption the requirements are also calculated by using the distribution of enterprises as weights for the different rating classes. The result of this homogeneous borrower assumption is a capital requirement of 6.36 per cent which is roughly 1 per cent higher than the heterogeneous case.

REFERENCES

Basle II (2002), 'Quantitative Impact Study 3: Technical Guidance', Basle, 1 October, www.bis.org.

Eller, R., W. Schwaiger and R. Federa (2002), *Bankbezogene Risiko- und Erfolgsrechnung* (Managing the Risk and Profit Profile of Banks), Stuttgart: Schäffer Poeschel Verlag.

Gordy, M. (2001), 'A risk-factor model foundation for ratings-based bank capital rules', 5 February, www.bis.org.

Moody's Investor Service (1999), 'Measuring private firm default risk', June, www.moodys.com/research.nsf/index/.

Schwaiger, W. (2002), 'Auswirkungen von Basle II auf den österreichischen Mittelstand nach Branchen und Bundesländern' (Consequences of Basle II for Austrian SMEs in Different Industries and Regions), *Zeitschrift für das Gesamte Bank- und Börsewesen*, **50**, June, S. 433–46.

10. The Basle Accord and macroeconomic activity

John-ren Chen*

1 INTRODUCTION

Due to externalities as well as imperfect information, banks as financial intermediaries have usually been regulated by national bank supervisory authorities. Minimum reserve ratios for deposits, interest rate ceilings, loan loss reserves as well as minimum capital requirements, deposit insurance and so on have broadly been used for bank regulation to protect against bank runs and insolvencies of banks. These measures apply to both nationally and internationally active banks (IABs). The latter need a well-functioning international payments system which has the character of a 'global' public good. The debt crisis in the 1980s brought the international financial system to the brink of collapse. The Basle Accord of international convergence of supervisory regulations governing the capital adequacy of IABs is the result of an effort initiated by the US and the UK to maintain the safety and soundness of the international financial system via an international cooperation system as well as to reduce competitive inequalities between IABs without detriment to the competitiveness of banks in relation to other kinds of financial intermediation. It explicitly mentions that it is to be applied to IABs. But according to a report of the Committee, since 1998 more than 100 countries worldwide have already adopted the Accord in their bank supervision structure. The Basle Accord was an agreement of the Basle Committee on Banking Supervision, a committee of banking supervisory authorities which was established by the central bank governors of the Group of Ten (G10) countries in 1975 after the breakdown of the Bretton Woods system. The Committee usually meets at the Bank for International Settlements (BIS) in Basle (the location of its permanent secretariat). On 15 July 1988 the Committee released a document (now known as the Basle Accord) under the title 'International Convergence of Capital Measurement and Capital Standards'. The 1988 Accord has two main features:

1. *Definition of capital* A two-tier capital framework is used: Tier 1 is confined to shareholder equity; Tier 2 includes

   a.   loan loss reserves,
   b.   up to 45 per cent of the unrealised gain on marketable securities, and
   c.   hybrid debt–capital instruments.

2. A minimum risk-adjusted capital adequacy standard of 8 per cent, half of which (4 per cent) had to be in the form of Tier 1 capital to be attained by the end of each bank's 1992 fiscal year.

A decade later, the Committee decided to introduce more detailed capital adequacy framework proposals, known as Basle II, which will replace the 1988 Accord. The Basle Accord has demonstrated an interesting example of providing a global public good: 'The Story of the Basle Accord may shed light on not just a financial regulation, but more broadly on the politics of rule creation in the international economy' (Kapstein 1994, p. 106).

What are the main impacts of the Basle Accord on the international financial system and on the national and international financial markets? Is the international financial system more safe and sound since the introduction of the 1988 Accord? A working group of the BIS led by Patricia Jackson has reviewed over 130 research papers by academics and research departments in the G10 central banks and regulatory bodies. In Section 2 of this chapter, a short survey of the main results on the impacts of the Basle Accord on financial market development is presented. The main changes in the new Accord will be summarised in Section 3. Important special characteristics of the Austrian economy are discussed in Section 4. The impact of the new Accord on macroeconomic activity in Austria will be discussed in Section 5. A short summary is given in Section 6.

2   SURVEY OF THE IMPACTS OF THE BASLE ACCORD ON FINANCIAL MARKET DEVELOPMENT

The main impacts of the 1988 Accord reviewed by the BIS working group (Jackson 1999) are summarised as follows:

1. The average capital asset ratio of bank industry has increased since the introduction of the Accord in 1988. There is an increasing trend from 9.3 per cent in 1988 to 11.2 per cent in 1996, but there is no conclusive claim that the capital requirements lead banks to hold higher capital ratios than they otherwise would. Note that there are various possibilities for increasing the capital ratio: (i) increase capital by accessing the capital

market or issuing equity; (ii) decrease credit; or (iii) increase capital and decrease credit.

2. In most cases (73 per cent) G10 banks have tended to augment their capital ratios by increasing both capital and risk-weighted assets, and only in specific circumstances by reducing lending. The bank's approach of adjusting balance sheets to capital requirements has been shown by raising equity capital and boosting retained earnings during booms and cutting back the loan base during downturns as well as moving away from high-risk-weighted assets. In general banks seem to fulfil the capital requirements in the least costly way, that is, when it is costly to increase capital, banks tend to adjust the composition or level of lending.

3. Minimum capital requirements (MCRs) in some periods have forced banks to cut back lending, particularly to small companies or real estate and this has contributed to the weakness of the economy.

4. The volume of 'regulatory' capital arbitrage is large and growing rapidly, especially among the largest banks. Securitisation has expanded enormously because of advantages of economies of scale, reduced costs of debt financing and better diversification of funding sources.

5. Bank holdings of government securities have increased by 54 per cent in the period between 1988 and 1993, while commercial and industrial loans have fallen by 24 per cent in the US (see Hall 1993).

6. There is no conclusive evidence whether the Basle Accord has encouraged banks to increase risk taking in some periods.

7. There is no (conclusive evidence of) significant correlation between the minimum capital requirements and financial stability. In addition to the impacts of the Accord reviewed by the working group, the following effects of MCRs to banks can be expected: (i) an increase in transaction costs of bank lending and therefore a reduction in earnings of banks; (ii) an increase in the external financial premium because of increasing transaction costs of bank lending; and (iii) the financial system may become more secure, and influence the portfolio decision of financial investors.

3   THE NEW BASLE ACCORD

The 1988 Accord prevented neither the Mexican nor the Asian crisis. Even more seriously it did not prevent the contagion effects caused by the financial crisis in Thailand. Therefore the Basle Committee on Banking Supervision (the Committee) has decided to amend the 1988 Accord by a more detailed capital adequacy framework. The new Accord is to be built on three mutually reinforcing pillars, that is, minimum capital requirements, a supervisory review process and effective use of market discipline, to contribute to a higher degree of security in the international financial system.

The First Pillar: Minimum Capital Requirements

The new Accord keeps both the existing definition of capital and the minimum requirement of 8 per cent of capital to risk-weighted assets with major changes in the measurement of risk. The 1988 Accord applies uniform risk weights assigned according to the type and perceived riskiness of the borrower. Three categories of borrower, that is, corporates, sovereigns and banks, are classified and assigned distinct risk profiles. Within each category the risk weights vary according to membership of the Organization for Economic Cooperation and Development (OECD) and the maturity (short or long term) of loans. The new Accord also introduces a more complex measurement of credit risk, but leaves the measurement of market risk unchanged and proposes a new framework for the measurement of operational risk. Three approaches to the measurement of credit risk are envisaged in the new Accord, namely: the standardised approach, the foundation internal ratings based approach and the advanced internal ratings based approach (a modified version of the existing approach).

The standardised approach

This approach is a modified version of the existing approach in the 1988 Accord. Major changes from the 1988 Accord are:

1. the distinction between OECD and non-OECD membership is abandoned;
2. creditworthiness is determined by external credit assessment institutions;
3. the sovereign floor is abolished, that is, banks and corporates may be assigned a better rating than the sovereigns. Weights will be determined by three categories of borrower: sovereign, bank or corporate.

Risk weights of the standardised approach are shown in Tables 10.1, 10.2 and 10.3. Table 10.1 lists those for sovereign borrowers.

Table 10.1   Risk weights for sovereign borrowers

Export credit agency ratings under sovereign creditworthiness	AAA AA–	A+ A–	BBB+ BBB	BB+ B–	B–
Risk weights	0%	20%	50%	100%	150%

To assign risk weights for bank borrowers, supervisors will choose between two options:

1. all banks in a given country will be assigned one category less favourable than the sovereigns;
2. the risk weights will be based on the assessment of export credit assessment (ECA) institutions as given in Table 10.2.

Table 10.2   Risk weights for bank borrowers

ECA of banks	AAA AA−	A+ A−	BBB+ BBB−	BB+ B−	Below B−	Unrated
Risk weights	20%	50%	50%	100%	150%	50%
Risk weights	20%	20%	20%	50%	150%	20%

Note that the new Accord differs from the 1988 Accord in its treatment of short-term claims. According to the 1988 Accord all claims on banks in the OECD are assigned a 20 per cent risk weight. For banks outside the OECD the risk weight was 20 per cent for short-term claims, but 100 per cent for other claims (that is, a duration of more than one year).

For risk weights for corporate borrowers, see Table 10.3. The 1988 Accord assigns a 100 per cent risk weight to claims on the private sector. Note that the 100 per cent risk weight for unrated corporate borrowers is designed to avoid an increase in the cost of funding for small/medium businesses.

Table 10.3   Risk weights for corporate borrowers

Credit assessment	AAA AA−	A+ A−	BBB+ BB−	Below BB−	Unrated
Risk weights	20%	50%	100%	150%	100%

The internal ratings-based (IRB) approach

According to an explanatory note of the Basle Committee on the New Basle Capital Accord:

> Under the IRB approach, banks will be allowed to use their internal estimates of borrower creditworthiness to assess credit risk in their portfolio, subject to strict methodological and disclosure standards. Under the IRB approach, a bank esti-

mates each borrower's creditworthiness and the results are translated into estimates of a potential future loss amount, which form the basis of minimum capital
requirements. The framework allows for both a foundation method and more
advanced methodologies for corporate, sovereign and bank exposures. In the
foundation methodology, banks estimate the probability of default associated with
each borrower, and the supervisors will supply the other inputs. In the advanced
methodology, a bank with a sufficiently developed internal capital allocation
process will be permitted to supply other necessary inputs as well under both the
foundation and advanced IRB approaches. The range of risk weights will be far
more diverse than those in the standarized approach, resulting in greater risk
sensibility. (Basle Committee on Banking Supervision 2002, p. 4)

The Second Pillar: Supervisory Review Process (SRP)

According to the explanatory note of the Basle Committee:

> The SRP requires supervisors to ensure that each bank has sound internal process
> in place to assess the adequacy of its capital based on a thorough evaluation of its
> risks. The new framework stresses the importance of bank management develop-
> ing an internal capital assessment process. This internal process would then be
> subject to supervisory review and intervention, where appropriate. (ibid., p. 5)

The Third Pillar: Market Discipline

> The new framework sets out disclosure requirements and recommendations in
> several areas, including the way a bank calculates its capital adequacy and its risk
> assessment methods. The core set of disclosures recommendations applies to all
> banks, with more detailed requirements for supervisory recognition of internal
> methodologies for credit risk, credit risk mitigation techniques and asset
> securitisation. (ibid., p. 5)

Adoption of the New Accord by Banks

To the question: 'Will banks be able to remain in the present system if they
wish?' (see Annex 1, Some Basic Questions, in ibid., p. 8), the Basle Committee has given the answer that it expects supervisors to start applying the
new framework to internationally active banks from 2004, but those banks
that choose its simpler options may continue to calculate capital requirements
in a way broadly similar to the current Accord. According to this answer
there must be some benefits for banks to adopt the new Accord. Three kinds
of benefit may be classified:

1. reduction of the credit risk by a better assessment of borrowers;
2. reduction of contagion effects caused by credit crunch of other banks; and
3. an increase in net earnings by improving loans to sound borrowers.

But the introduction of a more complex calculation of capital requirements also implies an increase in the costs of information collection and calculation of capital requirements.

4   SPECIAL PROPERTIES OF THE AUSTRIAN ECONOMY

The following special properties characterise the Austrian economy, especially the Austrian financial market.

First, it has a high share of small and medium-sized enterprises (SMEs). In 1994, there were about 73 200 craft and service enterprises in Austria. Their number is growing by about 2 per cent annually. They are particularly important as short distance providers for goods and services. About half of these enterprises have between one and 19 employees and comprise 3.6 per cent of the workforce. About 61.8 per cent of the workforce is employed in SMEs with between 1 and 499 employees. The annual investment of SMEs amounts to €3650 per employer. About one-third of this is used for building and premises, and two-thirds for equipment. The capital structure of SMEs is considered to be weak because of a low share of own equity and a high debt ratio.

Second, the house bank of Austrian firms characterises the borrowers' relationships with specific banks in the business community. Some indicators that represent the house bank tradition of Austrian firms are:

1. on average about 70 per cent of the total bank loans come from one bank. The share is about 84 per cent for the small firms and about 68 per cent for the large firms;
2. the share of long-term loans from one bank is about 73 per cent on average, about 88 per cent for small firms and 70 per cent for large firms; and
3. the share of short-term loans from one bank is about 82 per cent on average, about 87 per cent for small firms and 81 per cent for large firms.

Third, bank loans are the most important external financial source for Austrian SMEs:

1. loans from credit institutions have decreased from 40.9 per cent (1989) to 24 per cent (1999);
2. loans with maturity of less than one year have decreased from 25.5 per cent (1989) to 16 per cent (1999); and
3. loans with maturity of more than one year have decreased from 15.4 per cent (1989) to 8 per cent (1999).

Fourth, saving deposits have played a dominant role in the asset disposition of Austrian households and SMEs in the economy, therefore the stock market provides only a small share of capital in Austrian enterprises.

Fifth, trade credit has played an important role in the short-term credit to SMEs. Trade credit accounted for about 20 per cent of the liabilities of Austrian firms (1989) but this decreased to 11 per cent (1999). Trade credit has been broadly used in firm to firm business to reduce transaction costs.

Sixth is the system of capital returns tax whereby a '25 per cent tax' on all interest income and returns to capital has been implemented since 1993.

Seventh, the Austrian residential construction saving and subsidy systems have played a very important role in the housing sector.

5   IMPACTS OF THE NEW BASLE ACCORD ON MACROECONOMIC ACTIVITY IN AUSTRIA: ASSUMPTIONS AND LEMMATA

Assumptions

To study the impacts of the new Basle Accord on macroeconomic activity in Austria, the following assumptions are made:

- *Assumption 1*   There is a house bank relation between banks and corporates in Austria: this is a special characteristic of the Austrian financial market.
- *Assumption 2*   For some borrowers bank lending can only be offset by other sources of credit with unusually high costs if bank lending is the dominant form of external finance. Theoretically, there are several external financial sources for borrowers, especially enterprises, and the optimal combination between internal and external sources should be implemented. But for SMEs to have access to both internal and external sources, fixed costs are needed. This is true for every external source. Therefore bank lending cannot be offset by other sources of credit; nor can lending by one bank be replaced by that of other banks. This is especially the case if there is a house bank situation such as in Austria. In such a system, small firms which have a close relationship with a bank (a house bank) have greater access to the credit of the home bank than firms without such a relationship. In Austria about 70 per cent of loans are made by a bank to all firms on average, with about 84 per cent and 68 per cent for small and large firms, respectively. Therefore, for small Austrian firms bank lending cannot be offset or can only be offset with unusually high costs by other sources of credit

because bank lending is the dominant form of external finance (see Section 4, above). Hancock and Wilcox (1997 and 1998) studied the impacts of bank capital shocks on credit availability and activity in real estate markets and real activity in the small business sector. In the US these sectors have traditionally relied on bank lending. Their empirical results imply that a reduction in capital at small banks has a much larger impact on economic activity than a reduction at large banks in the US, because small businesses are more dependent on bank lending in the US.

- *Assumption 3*   The transaction costs of bank lending will be higher by adopting the new rather than the current Basle Accord (thus the external financial premium will be increased by adopting the new Basle Accord).

- *Assumption 4*   Neither the current nor the new Basle Accord has any significant influence on asset disposition (portfolio decision) of the Austrian economy, nor any significant effect on housing investment (see Tobin 1955; Chen 2002). Theoretically, higher capital requirements for banks may have negative effects on the competitiveness of banks compared to other financial intermediaries and financial suppliers. Empirical research on the competitiveness of bank versus other financial intermediaries in the US, the UK, Japan and so on does not find evidence of a loss of bank competitiveness. Empirical research about the influence of stock market reaction on the announcement of introduction of capital requirements in several G10 countries also fails to find clear effects and there is even less evidence about causality. The recent development of bank business has been influenced by the implementation of information and communication technology by banks. Therefore, we believe that assumption 4 can be made in our study on the impacts of the Basle Accord (both the current and the new one) on macroeconomic activity in Austria. The main reason for this is that the capital requirements for banks may have a negative effect on the profitability of bank lending but a positive effect on the soundness and safety of banks, the one cancelling out the other. Housing investment in Austria is mainly financed through the so-called 'Bausparvertrag' (construction saving contract) source which enjoys a high government subsidy. The interest rates for the Bausparvertrag are fixed long term at 6 per cent annually for financing construction and at 3 per cent for a savings deposit with a government subsidy. Additionally there are also construction subsidies for socially deprived households. The loans for residential construction are guaranteed with homes and premises as collateral.

Lending Decision of Bank to Corporate Borrowers with respect to MCRs

To study the impacts of the new Basle Accord on the macroeconomic activity in Austria we first have to show the influence of the new Accord on the lending behaviour of banks, especially to corporate borrowers. As reported above, instead of the same risk weight for all corporate borrowers as in the current Accord, a differentiation of risks weights for the corporate sector will be introduced in the new Accord. The minimal capital requirements (MCR) for banks remains the same at 8 per cent for the new Accord. Under the assumption that the bank maximises expected net yields from loans to corporate borrowers and that the probability of default is exogenously given, the bank lending decision can be described by the following maximization problem.

The objective function is given as:

$$E\sum_i (r_i X_i - f_i X_i = c X_i)$$

where

r_i = net interest yield per unit of loan of the risk groups, RG_i
X_i = loan of RG_i
f_i = probability of default which represents the percentage of loss of the ith RG
c = transaction cost of bank lending.

The MCR for a bank is represented by:

$$\sum_i w(f_i)X_i \leq K$$

where

w = the risk weights
K = given capital of a bank.

The house bank structure of Austrian enterprises can be described by the demand function of a corporate for bank loans:

$$r_i = h(X_i) \text{ with } h' = \frac{dh(X_i)}{dX_i} < 0.$$

Because of the house bank situation a bank has a monopolistic position with respect to its borrowers. The lending decision of a representative bank can be described by the following optimalisation problem subject to the constraint of capital requirements:

$$\text{Max } E\left\{\sum_{i=1}^{n}[h(X_i)X_i - (f_i + C)X_i]\right\}, s.t. \sum_i w(f_i)X_i \leq K.$$

The control variable is X_i, the loans to the ith RG. To show more clearly the effect of risk weights in the current and the new Accords on the loans and the interest yields rate r_i we present a case with the same demand function of bank loans for all RGs. The only difference between the RGs is their different probability of default.

$$h(X_i) = a_0 - 0.5a_1X_i, \text{ with } a_0 > 0, \ a_1 > 0.$$

Taking into account these loan demand functions, the lending decision of the bank is to maximise the expected net interest yields:

$$\text{Max } E\left[\sum(a_0 - 0.5a_1X_i)X_i - (f_i - c)X_i\right]s.t. \sum w(f_i)X_i \leq K,$$

where E is the expectation operator.

The solutions for two RG cases are given as follows (for details, see the appendix):

- Case 1: if capital requirements are constrained:

$$\sum_{i=1}^{2} w(f_i)X_i = K.$$

In this case we have

$$\lambda* = \frac{\sum_{i=1}^{2} w_i(a_0 - f_i - c) - a_1K}{\sum_{i=1}^{2} w_i^2}$$

$$X_i^* = \frac{a_0 - f_i - c}{a_1} - \frac{w_i}{a_1}\lambda*$$

$$r_i^* = 0.5a_0 + 0.5(c + f_i) + 0.5\frac{w_i}{a_1}\lambda*$$

for $i = 1, 2$. This proves that MCRs can reduce bank lending when banks are capital constrained.

Following G10 studies with respect to the contribution of the change in the capital base and risk-weighted assets to the overall change in the capital ratio in some countries and periods, banks have cut back lending in order to achieve capital requirements when banks are capital constrained. In these cases banks have several options to fulfil the MCR, that is, to cut lending, to increase equity or to cut lending and increase equity. But usually the periods when banks are confronted with constrained capital are those when they have to make substantial write-offs of provisions. At such time the credit demand may be weak or the credit quality of borrowers may deteriorate and the cost of increasing equity is usually higher than to cut lending. For instance in 1989, 1991 and 1992 among the G10, banks in Belgium, Canada, France, Germany, Italy and the Netherlands increased their capital ratio by increasing the capital base and decreasing risk-weighted assets. Although there is no evidence that the MCRs of the Basle Accord increased capital ratios of the G10 banks we believe that an increase in MCR can reduce bank lending when banks are capital constrained, because in this case in the short run, a reduction in lending is more cost effective than an increase in equity. The MCRs in the new Accord will stay the same as in the current one. Thus an increase in MCRs will not be expected. Therefore the impacts of the new Accord on macroeconomic activity will not be induced by an increase in capital requirements.

- Case 2: if capital requirements are not constrained. Thus

$$\sum_{i=1}^{2} w(f_i)X_i < K$$

and therefore in this case, $\lambda^{**} = 0$ and

$$X_i^{**} = \frac{a_0 - f_i}{a_1}$$

$$r_i^{**} = 0.5a_0 + 0.5f_i$$

for $i = 1, 2$.

The following propositions summarise these results:

Lemma 1: In a house bank environment the corporate borrower of bank lending with a higher probability of default will be faced with a higher interest rate and get a lower loan, either with or without effective capital constraint from the house bank.

Proof:

1. In the case of a capital constraint of the house bank:

$$r_1^* - r_2^* = 0.5(f_1 - f_2) + 0.5\frac{\lambda^*}{a_1}(w_1 - w_2)$$

thus $r_1^* \underset{>}{\overset{<}{=}} r_2^*$, if $f_1 \underset{>}{\overset{<}{=}} f_2$; since $w_1 \underset{>}{\overset{<}{=}} w_2$, if $f_1 \underset{>}{\overset{<}{=}} f_2$ and

$$X_1^* - X_2^* = \frac{f_2 - f_1}{a_1} + \frac{\lambda^*}{a_1}(w_2 - w_1).$$

Thus $X_1^* \underset{>}{\overset{<}{=}} X_2^*$; $w_1 \underset{>}{\overset{<}{=}}$, if $f_1 \underset{>}{\overset{<}{=}} f_2$.

2. In the case of no capital constraint of the house bank:

$$\lambda^{**} = 0, r_1^{**} - r_2^{**} = 0.5(f_1 - f_2) \text{ and } X_1^{**} - X_2^{**} = \frac{1}{a_1}(f_2 - f_1)$$

Thus $r_1^{**} \underset{>}{\overset{<}{=}} r_2^{**}$, if $f_1 \underset{>}{\overset{<}{=}} f_2$ and $X_1^{**} \underset{>}{\overset{<}{=}} X_2^{**}$, if $f_1 \underset{>}{\overset{<}{=}} f_2$.

Lemma 2: In a house bank environment the difference in the probability of default is the only determinant for the difference in lending interest rate and the bank loan for corporate borrowers with diverse probabilities of default, even if the same risk weight is applied to each corporate borrower as in the current Accord.

Proof: According to the current Basle Accord for each corporate borrower, $\bar{w} = w_i$ for all i where $\bar{w}$ is determined by the Accord. In this case:

$$r_1^* - r_2^* = 0.5(f_1 - f_2) \text{ for both } \lambda* > 0 \text{ and } \lambda* = 0$$

$$X_1^* - X_2^* = \frac{f_2 - f_1}{a_1} \text{ for both } \lambda^* > 0 \text{ and } \lambda^* = 0.$$

Lemma 3: The new Basle Accord will intensify the difference in bank lending interest rates and bank loans between corporate borrowers with different probabilities of default, if the house bank is capital constrained.

Proof: In this case according to the new Accord: $w_1 \overset{<}{\underset{>}{=}} w_2$, if $f_1 \overset{<}{\underset{>}{=}} f_2$. Therefore

$$r_1^* - r_2^* = 0.5(f_1 - f_2) + 0.5\frac{\lambda^*}{a_1}(w_1 - w_2)$$

and

$$X_1^* - X_2^* = \frac{f_2 - f_1}{a_1} + \frac{\lambda^*}{a_1}(w_2 - w_1).$$

Corollary 1 of Lemma 3: The difference in the bank lending interest rates and in the bank loans to different corporate borrowers with diverse probabilities of default will be higher, the lower the capital of the house bank in the case of capital constraint.

Proof:

$$\frac{d(r_1^* - r_2^*)}{dK} = \frac{0.5}{a_1}(w_1 - w_2)\frac{d\lambda^*}{dK} \overset{<}{\underset{>}{=}} 0$$

$$\frac{d(X_1^* - X_2^*)}{dK} = \frac{w_2 - w_1}{a_1}\frac{d\lambda^*}{a_1} \overset{<}{\underset{>}{=}} 0, \text{ if } w_1 \overset{<}{\underset{>}{=}} w_2$$

since

$$\frac{d\lambda^*}{dK} = -\frac{a_1}{\sum_i w_i^2} < 0.$$

Corollary 2 of Lemma 3: The new Accord will decrease (or increase) the difference in bank lending interest rate and bank loans between the corporate borrowers with diverse probabilities of default in a period of boom (or slump).

Proof: In a period of boom the Tier 2 bank capital is higher because of the higher value of unrealised gains of assets and vice versa.

Lemma 4: The new Basle Accord assigns lower capital requirements for corporate borrowers with low probability of default than those of the current Accord. Therefore the bank lending interest rate will be lower and the bank loans will be higher for those corporate borrowers with low probabilities of default. For at least one kind of corporate borrower the risk weight is increased by about 50 per cent. Therefore the corresponding corporate borrowers will face higher bank lending interest rates and lower bank loans after adoption of the new Accord.

Proof:

1. For those corporates with low probability of default the risk weights are lower than 100 per cent. Therefore in comparison with the current Accord the bank lending interest rates will be lower and the bank loans will be higher.
2. For those corporate borrowers with higher probability of default the effects are vice versa.
3. For at least one group of corporate borrowers the bank lending interest rates and the bank loans may remain the same as in the current Accord.

Lemma 5: The new Accord will reduce the risk weights of short-term bank loans, therefore the interest rate difference between the long- and short-term loans will increase in favour of the short-term loans and these will increase while the long-term loans may decrease, other things being equal. Note that the proofs given in lemmata 1 to 4 can be carried over to this lemma; a separate proof is not necessary.

A Macroeconomic Model: A Synthesis of Interest Rate and Credit Channels

Following the discussion in the last section the new Basle Accord will increase the bank lending interest rate spreads and bank loans between corporate borrowers with different probabilities of default. In order to emphasise the impacts of the new Accord on macroeconomic activities in Austria we shall present a model for an economy the real sector of which consists of two groups of enterprises with different probabilities of default. Using the usual framework of a short-run macroeconomic model, the goods market consists of four demand components: consumption expenditure (both durable and non-durable goods as well as residential construction), investment expenditure, public expenditure and net exports. Since we believe that the new Accord will not influence consumption, public expenditure or net exports, only the investment expenditure will be considered here.

The investment expenditure is jointly determined by the investment demand of enterprises and the supply of financial sources needed to carry out the investment projects (see Chen 1987). Since investment is a long-term decision the relevant interest rate is the long-term real interest rate, which is an important variable for the user's costs of capital. The demand for investment is derived by realising the optimal capital stock in the neoclassical sense and is a negative function of the long-term real interest rate. To specify the supply of finance for investment we take into account the problem of an imperfect financial market because of asymmetrical information, or moral hazard, as well as interest yields tax. The financial sources for investment can thus be classified as internal and external sources. The former are either equity or retained profits, capital depreciations, loss reserves or government investment support, while the house bank is the most important supply of external financial sources in Austria. The interest rate for internal financial sources is the net rate after interest tax received by the owner, while the interest rates for external sources are the buyers' price, that is, the interest rate paid by the borrowers which generally includes the interest yields tax. Therefore the interest rates of external sources are higher than those of internal ones. Because of this, an enterprise that carries out an investment project will first use the internal sources and if additional funding is needed it will then look for external funds. Thus, investment expenditures can be classified according to the following three cases.

First, investment projects are financed by using both internal and external sources. This case is described in Figure 10.1. The curves of investment demand and supply of sources are described by I_d and I_S, respectively. The

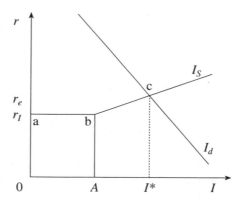

Note: I_S is investment funding; I_d is investment (demand) project.

Figure 10.1   Determination of investment

negative slope of I_d means that the investment demand depends negatively on the user's interest rates. The internal sources are described by the distance $\overline{ab}$ or $\overline{0A}$ at a supplier's interest rate after tax r_I; the supply of external sources is a positive function of the buyers' interest rate which is described by the positive slope of I_S. For the given investment demand the investment expenditure is determined at point C, that is, the intersection of the I_d and I_S curves. In this case, the investment expenditure is equal to $0I^*$ and the external interest rate is equal to r_e while the distance $r_e r_I$ is an external financial premium.

Second, investment projects are financed only by internal sources of the enterprises. This case is shown in Figure 10.2. The investment expenditure is just equal to the internal sources $I^* = 0A$.

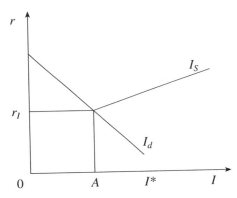

Figure 10.2   Determination of investment financed by internal sources

Third, investment projects are financed only by internal sources. In this case the investment demand is weak. Only a part of the internal sources, that is, $0I^*$ is used. The rest (I^*A) is not needed for financing own investment projects (see Figure 10.3).

The first case is the usual one in a higher aggregated macroeconomic model. In a disaggregated model consisting of several sectors all three cases can be expected. Expanding sectors are represented by the first case while shrinking sectors can be described by the last two. The interest rates for external sources are usually the net interest yield per loan in addition to the interest rate of refinancing the bank loans. This is strongly dependent on the monetary policy.

To show the impact of the new Basle Accord on macroeconomic activity in Austria we now consider the first case in a highly aggregated macroeconomic model with two groups of enterprises which differ by their probability of

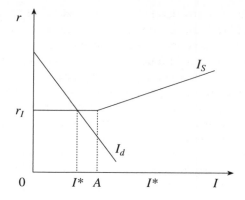

Figure 10.3   Deficit of investment demand for internal resources

default. For convenience of presentation the first group is said to have a lower probability of default. Both groups will invest I_1 and I_2 using AI_1 and AI_2 external sources and paying r_1 and r_2 external interest rates, respectively (see Figure 10.4).

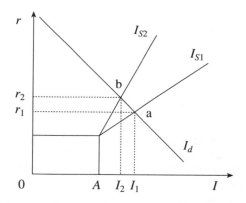

Figure 10.4   Impact of the Basle Accord on investment

The impact of the new Accord on macroeconomic activity in Austria depends mainly on the following three factors:

1. The effect of the new Accord on the transaction costs of bank lending to corporates in Austria: the higher the increase in transaction costs the higher will be the interest rates and the lower the use of external sources, that is, the lower the investment. A higher transaction cost of bank

lending can be represented by a higher slope of the supply curve of
investment finance.

2. The distribution of groups 1 and 2 in the Austrian economy: the adoption
   of the new Accord will improve the position of enterprises in group 1 and
   worsen that of group 2 with respect to access to bank loans, respectively,
   especially for the enterprises in group 1 if the increase in bank lending
   transaction costs is moderate.

3. The degree of impact of adopting the new Accord on changing the bank
   lending position of enterprises in groups 1 and 2, respectively.

Since these three factors produce opposite effects of adopting the new
Accord, the impact of the new Accord on investments depends on the relative
intensity of the three factors. Empirical research is therefore necessary to
estimate the impacts.

Theoretically, the following hypotheses of the impact of the new Accord
can be stated:

- *There are positive impacts* if the increase in transaction costs of bank
  lending is moderate and the share of group 1 is dominant in the economy.
- *There are no significant impacts* if the effects of an increase in transaction costs are compensated by the effects caused by the distribution of
  enterprises between groups 1 and 2.
- *There are negative impacts* if the effect of increasing transaction costs
  in bank lending is striking and the enterprises of group 2 have a
  substantial share in an economy.

The specifications of investment expenditures given in this chapter are
adapted to the special characteristics of the Austrian economy. Some empirical research, for instance Valderrama (2002), finds evidence for the role of
credit channels. The specifications of investment expenditures can be integrated into a conventional macroeconomic model to study the development
of the interest rate structure through the monetary transmission mechanism.
Investment expenditures are dependent, other things being equal, on the long-
term real interest rates, while the demand for money is explained by the
short-term nominal interest rates. This integration of short- and long-term
interest rates suggests a tentative synthesis of the interest rate and credit
channels in a macroeconomic model. Our study of the macroeconomic impacts
discussed above is static. In a dynamic business cycle model, different impacts
of the new Accord can be expected. Many experts have remarked on the
procyclical impacts of both the current and new Accords (Griffith-Jones and
Spratt 2001). One definition of a banker is that he is 'someone who lends you
an umbrella when the sun is shining and wants it back when it starts to rain'.

To summarise this section, it is likely that the new Accord will have a moderate impact on macroeconomic activity in Austria but, as the old saying goes, 'the proof of the pudding is in the eating'. The propositions of lemmata 1 to 5 have important implications for economic growth and development policies. According to these propositions a corporate borrower who has a higher probability of default will have to pay a higher lending interest rate and will receive smaller loans. The empirical assessment of the creditworthiness or credit rating (scoring) shows that a new enterprise usually, other things being equal, has a higher probability of default and therefore has a higher risk weight for bank lending; therefore it has to pay a higher bank lending interest rate and will receive smaller loans from its house bank. These less favourable conditions will make it more difficult for a new enterprise to be competitive. However, new enterprises are important for economic growth and development because they are innovators, introducing both new products and new technology. Therefore it is imperative, and also reasonable, to support the set-up of new enterprises via so-called 'venture capital' and other measures.

6   SUMMARY

The Basle Accord, under the title 'International Convergence of Capital Measurement and Capital Standard', was released by the Basle Committee on Banking Supervision on 15 July 1988 after intensive negotiation and consultation initiated by the US following the debt crisis in the 1980s. The aim was to maintain the safety and soundness of the international financial system as well as to reduce competitive inequalities between internationally active banks. The Accord has been adopted by about 100 countries since 1988. The Basle Committee has initiated new consultations to release a new Accord which is to be built on three mutually reinforcing pillars, that is, minimum capital requirements, a supervisory review approach and effective use of market discipline. The new Accord keeps both the existing definition of capital and the minimum requirements of 8 per cent of capital to risk-weighted assets assigned according to the type, and perceived riskness of the borrower. But it makes some changes as well as introduces some new approaches to the measurement of credit risk and new classifications of risk weights. The new Accord will be implemented in 2004.

In this chapter, some results of research on the impacts of the Basle Accord 1988 are summarised. The main changes in the new Accord are examined. After a discussion of some special characteristics of the Austrian financial market and economy our study focuses on the impacts of the new Accord on macroeconomic activity in Austria. In a house bank environment, which is one of the special properties of the Austrian financial market, optimal bank lending policy in the sense of maximisation of expected net interest yields is characterised by a differentiation of lending interest rates and loans with respect to the probability of default. The corporate borrower with a higher probability of default has to pay higher interest rates and receives smaller loans. The change in the risk weights in the new Accord will increase the difference in the lending interest rates and loans between the corporate borrowers who have a different probability of default if bank capital is constrained. The construction saving system 'Bauspar-Vertrag' in Austria, with high subsidies for housing, is the main reason why the Basle Accord has had no significant influence on residential construction in Austria. The special portfolio behaviour of Austrian households also seems to be responsible for the insignificant impact of the Basle Accord.

The main influence of the new Accord on macroeconomic activity will be on investment expenditure. In a static model, in which we propose a monetary transmission mechanism that is a synthesis of interest rate and credit channels, we study the impact of the new Accord on macroeconomic activity in Austria. Three factors with opposite effects on investment expenditures are responsible for the total effect of the new Accord. These factors can be identified by

1. the effect of the new Accord on the transaction costs of bank lending to corporate borrowers;
2. the distribution of corporations between low and high probability of default; and
3. the degree of impact on the changing position in bank lending of enterprises with a different probability of default.

Because of opposite effects and the different strength of each impact it is necessary to carry out empirical studies in order to estimate the net total macroeconomic impacts of the new Accord. Our study in this chapter is undertaken within the framework of a static macroeconomic model. The capital requirements of banks for risk assets have different impacts in periods of boom and slump, that is, during the business cycle. In the period of slump the capital requirements of banks are more constrained because of a reduction in Tier 2 capital through the unrealised gains on marketable securities. In a period of boom the capital requirements are less constrained. Therefore in this sense the impact of the Basle Accord (both current and new) on macroeconomic activity is expected to be procyclic.

Following the propositions proved by lemmata 1 to 5, those enterprise borrowers with a higher probability of default have to pay a higher lending interest rate and receive smaller loans. This implies that new enterprises which according to Creditreform, the most important credit rating supplier in

Europe, have a higher probability of default, other things being equal, are weakly competitive compared to established ones. However, new enterprises are important innovators, introducing either new products or new technology into an economy. Therefore to promote economic development and growth it is important to support new enterprises either by means of venture capital or through other measures.

NOTE

* I am deeply indebted to my colleagues Karl Socher and Richard Hule for their valuable comments.

REFERENCES

Basle Committee on Banking Supervision (2001), 'Consultative Document: Overview of the New Basle Capital Accord', Bank for International Settlements, Basle.

Basle Committee on Banking Supervision (2002), 'The New Basle Capital Accord. An Explanatory Note', www.bis.org/publ/bcbsca01.pdf, January 2001.

Chen, John-ren (1987), *Ein makroökonometrisches Modell für Taiwan*, Saarbrücken: Verlag Breitenbach, Chapter 6.

Chen, John-ren (2002), 'Asset disposition and economic development', in F. Bolle and M. Carlberg (eds), *Advances in Behavioural Economics*, Heidelberg: Physica Verlag, Chapter 12.

Griffith-Jones, S. and S. Spratt (2001), 'Will the proposed new Basle Capital Accord have a net negative effect on developing countries?', mimeo, Institute of Development Studies, Sussex.

Hall, B.J. (1993), 'How has the Basle Accord affected bank portfolios?', *Journal of the Japanese and International Economies*, **7**, 8–44.

Hancock, D. and J.A. Wilcox (1997), 'Bank capital, non-bank finance and real estate activity', *Journal for Housing Research*, **8**, 75–105.

Hancock, D. and J.A. Wilcox (1998), 'The "credit crunch" and the availability of credit to small business', *Journal of Banking and Finance*, **22** (6–8), 983–1014.

Jackson, Patricia (1999), 'Capital requirements and bank behaviour: the impact of the Basle Accord', Basle Committee on Banking Supervision Working Paper No. 1, Bank for International Settlements, Basle.

Kapstein, Ethan B. (1994), *Governing the Global Economy: International Finance and the State*, Cambridge, MA: Harvard University Press.

Tobin, James (1955), 'A dynamic aggregate model', *Journal of Political Economy*, **LXIII** (2), 103–15.

Valderrama, Maria (2002), 'Credit channel and investment behaviour in Austria: a micro-econometric approach', Working Paper No. 58, Oesterreichische Nationalbank.

APPENDIX   LENDING DECISION UNDER UNCERTAINTY OF CREDIT DEFAULT

$$L = r_1 X_1 + r_2 X_2 - f_1 X_1 - f_2 X_2 + \lambda(K - w_1 X_1 - w_2 X_2)$$
$$= a_0 X_1 - 0.5 a_1 X_1^2 + a_0 X_2 - 0.5 a_1 X_2^2 - fX_1 - fX_2 - 2cX$$
$$+ \lambda(K - w_1 X_1 - w_2 X_2)$$

under the loan demand function $r_i = a_0 - 0.5 a_1 X_i$

$$X_i \left(\frac{\partial L}{\partial X_i} \right) = X_i (a_0 - a_1 X_i - f_i - c - \lambda w_i) = 0, \text{ for } X_i \geq 0 \; i = 1, 2.$$

$$\lambda \frac{\partial L}{\partial \lambda} = \lambda(K - w_1 X_1 - w_2 X_2) = 0$$

$$X_i^* = (a_0 - f_i - c - \lambda w_i)/a_1, \text{ for } X_i > 0 \text{ for } \lambda > 0$$

$$w_1(a_0 - f_1 - c - \lambda w_1)/a_1 + w_2(a_0 - f_2 - c - \lambda w_2)/a_1 = K$$

$$w_1[a_1^{-1} a_0 - a_1^{-1}(f_1)c] - a_1^{-1} w_1^2 \lambda + w_2[a_1^{-1} a_0 - a_1^{-1}(f_2) - c - a_1^{-1} w_2^2 \lambda] = K$$

$$(w_1^2 + w_2^2)\lambda = w_1(a_0 - f_1 - c) + w_2(a_0 - f_2 - c) - a_1 K$$

$$\lambda* = \frac{w_1(a_0 - f_1 - c) + w_2(a_0 - f_2 - c) - a_1 K}{w_1^2 + w_2^2}$$

$$X_i^* = \frac{(a_0 - f_i - c)}{a_1} - \frac{w_i}{a_1} \cdot \left[\frac{w_1(a_0 - f_1 - c) + w_2(a_0 - f_2 - c) - a_1 K}{w_1^2 + w_2^2} \right]$$

$$r_i^* = 0.5 a_0 + 0.5(f_i + c) + 0.5 \frac{w_i}{a_1} \left[\frac{w_1(a_0 - f_1 - c)w_2(a_0 - f_2 - c) - a_1 K}{w_1^2 + w_2^2} \right]$$

if $\lambda* = 0$ then $X_i^* = (a_0 - f_i - c)/a_1$

$$r_i^* = a_0 - 0.5(a_0 - f_i - c) = 0.5 a_0 + 0.5(f_i + c).$$

Index